CRITICAL INCIDENT MANAGEMENT

A Complete Response Guide

Second Edition

CRITICAL INCIDENT MANAGEMENT

A Complete Response Guide

Second Edition

Vincent Faggiano • John McNall • Tom Gillespie

CRC Press
Taylor & Francis Group
Boca Raton   London   New York

CRC Press is an imprint of the
Taylor & Francis Group, an **Informa** business

CRC Press
Taylor & Francis Group
6000 Broken Sound Parkway NW, Suite 300
Boca Raton, FL 33487-2742

Library of Congress Cataloging-in-Publication Data

Faggiano, Vincent.
   Critical incident management : an on-scene guide for law enforcement supervisors / Vincent Faggiano, John McNall. -- 2nd ed.
      p. cm.
   Includes bibliographical references and index.
   ISBN 978-1-4398-7454-7 (hardcover : alk. paper)
   1. Organizational effectiveness. 2. Risk management. 3. Management. I. McNall, John. II. Title.

HD58.9.F334 2012
363.2'3--dc23   2011039386

Visit the Taylor & Francis Web site at
http://www.taylorandfrancis.com

and the CRC Press Web site at
http://www.crcpress.com

This book is dedicated with respect and admiration to the memory of

Tom Gillespie

Brother, Partner, Teacher, Friend

May your voice continue to be heard through these pages

Table of Contents

Preface

More than a dozen years ago I participated in a presentation and training program on emergency management by Vincent Faggiano, John McNall, and the late Thomas Gillespie. By that point in my career, I had been a patrol officer, police academy administrator, and chief of police and thought that I had a decent understanding of what to do, how to do it, and when to do it. Yet, what I heard that day changed my very understanding of managing critical incidents, and shifted my thinking on how we operationalize our efforts to save lives, protect property, and restore normalcy.

The authors have gone to great lengths to ensure that their evidence-based, tested and proven methodologies for managing critical incidents are applicable across demographics. Police, fire, EMS, elected officials, federal agencies, municipalities, state agencies, universities, marine, air and rail organizations, First Nations, and the private sector will each find the concepts and tactical directions in this book applicable to their environments. This is possible because the authors understand the common characteristics across critical incidents, and have identified a series of tasks to address the shared challenges that arise. Many emergency management texts describe the larger concepts with little practical direction for tactical leadership and functional management. This book provides time-tested methodologies to ensure that emergencies and critical incidents are prevented (when possible), contained, managed, and resolved efficiently and effectively. Their 7 Critical Tasks© have become the industry standard for emergency management and response. Having managed just about every genre of critical incident, and no matter the crisis, what I learned from them became seminal in my leadership and management skills toolbox. They teach more than response strategies. They teach prevention and mitigation, and the tactical leadership and functional management they embrace is relevant in planning and mitigation.

Lastly, I have long admired the attention that Vinny, John, and Tom pay to the psychological impact critical incident management has on the first responders and executive decision makers. They have incorporated the tenets of mental health into their writing and counsel, and do so in such a way that makes it acceptable and easy to discuss. In this book, you'll learn why this is so important and how to take care of those who take care of others; doing so is at the very core of effective crisis response, management, and mitigation.

Ultimately, beyond the teachings and experience within and combined with good training, what you will get from this book is the confidence to manage whatever crisis lands on your doorstep. Learn well these lessons and you are guaranteed to make the difference you seek.

Dr. Gary J. Margolis
Managing Partner, Margolis, Healy & Associates, LLC
Research Associate Professor, University of Vermont
Chief of Police (ret.)

Introduction

The forerunner to this book was geared toward law enforcement responders. There are issues unique to police responses that simply do not apply to others, and we have retained and updated this information.

A critical component in major incidents is integrating with other agencies, disciplines, and levels of the response. Communication, cooperation, and a clear understanding of roles from the Scene Command Post through the Emergency Operations Center (EOC) to the Executive Policy Group is one of the driving forces behind this book.

The other need we have identified in 30+ years of training and field experience is that "nontraditional" organizations (campuses, businesses, utilities, school districts, etc.) have been largely left out of the discussion. If you are a member of a nontraditional organization, this text will serve as a guidepost to organizing your emergency management structure and response strategies.

Pop quiz time:

- It's been a quiet night; you're heading back to the station to close out when you receive a call on a motor vehicle accident. As the first-arriving police officer, firefighter, or emergency medical technician (EMT), you know you are the Incident Commander. With no other information available, it seems routine. You roll up on scene only to find a school bus full of children overturned and wrapped around a ruptured tanker truck.
- As president of your organization, you are often working well after others have left. Suddenly you are shaken by what sounds like an explosion and look out to see smoke pouring out a broken window of one of your buildings where your facilities personnel and some contractors have been working.
- As a shift supervisor for buildings and grounds, you are checking building access after the record snowfall. Just as you are entering the building, you hear a loud crashing noise and discover that the roof of the activities room has collapsed, trapping multiple individuals who were in the room.
- As the director of Human Resources, you have just returned to your office from lunch. Suddenly you hear what sounds like gunshots coming from inside your building.

For each of these scenarios:

1. Where do you go?
2. What immediate actions do you take?
3. What resources will you need?
4. What will be your role: in the next few minutes, in the hours to come, days from now?

Critical incidents usually happen when you least expect them. But they needn't happen when you're least prepared.

That's where this book comes in. It gives traditional first responders a workable game plan for handling the unexpected. Since 1990, the authors have provided critical incident management instruction to tens of thousands of responders and supervisors of all types throughout North America. Time and time again, students have praised the practical information provided in these programs for its simplicity and effectiveness.

All critical incidents share some common characteristics. The basic premise of this book is that if critical incidents have common characteristics, then we can establish a common set of response strategies to address these characteristics. There are certain steps or tasks you can always apply at the onset of a critical incident to quickly and effectively manage the scene. Of course the incident elements may vary from scene to scene, but the core tasks remain the same regardless of the event you face.

The second premise is that incidents go through predictable phases. Recognizing those phases and their characteristics, as well as knowing your strategies, goals, and outcomes, will allow you to act quickly and effectively.

Training others in your organization regarding both the common issues and the incident phases will reduce confusion and end up saving lives and property.

While no book can replace training and experience, the information provided here will give you a major head start on understanding basic management tasks. These guidelines lead you through every aspect of a critical incident: from taking initial scene command, to managing resources, to resolution, and finally to recovery and mitigation from the incident.

Who Should Read This Book?

A basic premise of the Incident Command System (ICS) is that the first person on-scene is the Incident Commander until properly relieved. This person may well be a traditional responder, such as a police officer, firefighter, or EMT, or may be a nontraditional responder. If you are first on-scene at a critical incident, *you* are the Incident Commander. Hopefully, if you are not fully trained, you will soon be relieved by a person with more experience and expertise. The actions taken or not taken in the first few minutes of an incident may well determine the length and severity of an incident. You will find we constantly refer back to this premise.

Increasingly we are training nonpublic safety personnel from private and public organizations who want to know their role in an emergency. The individuals who are part of the Incident Management Team are eager to know where they fit into the organization's "emergency concept of operations" or Emergency Operations Plan (EOP). Dozens of relevant questions are articulated at the beginning of each session, such as: Where do I report? What do I do when I get there? Who's in charge? How do I interact with responding emergency personnel?

Once again, this updated text has been designed to retain the value to law enforcement while expanding these concepts to other individuals who find themselves in a new role as responders and members of a private or public organization's Incident Management Team.

As you will discover, we will cover initial response, scene management, executive management, and recovery and mitigation. Whether you are in the president's office, facilities, information technology, health, or public safety, your role will become clear.

Whether you have years in your position or are new to this role, this information will improve your ability and confidence to manage any type of major incident.

Experienced responders will recognize many of the book's recommendations as part of their current management style, but they will gain valuable information from our examination of various types of critical incidents. These individuals have the opportunity to learn from the experiences—both good and bad—of thousands of responders who have managed critical events.

As well as applying to all incident types, the tasks and techniques discussed in this book apply to all types of agencies. Although a large urban police force, federal agency, or other organization will have numerous resources available for prompt response, it is the proper *management* of these resources that is crucial to incident stabilization. The only difference for the smaller organization is that a first responder may have to wait a few minutes longer for support. You will quickly find that when it comes to critical incident response, the actions you must initiate are similar for all sizes and types of agencies and organizations.

Appropriate Initial Response

The initial actions taken by a first responder determine whether a critical incident is allowed to accelerate out of control or is quickly stabilized. Law enforcement officers are usually first to the scene in the vast majority of critical incidents. You will read this repeatedly: It's up to *you* to make decisions and take early, appropriate action.

Interestingly enough, this also applies to "first-first responders," which is a term coined by the 9/11 Commission. First-first responders are those individuals who are already at ground zero when an event occurs and must respond out of necessity.

In most cases you will not know that you are responding to a major incident until you arrive on-scene. Often critical incidents are not reported as such. A seemingly routine call can quickly escalate into a major critical event. For example:

- One of the first calls received in the 1999 Columbine High School tragedy in Littleton, Colorado, was to check for a student down in the parking lot.
- In the 1993 bombing of the World Trade Center, the initial emergency call came in as a transformer fire.
- The taking of 28 hostages at Fairfield University in Connecticut involving a person with purported explosives strapped to his body was initially reported as "book bags being thrown from a third-story window."
- The initial call at Virginia Tech was to "check for a student who has fallen out of bed."

The point is not so much to "always expect the unexpected" but to simply be prepared to implement a strong response plan if called upon.

The following chapters will examine various types of critical incidents. If you implement the "game plan" outlined in this book, you will improve your ability to limit the growth of those incidents, stabilize your scenes, resolve incidents, and recover more quickly.

NIMS and ICS: Beyond the Initial Response

Let's look at the big picture for a moment. The National Incident Management System (NIMS) is a federally mandated program of incident response, management, training, and publications. NIMS emanates from the National Response Plan and represents a national policy for critical incident response and management. Its recommendations and guidelines provide a framework for coordinating federal, state, local, and, in many cases, privately held resources.

A primary component of NIMS (and of any critical incident response) is the ICS. This book is *not* a theoretical discussion of NIMS and ICS. Although you will read about ICS components and implementation, it will be in a real-world context: you pulling up on the scene of a school bus/tanker truck accident with limited resources at 0800 on a foggy and rainy morning, or in any of the other scenarios listed in the pop quiz in the beginning of this chapter.

But make no mistake: Whether you are a patrol officer, supervisor, or the only adult representing your organization, if you are the first on-scene at an incident, *you are in command*. Somebody has to be. It will be you or nobody until a supervisor or other trained professional can relieve you.

This book will introduce you to the primary functional areas of NIMS and some of the requirements incumbent on you as a critical incident commander. Critical incident management, and particularly crisis phase management, is the working end of the whole NIMS/ICS structure—the point of the spear, if you will. It's where these high-level concepts meet the barricaded terrorist and the ruptured tanker car. It's where *you* make the whole system work.

Through NIMS, we will also explore a *commonsense* concept of operations for your organization. If you do not have an EOP that describes how you organize and communicate during and after a crisis, then your operations are at risk. More importantly, if that EOP is simply "holding down a shelf" and is not understood by all employees, then you really don't have a plan.

All members of the organization should be able to describe how they would initially handle and report an incident of any type and then describe where they would report and what they would do when they got there.

Where do you fit into the plan? Would you go to the command post near the scene or the EOC at a predesignated location? Or are you a part of the Executive Policy Group? Can you describe the basic function of each of these levels of management?

Most institutions, agencies, and authorities still rely on "round table management," using the committee approach for their normal everyday business process. As you will discover, the round or conference table is the enemy of effective emergency management. NIMS/ICS brings a very sensible "functional" approach to management where everyone has a very clear mission to perform. Breaking the committee mentality during crisis management is essential.

The only way individuals will understand this and respond appropriately is if they have been trained, exercised, and have appropriate guides and checklists to work with.

The Importance of Training

This book will focus on the *stages* of critical incident supervision and management: **prevention, preparedness, response**, and **recovery** and **mitigation**.

It will further define the *three phases* of the response stage: **crisis phase, scene management phase**, and the **executive management phase**. You'll learn how to assess an event and to order and deploy resources effectively.

Hopefully your organization has an NIMS-compliant "operational plan" as well as "procedural plans" for specific events already in place. But appropriate response is more than just planning:

> A plan is only as good as the training that backs it up! You must educate yourself and your organization to implement an appropriate critical incident response.

We can give you an overview of the issues you will face and the thought processes you must go through, but a book is no substitute for training, and training is no substitute for experience. Would you attempt an armed SWAT assault after reading one book on the subject? Of course not. You must practice the tasks and techniques outlined in this book on a regular basis.

Most responding officers relate that they "flash back" on similar incidents they've handled to guide their actions. The same is true for all of us; under stress we will go back to our closest similar experience and start to respond in a similar fashion. But what if that previous response was completely wrong or you've never managed a critical incident? You have only your training to rely on. Get it if you can. And make sure it's as realistic as possible.

Our classroom training, for example, involves complex scenarios played out on a large Model City Simulator™. Each participant actually manages an incident on the simulator, giving orders, making requests for resources, and so on. Many of our students have told us that the incidents they managed on the model city (in front of their peers) were identical to real-life critical events with which they've been involved. It's only through training and experience that a plan can be expected to actually work in the field.

What You'll Find Inside

Over the next several chapters, you'll be introduced to a unique perspective on critical incident management. Much of it is common sense, but other recommendations are a departure from traditional response strategies. If you are like thousands of others, you will find the information thought provoking and easy to implement. We pride ourselves on making the complex easy to understand, and we hope that by the end of this read we will have accomplished this for you.

- You are not alone. The first chapter discusses many of the issues identified by our students over the years as having impacted their responses. Subsequently, each concern is addressed with problem-solving techniques and winning attitudes.

- You will read about the phases of a critical incident response and the tasks you must implement to stabilize the scene. And because all responders are storytellers, you'll find real-life incidents throughout the book to reinforce concepts.
- What makes a good tactical leader? You'll learn the leadership style and techniques required to manage a critical incident successfully in the early crisis phase.
- There are tasks you must always do and do quickly. These Seven Critical Tasks™ serve as your game plan for managing any type of critical incident.
- From the crisis phase we move to managing the scene and resolving the incident. We will introduce you to NIMS and describe in some detail the simplicity, flexibility, and importance of the ICS.
- We all know the world is full of dangerous chemicals that can seriously injure or kill you and the public through accidental or deliberate release. Chapter 7 provides need-to-know information about responding to hazardous materials and weapons of mass destruction incidents.
- Our number one priority, whether in the classroom or in writing this book, is to save lives—the lives of those who find themselves in the middle of a critical incident or those who are responding to the incident. In order to do so effectively, we must examine the actions during the incident and also subsequent to the incident. Unfortunately, all too often lives are lost long after an incident has been resolved due to critical incident stress issues that go unaddressed or ignored. Therefore this book also examines critical incident stress management. If not identified and handled properly, acute or cumulative stress can have devastating effects on responders.
- Our experience working with organizations from both the training and emergency planning perspective is that there is a natural tendency at all levels to focus on the scene, much like a moth is drawn to the flame. We will advocate strongly that your concept of operations needs to separately take into account the continuity of business and delivery of products or services in the face of a crisis.
- This tendency to be drawn to the "scene" extends to the level of elected official, CEO, and/or the office of the President. Executives at this level have a much more valuable role to play away from the scene in terms of setting policy and direction for the response and recovery efforts.

As you can see, we'll be covering a lot of information. Critical incident response is a complex topic. You, as the response leader, are under pressure from all sides and frequently under intense public and professional scrutiny to take decisive action. You get only one chance to do the job right.

Throughout this book we reference incidents that you may have read about or perhaps even been involved in. Understand that it is never our intent to criticize or critique agency responses. We perform analyses based exclusively on official reports and firsthand interviews of individuals who were involved. This is how the emergency management community continually learns from its experience.

We have tremendous respect for first responders who take charge of critical incidents as they set the table for the rest of what follows. We've all had to make tough and immediate decisions with little information and high risk. Our passion for this topic is fueled by the belief that the information contained in this book will save lives—those of first responders and those of citizens. There is no more important purpose.

Vincent F. Faggiano
Thomas T. Gillespie
John W. McNall

About the Authors

Vincent F. Faggiano retired from the Rochester Police Department (RPD) after 32 years of service. As the patrol division commander, he was directly responsible for the management of seven patrol sections and over 450 sworn patrol officers. During his tenure with the department, he held numerous command positions in the patrol, investigations, and administrative divisions of the RPD, including the command of the Monroe County Drug Task Force, a multiagency countywide enforcement unit.

Vince was responsible for the initial development of the BowMac Critical Incident Response training courses, for both first responders and the Command Post programs. He has delivered numerous critical incident programs to thousands of law enforcement personnel, firefighters, emergency medical technicians, and elected and appointed officials, both in the United States and abroad. He was selected by the U.S. Department of Justice to deliver critical incident management courses to the Panamanian National Police Force and members of the presidential cabinet shortly after Operation Just Cause reinstated a democratic government in Panama. The initial response guidelines, which he is responsible for developing, have been formally adopted and are currently being trained in seven states: Connecticut, Florida, Illinois, Massachusetts, New Mexico, New York, and Wisconsin. The unified command program he co-developed has been delivered throughout the United States and Canada. He has been a featured speaker at numerous seminars throughout North America.

During his career, he responded to and was directly responsible for managing the response to numerous critical incidents. His former department, other governmental agencies, and community groups have officially recognized him for his actions at these events, which included the awarding of the Medal of Valor for his lifesaving actions at the scene of a barricaded gunman/hostage police-shooting incident.

Vince is the founder and lead singer of the official New York State D.A.R.E. band, Lightning. He has composed several songs including "Just Say No," an anti-drug abuse song, and "Do the Right Thing," the theme song for the national program of the same name.

He has authored articles in the critical incident genre. He holds a bachelor's degree in organizational management from Roberts Wesleyan College.

John W. McNall has dedicated 40+ years to education, service, training, and consulting in the public safety field. He currently serves as the president of BowMac Educational Services, Inc., and BowMac Software, Inc. BowMac Educational Services, Inc., is a nationally recognized provider of high-quality public safety training. BowMac Software, Inc., is a market leader in providing Web-based emergency management solutions to private and public organizations to assist them in their NIMS compliance.

After graduating from the University of Dayton with a degree in criminal justice, he started his career in Detroit, graduating from the Detroit Police Academy in 1968. In 1975, Mr. McNall was offered the position of associate director at the Regional Criminal Justice Training Center in Rochester, New York, where he served until 1984. He assisted in the founding and growth of this nationally recognized training agency, supervising the day-to-day operations of the Police Academy's staff.

In December 1984, Mr. McNall left the Training Center to pursue a full-time career with BowMac Educational Services, Inc. The overriding philosophy of its training programs is to provide the participants with reality-based training, utilizing working professionals and hands-on exercises designed to improve performance. Mr. McNall has conducted executive training and other sessions in major cities such as New York, Boston, Philadelphia, and Chicago, as well in the smallest communities in New York, Pennsylvania, Colorado, and New Mexico. BowMac was selected to conduct its unique critical incident management training in Panama and other Central American countries by the U.S. Justice Department. BowMac currently has five simulation-based command and initial response courses certified by the Department of Homeland Security, making them eligible for grant funding.

In 1998, BOWMAC Software, Inc., was created to market a unique software product in emergency management for school districts. This effort has been expanded to include comprehensive Web-based planning tools for municipalities, campuses, public authorities, businesses, and utilities. These software tools are designed to allow easy compliance with the NIMS and to support the "concept of operations" presented in this book.

Mr. McNall also served as executive director of the International Organization of Youth Courts (IOYC) from 1989 to 1992. The IOYC is a not-for-profit organization whose mission is to promote and assist in establishing youth courts in communities across the nation. Youth courts are peer courts operated by youth that, with training and adult advisement, hear and adjudicate actual cases involving other youth.

Notably, he presented to and was a member of the FBI's National Symposium on School Violence, and consulted to the IACP Private Sector Committee on School Safety and the National School Safety Center's Curricula Committee on School Resource Officer training.

Thomas T. Gillespie (deceased) began his law enforcement career in Detroit, Michigan in 1970 and worked as a patrol officer and as a sergeant-field supervisor. During 1971–1974 Tom served in the US Army as a military police officer and subsequently with the Army's Criminal Investigation Division. Tom returned to Detroit after his military service and in 1979 was selected to serve as the Chief of Police for the City of Las Vegas (New Mexico) Police Department. In 1984 he became the Director of the New Mexico Law Enforcement Academy as well as the Director of the New Mexico Department of Public Safety's Training and Recruiting Division. Tom then served as the Director of the State of New Mexico Attorney General's Investigative Division.

In 1987 Tom began offering training and consulting services as the owner of Criminal Justice Training & Consulting Services (CJTC). Through CJTC, Tom conducted agency management audits, policy and procedure development, management of the investigative function programs, entry level and promotional process, strategic and project planning seminars, and executive and supervisory training programs. Tom provided training for the US Department of Justice and the US Department of State, conducting programs in several countries in Central and South America.

Tom delivered more than 400 critical incident training programs in 36 states, training over 8,000 law enforcement, fire, and EMS personnel in initial response and command post operations. These programs were delivered in partnership with BowMac Educational Services, Inc. of Honeoye Falls, New York.

Tom also served as an expert witness in deadly physical force cases and was qualified as a law enforcement expert in both state and federal court. He was retained in over 300 civil and criminal actions. Tom is also the co-author of *Police Use of Force: A Line Officer's Guide.*

About the Company

BowMac.com represents two companies, **BowMac Educational Services, Inc.** (established 1980) and **BowMac Software, Inc.** (established 1998), which are dedicated to increased public safety on a national basis. We are comprised of a group of individuals, each with between 20 and 40+ years of policing, training, and management experience in public safety.

BowMac Educational Services, Inc., delivers high-quality training programs to communities in three main areas: critical incident management, community policing, and interviewing and investigative strategies.

BowMac Educational Services, Inc., has five simulation-based training courses certified by the Homeland Security Department's Office of Domestic Preparedness, rendering them eligible for federal and state terrorism funding. These courses can be found in the State-Sponsored Course Catalog at https://www.firstrespondertraining.gov/odp%5Fwebforms/, reference numbers NM-001 RESP through NM-005 RESP.

We have provided major "turnkey systems" of our simulation-based critical incident management command post and initial response courses to the states of New Mexico, Connecticut, Wisconsin, Illinois, and Massachusetts, as well as to the Metro Dade and Savannah Police Departments. BowMac just completed a highly successful three-year project with the International Association of Campus Law Enforcement Administrators (IACLEA), which provided command post training to hundreds of campuses across the United States. We conducted numerous courses with Panamanian government officials and national police through the U.S. Justice Department post Noriega. Thousands of police, fire, and emergency medical service (EMS) command personnel from hundreds of agencies across the country have benefited from this training. Our focus has always been to build useable skills through innovative simulation and role-play exercises, rather than classroom lecture.

BowMac Software, Inc., initially in collaboration with the National League of Cities Risk Information Sharing Consortium, developed an automated, online source for community emergency planning. Our Web-based tools are designed to allow the customer to take control of the planning process absent costly consultants. These products represent years of training and consulting with clients in various organizations to make their environments safer. Our REDI for Emergencies™ planning tools have six modules designed to assist municipalities, school districts, colleges, universities, and businesses in their National Incident Management System (NIMS) compliance.

As both of our companies grow and evolve, we find a natural interweaving of services emerging. Our software customers are seeking training that will make their plans more effective, and our training customers realize that the skills and techniques taught need to be reflected in their planning. Too long have police trained with police, fire with fire, EMS with EMS, and so on, setting up natural barriers to effectiveness when they are called upon to work, plan, and act together. *At the very core of our philosophy is the fundamental belief that integration of disciplines in the planning and training process is what brings about rapid and lasting change.*

This book represents the philosophy and passion that we bring to our other endeavors.

For additional information on our critical management courses and/or REDI for Emergencies™ software, see our Web site at www.bowmac.com and contact us by either e-mailing johnmcnall@bowmac.com or calling BowMac at 585-624-9500.

The Nature of
Critical Incidents

1

Objectives

After completing this chapter, you should be able to:

- Recall the most common characteristics of critical incident response.
- Describe the three universal criteria for agency response plans.
- Recognize the impact of politics on agency response.
- Differentiate between controllable and uncontrollable incident factors.

So what is a critical incident? This book uses a broad definition that covers every conceivable type of occurrence:

> A critical incident is an extraordinary event that places lives and property in danger and requires the commitment and coordination of numerous resources to bring about a successful conclusion.

Within the definition lies the greatest obstacle to success. As emergency responders, we train to respond to a scene, resolve it, and return to service. The majority of calls for service are handled in this manner. However, when the first responders are not capable of resolving the scene and it will require numerous resources, sometimes from multiple agencies, problems arise. It is the coordination of these resources and their integrated response that are key to success.

You can probably recall a few responses that fit this definition. It is deliberately inclusive. Within the critical incident category, there are several types of events that you could be called upon to manage. A short list includes the following:

- **Terrorist Activities (Weapons of Mass Destruction):** Weapons of mass destruction can range from biological (think anthrax or small-pox) and chemical to nuclear, radiological, and explosive.
- **Natural Disasters:** In the event of earthquake, hurricane, tornado, flood, ice storm, or blizzard, the problems are often magnified due to the size of the incident. A different type of natural disaster may involve health issues. Both the SARS incident in Toronto, Canada,

and a MRSA, influenza, or meningitis outbreak are natural disasters, which can impact entire communities.

- **Transportation Accidents:** These can range from mass-casualty bus accidents and train derailments to airplane crashes and shipping mishaps. Each classification has its own hazards. Additionally, any transportation accident has the potential to involve hazardous materials. Basically any transportation accident that fits the definition of requiring large numbers of resources from numerous agencies to resolve would qualify as a critical incident.
- **Criminal Activities:** This broad category can include bombings, arsons, active shooters, barricaded gunmen, and hostage situations.
- **Fires/Hazardous Materials Incidents:** Hazardous-chemical spills and explosions, industrial fires, high-rise fires, and multiple-dwelling fires can quickly become the most dangerous events of all. In the vast majority of HazMat situations, a police officer is first on-scene.

Incident Types

Incidents may be typed on the following five levels of complexity in order to make decisions about resource requirements:

Type 5

- The incident can be handled with one or two single resources with up to six personnel.
- Command staff and general staff positions (other than the Incident Commander) are not activated.
- No written Incident Action Plan (IAP) is required.
- The incident is contained within the first operational period and often within an hour to a few hours after resources arrive on scene. Examples include a vehicle fire, an injured person, or a police traffic stop.

Type 4

- Command staff and general staff functions are activated, only if needed.
- Several resources are required to mitigate the incident.
- The incident is usually limited to one operational period in the control phase.
- The agency administrator may have briefings and ensure that the complexity analysis and delegation of authority is updated.

- No IAP is required, but a documented operational briefing will be completed for all incoming resources.
- The role of the agency administrator includes operational plans with objectives and priorities.

Type 3

- When capabilities exceed initial attack, the appropriate ICS positions should be added to match the complexity of the incident. Some or all of the command staff and general staff positions may be activated, as well as division/group supervisor- and/or unit leader-level positions.
- A Type 3 incident management team (IMT) or incident command organization manages initial action incidents with a significant number of resources, an extended attack incident until containment/control is achieved, or an expanding incident until transition to a Type 1 or 2 team.
- The incident may extend into multiple operational periods.
- A written IAP may be required for each operational period.

Type 2

- This type of incident extends beyond the capabilities for local control and is expected to go into multiple operational periods. A Type 2 incident may require the response of resources out of area, including regional and/or national resources, to effectively manage the operations, command, and general staffing.
- Most or all of the command staff and general staff positions are filled.
- A written IAP is required for each operational period.
- Many of the functional units are needed and staffed.
- Operations personnel normally do not exceed 200 per operational period, and total incident personnel do not exceed 500 (guidelines only).
- The agency administrator is responsible for the incident complexity analysis, agency administrator briefings, and the written delegation of authority.

Type 1

- This type of incident is the most complex, requiring national resources to safely and effectively manage and operate.
- All command staff and general staff positions are activated.
- Operations personnel often exceed 500 per operational period, and total personnel will usually exceed 1000.
- Branches need to be established.
- The agency administrator will have briefings and ensure that the complexity analysis and delegation of authority are updated.

- Use of resource advisors at the incident base is recommended.
- There is a high impact on the local jurisdiction, requiring additional staff for office, administrative and support functions.

The ability to effectively categorize incidents will allow a clear understanding of the size, scope, and seriousness of an incident, especially when ordering assets from other levels of government. Although an incident may not be able to be categorized specifically during its inception, this becomes critically important in the after-action reporting phase.

That's a wide range of incident types, but they have more in common than most people would imagine.

Common Characteristics

As we mentioned in the Introduction, we have had the opportunity to share the management strategies discussed in this book since the mid-1980s with tens of thousands of emergency responders. Participants have included:

- Law enforcement personnel, from patrol officers to police chiefs
- Fire service personnel, from firefighter lieutenants to chiefs
- Emergency medical technicians and supervisors
- State, local, and federal authorities
- Emergency management personnel
- Elected officials
- K–12 officials
- Campus personnel including faculty, staff, administrators, and executive-level management

In one classroom exercise, students identify common issues that have caused them problems in managing critical incidents, especially in the crisis phase. The similarities among the lists from each session are truly amazing. Geography doesn't matter. Agency representatives from every corner of the United States and beyond identify the same issues. Think the size of your organization makes a difference? Similar issues apply regardless of whether respondents work in small, midsize, or large departments—rural or urban, for that matter. They are the tasks that, if accomplished well, usually result in an excellent response, but they are also the issues that can be problematic at a scene—the issues raised in the after-action and media reports of the incident.

Most interestingly, responses are generally the same regardless of the *specific nature* of the incident. It does not matter what type of incident you face. The issues described in this chapter apply equally to all, be they barricaded gunmen, hazardous-material spills, or mass-casualty incidents.

Common issues fall into the following broad categories:

- Communications
- Who's in charge?
- Resources and resource coordination
- Intelligence gathering and problem assessment
- Crowd and traffic control (perimeters)
- Environmental issues
- Planning and training
- The media

Politics

As you read through these, think of an incident you have responded to. Try to recall if any or all of the identified issues had an impact—positive or negative—on your response.

Communications

Communications encompasses so many areas that responders almost always identify it as the number one issue that impacts their incident response. Specifically, concerns usually break out into technical, personal, and organizational communication.

Line officers and supervisors usually identify communications concerns in terms of equipment or technical issues such as:

- Poor radio equipment
- Lack of quality power sources (i.e., batteries dying in the field)
- Lack of a common radio frequency that can be shared by all responders. The term "interoperable communications" has become a mainstay of grant writers subsequent to the events of September 11, 2001. The need to be able to communicate not only between local responders but with state and federal assets has become an issue that almost all communication units have either addressed or are in the process of doing so.
- Garbled or unreadable transmissions from the scene due to poor reception or transmission (weak signals and dead spots)

Obviously, any or all of the these equipment issues can have a direct effect on problem assessment and deployment of personnel to stabilize the scene. What can you do to limit technical communications problems on-scene? Prepare. Plan. Procure!

Personal communication issues, such as the ability to communicate effectively in spite of the high-stress conditions at the scene, are also identified as key. Can you organize your thoughts and give critical orders under pressure? We will discuss leadership issues, including tactical communication, later under "Who's in Charge?" and in Chapter 4.

Administrative personnel tend to identify organizational communication issues that go beyond technical considerations. These issues can have as great or greater impact at a scene. These concerns include:

- Departmental sharing of expectations with responders
- Communication of response plans to those responsible for implementing the plans
- Communication with other responding agencies—other law enforcement, fire, EMS, utility agencies, and so forth
- Use of 10-codes

All of the areas just listed directly impact the effectiveness of the first-responding units. Do you know what your organization expects of you in a crisis? Do you know what plans are available? Can your organization effectively coordinate with fire and EMS services? Most of these issues touch on training, which we will address shortly.

It is easy to see why such a broad area as communications can have the single greatest impact on the initial response to a critical incident. Doubtless, you can recall many instances in which communications (both good and bad) affected your response.

Who's in Charge?

The dilemma of command turns up in every problem assessment exercise. This is cited as a major issue at *every* scene—even in single-agency responses! The standard answer to the question "Who's in charge?" is a simple one: "You are!" Clarity of command—to those on-scene and those involved off-site, such as dispatchers—is imperative to prevent confusion and the potentially tragic results that confusion can cause.

Multiple-agency and *multidisciplinary* (police, fire, public works, and EMS) responses add a whole new spin to the command issue. Of course, the question of a scene's overall management and the assumption of command can be complex. In Chapter 6 we will discuss the implementation of a unified command structure as outlined in the national ICS model. For response to an incident in the crisis phase, however, use a much simpler approach: *Each discipline is in charge of and responsible for its own particular area of expertise.*

Simply put, the folks with the hoses are responsible for fire suppression. The folks with the ambulances and medical equipment are responsible for treatment and victim transport. Law enforcement is responsible for traffic and crowd control, site security, and police-related activities. Public health officials will assume responsibility for health issues, and so on.

Focus on your tasks. Don't make command more complicated than it has to be.

Resources and Resource Coordination

Not surprisingly, when participants talk about resources as a problem, what they usually mean is that they *lack* resources. Such a lack may well hamper the initial management of a spontaneous critical incident. Expect your initial response to be less than what you need or request.

An unusual characteristic of critical incidents, however, is that the lack of resources in the crisis phase of an incident is usually offset by an *enormous* resource response in a very short period of time. This applies whether you are in an urban or a rural setting. Your ability to shift gears from directing an understaffed response to directing a large response is an essential part of effective critical incident management.

When we do not coordinate resources in a major response efficiently, our management appears unorganized, disjointed, and confused. The arrival of resources requires us to bring order to chaos. The ICS discussion later will provide a time-tested method to accomplish this feat. Also, one of the Seven Critical Tasks™ is devoted to establishing a staging area for responding resources. This is a central location where resources respond and wait to be assigned duties by the scene supervisor.

Intelligence Gathering and Problem Assessment

There are questions that you need answered at any incident scene:

- What happened?
- What am I dealing with?
- What are the dangers?
- What can impact and worsen this scene?
- What needs to be done to stabilize and ultimately resolve this incident?

The decisions you make depend on the availability and quality of the answers to these questions. And in turn, your ability to *get* answers, and the *quality* of those answers, is affected by the panic and confusion that characterize the crisis phase of an incident. Add to that the urgency to take action during the crisis phase, and intelligence gathering may become your most difficult task.

We will discuss the need for good problem assessment skills on the part of the first-responding crisis manager in the following chapters. Poor problem assessment or intelligence gathering will result in poor decision making and may inflame a situation rather than stabilize or resolve it.

The better your intelligence, of course, the more informed and appropriate your decisions will be.

Crowd and Traffic Control (Perimeters)

We must limit access to a scene and prevent gridlock. It is our responsibility to prevent unwitting individuals from endangering themselves by entering areas that may pose a threat to their safety. We must also provide a controlled area that allows emergency workers to perform their duties unimpeded by bystanders or crowds.

The term "crowd" applies to swarms of emergency responders as well as civilians. A scene gridlocked by an overresponse of emergency workers is just as inaccessible as a scene gridlocked by a mob of civilians. It is our responsibility to provide both access and egress for a scene. Exerting crowd and traffic control by establishing perimeters is without question one of the primary law enforcement tasks at any emergency scene.

Environment

This one may seem pretty obvious, but it needs to be mentioned. As you will see shortly, critical incidents are made up of controllable and noncontrollable factors. Weather and the area in which you encounter an incident are definitely uncontrollable. However, since most of our responses are outdoors, we must all contend with our environments!

You may work in rain, fog, snow, blazing heat, or dust storms. You may be on the plains or a cliff, in the desert or a swampland. Regardless, you must manage *around* the environmental conditions in your jurisdiction. Take into account the impact weather and topography may have on your planning and your resource requirements, such as communications and shelter. At a minimum, for example, you must protect your command post from the elements. It's hard to make calm, informed decisions while shielding your face from driving sleet.

Planning and Training

The planning an agency does to organize and prepare for critical incidents is a key first step to having a viable response strategy. Although planning is critical, it is effective only if responders understand and can implement those plans. If they don't, you're left with notebooks upon notebooks filled with orders and procedures holding a shelf down.

Agencies often spend hundreds of hours developing specific plans for specific incidents. It is not unusual for an agency to have procedural plans for a barricaded gunman plan, a hostage plan, a hazardous-material spill plan, an airplane crash response plan, a natural disaster response plan, and so on. This information is valuable when we move to incident resolution with an expanded incident command-based team.

Procedural plans are also great for evaluating an agency's response postincident, but may not be accessible by the newly promoted supervisor working alone on the midnight shift. Are your plans fully understood and capable of being implemented?

Plans must be able to make the transition from the tranquility of the administrative offices where they are conceived to the chaos of a critical incident in the field where they are used. Therefore they should be simple, flexible, and clearly understandable by field personnel. Strategies must be tested through training and practical application. The plan we set forth in this text is truly an "all hazards operational approach." That is to say, one that can be applied to any critical incident regardless of its specific nature.

If your organization has an NIMS-compliant operational (organizational) plan in place and everyone knows where they fit into it, then you are well on your way. If not, you will want to carefully evaluate the approach we are presenting throughout this book.

It continues to amaze: We in emergency response take an area with the greatest ramifications—the potential life and death of our responders and the public—and do little or no related training. Then we expect our people to perform well under the most trying conditions imaginable. In the past we failed to train with our counterparts from other disciplines, but we are expected to integrate our tactics and strategies with them in a unified response. This is changing and must continue to do so.

It is imperative that all Emergency Operations Plans meet the following criteria:

- The plan must be simple.
- All responders must understand the plan.
- All responders must practice that plan through scenario training.
- The plan must be NIMS compliant.

The rest of the information in this book, particularly the Seven Critical Tasks™, will provide the fundamental steps you can apply to any situation.

The Media

Reporters are drawn to critical incidents like bears to honey. Traditionally, our profession has not incorporated media representatives into emergency response. The media has therefore been left on their own to gain information and report on events. As a result of their independent actions, there have been occasions when they have been counterproductive to resolving critical incidents. We have all been on or heard of scenes where media coverage was incomplete or inaccurate. At other scenes, members of the media have been an intrusive presence that simply added to the work of responders.

As we will see later, it doesn't have to be this way. There have been numerous occasions in which the media have been well informed and incorporated into emergency response plans. "Amber alerts" are a good example.

Politics

Many consider politics too "sensitive" for official discussion in a classroom or response book. We feel politics is a topic too important *not* to be discussed. It is something that field personnel feel they should not have to consider, yet it frequently dominates the thoughts of their upper-level command officers.

Simply put, if a field commander has a tactical solution to a problem, but that solution is politically unacceptable, that commander does not have a solution.

You can think of politics as falling into three broad categories:

- Traditional external political influences brought about by elected officials, community members, or others outside our specific agency
- Internal politics within our own agency
- Interagency politics

Each category can impact our response to critical incidents.

Regarding **external politics**, a basic tenet of American civilian policing is that we serve and protect the communities that hire us. Therefore we are answerable to those communities and their elected officials. Such external influences are an undeniable factor of critical incident management. This is especially true during the executive management phase of a critical response, which we will get into in Chapter 3.

As a critical incident supervisor, the overall quality of the relationship between your department and your jurisdictional government is probably not your direct responsibility. Hopefully, it's a good working relationship. If each department member does his or her job professionally, there should be no cause for friction.

Never underestimate the impact of **internal politics**. Agencies in turmoil and/or transition tend to respond differently to critical incidents than stable organizations do. Individuals vying for recognition or "jockeying for position" can bring hidden agendas to the management team. This can manifest itself in a variety of ways, from inappropriate assumption of command to unjustifiable decision making at the scene. Any ulterior motive beyond public and responder safety can greatly jeopardize a response (and lead to external political problems!).

Departments rarely discuss or acknowledge these internal conditions. Instead, gossip grinds through the rumor mill and can have a destructive effect on both moral and confidence.

If these conditions exist within your organization, the top management team must be willing to recognize, acknowledge, and minimize their impact on your agency's response. This responsibility falls *squarely* upon the upper-level command staff. Failure to address the distractions of internal politics can have disastrous effects on both the organization and the community.

And lastly, **interagency politics** have a long and storied history. If you've been around for a while, you've probably seen the effects of tension among local, state, and federal agencies. The issues are too numerous to deal with here, but most problems can be addressed with a few simple techniques:

- **Focus on the scene.** You and your mutual response agencies all want the same thing: a swift and safe resolution. Keep your eye on what's best for incident response.
- **Ignore personality issues.** Don't give in to personal antagonism for someone you find abrasive or with whom you've had difficulties in the past.
- **Recognize competence.** Other agencies may have special competencies to deal with your situation. Give them the benefit of the doubt.

You have your own areas of competence, which may include a more detailed knowledge of an incident scene or participants. Work *with* responders from other agencies. Don't work against them or give them reason to work against you.

It is often said that from tragedy good things may flow. There is now widespread recognition that we need to work cooperatively should our communities come under attack. We have seen firsthand the crumbling of barriers that have existed for years. Organizations that have not traditionally interacted well are now training together and will therefore be better prepared to respond together. We can no longer allow petty difference to compromise the protection of our communities.

Uncontrollable versus Controllable Factors

Needless to say, a critical incident can happen any time, any place, without warning. Incidents accelerate or decelerate based on a variety of uncontrollable and controllable factors. It is your job as a first responder to focus on the aspects *you* can control. Remember, the less time an incident has to develop in the crisis phase, the more likely you are to gain control of the scene.

We all know that elements beyond our control can greatly impact (and in some cases determine) our strategies. You will not be able to change the **uncontrollable factors** listed next, but you can make informed decisions to lessen their impact.

- **Time:** Day or night? In the middle of rush hour, perhaps? If at night, you may need to obtain portable lights to manage the scene effectively.
- **Weather:** Sunny and dry or sleeting, snowing, and foggy. A balmy 70°, a sweltering 102°, or a frigid –5°. The safety and well-being of your officers is *your* responsibility. If it's cold or raining, make sure your personnel have the proper equipment to allow them to do their jobs. If it's 120° on the asphalt, make sure those directing traffic have access to shade, fluids, and frequent relief.
- **Location:** Are you operating in an urban environment or do you find yourself miles from the nearest stoplight? What kinds of terrain are you dealing with? You could be in the flats or looking down at a school bus at the bottom of a 50-foot ravine. Once on-scene, you need to quickly assess obstacles and call for the proper resources to deal with them.
- **Initial Injuries/Death:** Certainly, a large number of injuries or deaths can impact you and your responders. All you can do is try to keep a situation from deteriorating. Your job is to reduce further harm.
- **Weapons:** Concerns include the number of weapons, the caliber, whether they are semi or fully automatic, and whether any heavier ordnance is involved. You may find yourself "outgunned" at a scene. When this happens, your first job is to ensure the safety of your people: Back them off, get them behind proper cover, and then order up appropriate reinforcement.
- **Chemicals:** If you respond to the scene of a HazMat spill, the agents involved could be toxic, poisonous, corrosive, explosive, and so on. The list is depressingly long. You must determine as quickly as possible the type of chemical, and take action to protect your personnel and citizens.

A key theme of this book is that you must focus your energies on **controllable factors**. In the early stages of an incident, these are the elements that can make or break your response. They include the following:

- **Access to the scene:** It's up to you to prevent gridlock caused by the public and a potentially overwhelming emergency response. Make sure *your* personnel have proper access and do not contribute to gridlock. This involves establishing proper perimeters and a staging area.
- **Limiting crowd size:** The task of controlling crowds for their safety is a primary police function. You can expect crowds at any critical incident. You must make sure those crowds do not become unmanageable. This is especially applicable to civil disturbances. While you may not be able to control the size of the crowd before your arrival, you certainly want to limit others from joining in once you establish scene control.
- **Evacuating adjacent areas:** Most critical incidents involve threat to civilians in the immediate area. If evacuation is not an option, you may "shelter-in-place" homes, businesses, and facilities such as schools and hospitals. The sooner you define who might be endangered and protect them from harm, the quicker you will be able to stabilize the scene.
- **Rerouting traffic flow:** You must swiftly ensure the safety of motorists and others in the area. If possible, keep traffic flowing some distance from the scene. Your perimeters must be far enough away from the incident to ensure citizen and responder safety, but close enough so that you can effectively manage citizen and responder movement. In other words, don't establish an outer perimeter that you don't have the resources to control.
- **Ordering additional personnel and equipment:** Try to recognize potential resource needs as soon as possible. Err on the side of caution: If you think you might need additional resources or support from other agencies, get them rolling. Specialists such as HazMat or SWAT (special weapons and tactics) teams usually won't arrive immediately. An early request will reduce their response time to the scene.
- **Where and how you use your personnel:** You must take charge. As the leader, you allocate and position resources as you see fit. Make sure your decisions contribute to the stabilization of the scene. If all of your people are engaged in assisting EMS personnel rescuing injured persons at a mass-casualty incident, you may be neglecting perimeter control and allowing road and foot traffic into what you will come to know as the "hot zone." We call this focusing on "resolution" rather than "stabilization" during the crisis phase of an incident.

- **Establishing communication with personnel:** Unless you are experiencing technical difficulties, it's up to you to maintain communication with all responders on the scene. Make sure they know what you expect from them. The best-laid plan can be quickly compromised by a shot fired in error or a unit simply moving out of position without orders.
- **Your own command presence:** Your ability to take charge and issue clear and concise orders is crucial. The decisions you make and your attitudes dictate events and the response of your subordinates.

Summary

As you've read through this chapter, did you compare the issues raised against your own critical incident experience? If you have, you undoubtedly found many of the issues familiar. Knowing the potential hurdles is the first step to overcoming them. Focus on the factors you can control, and work around those you can't. And remember: You are not alone. *We all face the same issues.*

Review Questions

- Can you recall several of the most common obstacles to critical incident response?
- Can you distinguish between "procedural" plans and "operational" plans?
- Can you differentiate internal, external, and interagency politics?
- Can you explain the difference between controllable and uncontrollable incident factors?

First-First Responders

2

Objectives

After completing this chapter, you should be able to:

- Define and describe a "first-first Responder."
- List and describe the three goals of a first-first responder in the first few minutes of an incident.
- Explain the impact that acting quickly and appropriately can have on an incident.

We've all heard of "first responders," those brave police, fire, and EMS personnel who are first called to critical incident scenes. We have worked with first responders for over 30 years in our training programs. But who are first-first responders? The term "first-first responders" was initially used in the 9/11 Commission Report to describe those individuals outside of the traditional public safety sector who are already at ground zero when an event occurs and must respond out of necessity.

At a critical incident, responses can be driven by self-preservation, previous experience (such as the military, etc.), purposeful training and mental preparation, or fear. Effective first-first responders distinguish themselves from others on-scene who fail to act out of fear, lack of previous experience, or lack of mental preparation. In an incident, you will have the option to act or freeze up. We hope that this book will assist in purposeful preparation. If it does, it will assist in saving lives.

A True Story

"Remember Rick Rescorla"
  U.S. intelligence could learn from his valor and leadership.

By Bill Gertz

Editor's Note: This is an excerpt from Breakdown: How America's Intelligence Failures Led to September 11.

Rick Rescorla began the day as he usually did. He got up at 4:30 a.m., kissed his wife goodbye, and took the 6:10 train to Manhattan. A combat veteran who fought in Vietnam's bloody Ia Drang Valley, Rescorla was at his desk in a corner office of the World Trade Center by 7:30. It was September 11, 2001, and outside the day was clear and bright. Rescorla was on the forty-fourth floor of the South Tower when the first hijacked airliner slammed into its nearby twin. Rescorla sprang into action. Grabbing a bullhorn, he went to work in the same calm fashion that he showed under intense combat fire in Vietnam.

Born Cyril Richard Rescorla in Hayle, Cornwall, England, Rick was vice president for security at Morgan Stanley Dean Witter, one of Wall Street's largest brokerage houses. The company had 3,700 employees in the World Trade Center—2,700 employees in the south tower on floors forty-four through seventy-four and 1,000 employees in Building Five across the plaza. There was no hesitation. He ordered everyone to evacuate the building immediately. A short time after the aircraft hit, an official of the Port Authority of New York and New Jersey, which owned the Trade Center towers, called. Everyone in the building should stay put because there was no danger, the Port Authority man said. Rescorla shot back: "Piss off, you son of a bitch. Everything above where that plane hit is going to collapse, and it's going to take the whole building with it. I'm getting my people the f*** out of here." He recounted the exchange in a telephone call to his longtime friend Dan Hill, then ran off and began helping the evacuation.

As a security professional, it was Rescorla's job to think like a terrorist. In 1990, he saw that the World Trade Center was a likely target for a terrorist attack because it was a symbol of American economic power. He did a security survey of the building and concluded, with Hill's help, that driving a truck bomb into the basement near a key supporting column would bring down the entire complex. On February 26, 1993, that exact scenario almost played out. Islamic terrorists set off a homemade chemical bomb packed inside a rental truck that was parked in the basement in an attempt to make the towers collapse.

Rescorla knew the Islamic terrorists who failed the first time would try again. He thought the terrorists' next attempt would be to fly a plane, possibly filled with chemical or biological weapons, into the towers. He had advised Morgan Stanley executives that the company should move from the Twin Towers to a safer location. But the company's lease went until 2006. The next best thing, Rescorla thought, was to practice evacuation drills. He pressed the company to conduct regular drills even though some employees grumbled and joked about them. Every few months, all 2,700 employees in the South Tower would be marched, with Rescorla at the bullhorn, in an arduous trek down the long winding stairwell of one of the world's highest skyscrapers and out of the building, just for practice. Another 1,000 employees would be evacuated from the Morgan Stanley offices nearby.

On September 11, the evacuation was real. A fireball erupted in the nearby tower, and all of Morgan Stanley's employees were making their way down and out of the other tower. By the time the second hijacked airliner hit the south tower at 9:07 a.m., most of the company's employees were out. But Rescorla's work was not finished. Three employees were missing. Rescorla and two assistants went back to look for them. Rescorla was last seen on the tenth floor of the burning tower. He died when the building collapsed a short time later. But he had saved thousands of lives. Out of 3,700 employees, Morgan

Stanley lost only six, including Rescorla. R. James Woolsey, former director of Central Intelligence, sees Rescorla as the kind of person urgently needed by U.S. intelligence. An iconoclast and strategic thinker who wasn't afraid to buck the system, Rescorla "is an example of somebody who should have probably been at the top of the intelligence community, but wasn't," Woolsey told me. "He's a perfect example of the kind of guy that the Germans say has fingerspitzengefühl—fingertip feel" or intuition, he said. "God, it would have been wonderful if he had been the head of the DO's [the CIA's Directorate of Operations] counterterrorist operations, but at least he saved 3,700 people."

Aside from his military experience, Rescorla, sixty-two, had worked for British intelligence conducting special operations in some dangerous places. And while his specialty was corporate security, intelligence and security are symbiotic. On September 11, they were hopelessly divided.

—Bill Gertz has been defense and national-security reporter for the Washington Times since 1985.

Rick, unlike others at Morgan Stanley, was tasked with "security" as his profession, but it was his exceptional mental preparation that separated him from the other employees and perhaps his peers at other companies. He had a plan, recognized the immediate danger, and took action even in the face of countermanding instructions from "authorities."

First-first responders can of course be anyone in your organization, including yourself. There are some categories of personnel, like facilities and maintenance, coaches, teachers, nonsworn security, and so forth, who may have a higher probability of coming across an incident, but literally it could be anyone from the CEO down. Often in schools, campus settings, and other organizations, high-level administrators and maintenance employees are some of the only people at a facility during off hours and vacation periods, which increases their probability of having to take initial charge of an event.

Increasingly we are training nonpublic safety personnel from private and public organizations who want to know their role in an emergency, individuals who are part of the "incident management team." They are eager to know where they fit into the organization's "concept of operations" or Emergency Operations Plan (EOP). Where do I report? What do I do when I get there? Who's in charge? How do I interact with responding emergency personnel? These and dozens of other relevant questions are articulated at the beginning of each session.

First-first responders will set the table for the traditional first responders from police and fire agencies. That table can be messy and disorganized, slowing down and distracting responders in the critical first few minutes, or it can be efficiently set so as to aid and speed the response efforts. Understanding the dynamics of critical incidents, such as the "common issues," which were presented in the last chapter, and the strategies and goals of initial response by public safety responders will assist in helping you "set the table" efficiently and will ultimately lead to saving lives.

We will explore the role of first-first responders from an individual point of view as well as an organizational perspective. Individuals can apply these skills in any circumstance in or out of the workplace. If you are reading this book because you are involved with crisis management from an organizational point of view, then you need to evaluate the readiness of your workforce in terms of response. If you are just personally concerned about "What can/should I do in a crisis?," then you need to internalize these response strategies and practice some "mental rehearsal" regarding your response in and out of the workplace.

In upcoming chapters, we will also explore in depth the response strategy for formal first responders outlining a detailed list of Seven Critical Tasks™. Even if you are not a formal first responder, you may want to delve into how the "professionals" manage scenes. In this chapter, however, let's walk before we run. We will describe what your commonsense goals should be as a first-first responder if you should find yourself in that situation and what the consequences can be if you fail to act.

Let's revisit the scenarios presented in the pop quiz in the Introduction of the book. Explore each response option for the individuals (and yourself) who found themselves at their own ground zero as we move through the rest of the chapter:

- As president of your organization, you are once again alone in your office long after everyone else has left for the weekend. Suddenly you hear an explosion and see smoke and glass flying from the building next to yours, where outside contractors and your facilities personnel are involved in weekend repairs.
- As a supervisor in the maintenance and grounds crew, the last few days have been exhausting given the record snow fall. The institution has reopened and you are checking the heating system in the physical education complex when you hear a loud crash. You quickly discover that the roof has collapsed from the weight of the snow in one of the large workout rooms, trapping the students and staff that were in the area.
- You are the Director of Human Resources. You're in your office shortly after returning from lunch, and you hear what sounds to you like gunshots in your building.

First of all, think of your initial response in terms of the next 5 to 20 minutes. We will transition your role in these events to the next hours, days, and perhaps even weeks later in the book.

What your goal is in the next few minutes may go counter to your intuition and emotion. We are going to ask you to weigh your options and then think about the consequences of your options, both positive and negative.

As a first-first responder you are already on-scene and involved. Your choice in the ensuing minutes is to be part of an overall solution or part of the problem. Of course, we want to be part of the best possible outcome, which means that we need to be mentally prepared with a commonsense plan.

First and foremost, you need to think about working toward stabilizing and isolating the scene of the event as best you can, ahead of the formal professional response. This means that you need to **assess** the situation in terms of its danger to yourself and others, and *report* your findings to 911 or whatever internal response organization you have on site.

Next, you need to *identify areas that are dangerous* to yourself and others, and take measures to *isolate that area* so as to reduce potential future victims. You will do this utilizing bystanders, yellow tape, your vehicle, barricades, or whatever creative means are at your disposal. Again, your objective here is to reduce future victims by not allowing them into a dangerous area.

But what about the current victims? This is where your strategy may bump into your intuition and emotion. You will often feel that your best course of action is to rush into the heart of a scene so you can find and assist injured or trapped individuals. You are not alone in this feeling. We have spent our careers training law enforcement and other responders not to take independent action in unstable environments.

But why not attempt to locate and save the injured first? Aren't people our first priority? They absolutely are. But as you will learn in other chapters, there will always be a rush to the scene (think of a fight in a hall or other public area or an auto accident; it doesn't take but a minute to attract a crowd). If this crowd is allowed to act on emotion versus a plan, then dozens of new individuals will be introduced to the dangerous area and will become victims as well.

So what actions should the President and the Maintenance Supervisor take? We will save the HR Director's actions for a moment as an active shooter situation has some special considerations that are unique.

Remember, the President was working off hours next to an adjacent building, when she heard an apparent explosion and saw evidence of flying debris and fire.

What is the strategy and what actions should she take?

- First is to *assess* what just occurred and *report* it to 911. "I am _____ and I just observed an explosion in the _____ building located at _____. I know there are numerous contractors and maintenance workers on the site."
- "I will be located outside the building attempting to *prevent any entry* to nonemergency personnel. My cell number is _____."

- Next the President takes up a position at a safe distance from the building and *stops* several individuals who were rushing toward the scene. She tells them 911 was notified and help is on the way. She *directs* them to secure the other sides of the building from a safe distance and to prevent entry by nonemergency personnel.
- Using a cell phone, the president *notifies* the maintenance director and safety director, who are at home.
- Police arrive and start to take over perimeter positions as fire/EMS also begin to arrive. There were nearly 50 people being held in check on various sides of the building within the 6–10 minutes of the formal response.
- A small but secondary explosion and some additional fire are observed at this time.

What was accomplished using this strategy of **assess**, **notify**, and **isolate**? What would have been the consequences of inaction, delayed action, or an emotional response of entering the facility in search of victims?

The President with little or no equipment, only mental preparation, was able to initiate an immediate 911 response and to create an inner perimeter using direct commands to ordinary individuals who wanted to assist, but who needed direction from someone "in charge" during a crisis. The table was set for arriving public safety units to take over and expand the perimeter for safety and effective working space. Having a relatively secure and stable scene on arrival saved the first responders precious minutes.

The alternative:

- An emotional rush to the scene would have delayed the 911 call and response, giving the resultant fires a larger head start.
- An entry into the scene by the president would have put her in danger and left the scene leaderless until the arrival of the first police/fire units.
- A leaderless scene would have been unsecured, and numerous other individuals would have no doubt attempted a "heroic" entry, resulting in a large increase in individuals who needed assistance by first responders.

Then there was the maintenance supervisor who after the record snow fall and resultant cleanup heard the roof collapse at the institution's physical education facility.

What is the strategy, and what actions should he take?

- In *assessing the scene,* he quickly realizes the roof has collapsed on the workout wing of the facility, where he knows there are faculty, staff, students, and others using the equipment.

- He immediately *reports* it to 911. "I am _____ and I just observed a roof collapse at the north end of _____ building located at _____. I know there are many individuals who were in the site at the time of the collapse."
- "I will be located in the main building attempting to *prevent any entry* to the workout area by nonemergency personnel. My cell number is _____."
- He notifies his nearby workers via his portable radio that he wants them to position themselves so as to prevent any entry through the exterior doors of the workout facility by nonemergency personnel. He also issues a directive that no one is to enter that area of the building. Over a hundred people from the campus gathered outside the building within 10 minutes of the beginning of the event
- He then requests that his dispatch notify the institution's Emergency Manager of the situation and requests that yellow emergency tape be delivered to his personnel on-scene.
- He then requests that maintenance vehicles be positioned to prevent any nonemergency vehicles from entering that area of the campus.
- Police, fire, and EMS begin to arrive on-scene.

What was accomplished using this strategy of **assess**, **notify**, and **isolate**? What would have been the consequences of inaction, delayed action, or an emotional response of entering the facility in search of victims?

A collapse like this creates a very unstable environment inside that facility. Any movement, untrained people rushing in to search and rescue trapped individuals, or even the trapped individuals themselves can dislodge key pieces of rubble that can cause a further collapse, resulting in additional casualties and/or property damage.

The supervisor was able to make a quick assessment and notify 911, maximizing the efficiency of the response with precise information about the situation and location. Knowing people are trapped maximized the response in terms of equipment, personnel, and specialties being dispatched.

Taking charge and securing the immediate area of danger prevented untold numbers of individuals from entering this fragile and unsafe area. His notifications allowed others to reduce needless congestion in the larger working area, which was already compromised due to the snowstorm.

Having his dispatch initiate the larger institutional response plan will aid in unifying and maximizing the resources needed at this type of event. This quick notification will ripple, paying dividends down the road with regard to required notifications, managing the media, and numerous other tasks that need to be accomplished outside of the immediate rescue effort.

The alternative:

- An emotional rush into the fragile scene would have delayed the 911 call and response, allowing any and all movement in this area to compromise all the trapped victims.
- An entry into the scene by the supervisor would have put him in danger and left the scene leaderless until the arrival of the first police/fire units.
- A leaderless scene would have been unsecured, and numerous other individuals would have gained entry, resulting in a large increase in individuals who needed rescue and/or assistance by first responders.
- Failure to make the radio requests regarding traffic control would have resulted in potential gridlock, where emergency vehicles would have been hard pressed to access the scene, or worse yet, exit with the injured.
- Failure to notify the Emergency Manager (through the dispatcher) would have delayed the institutional response, which is key to relieving scene personnel from unnecessary tasks beyond the scope of life/safety.

Internalize these ideas and spend a few minutes thinking about the various places you find yourself on a regular basis. Then mentally rehearse how you would respond and "take charge" if an incident occurred there. This visualization and mental preparation will prepare you to act quickly and effectively and put you in a position to save lives, even perhaps your own.

As you read further chapters, you will see this strategy formalized for first responders and referred to as the Seven Critical Tasks™. Even if you are not a paid professional first responder, take the time to study how they are expected to respond and how similar it is to the commonsense approach presented here.

What about the Director of Human Resources who heard what sounded like shots being fired? We will explore the newest strategies for an "active shooter" situation in Chapter 5. You will learn the differences between an armed "hostage" situation and an active shooting situation and how your response may differ from most other situations you might find yourself in.

Review Questions

- Can you describe a "first-first responder"?
- What actions do they need to take?
- If they take the appropriate actions what impact does it have on the formal first responders?
- What is the impact on the first responders and the incident outcome if the fail to act correctly?

Stages, Phases, and Strategies

3

Objectives

After completing this chapter, you should be able to:

- List and explain the stages in the emergency management life cycle.
- Identify the main characteristics of each phase in the response stage.
- Identify the response goals for each phase in the response stage.
- Describe the appropriate strategies for each phase in the response stage.

All critical incidents—from hostage situations to HazMat releases—share certain common traits. There is also a commonality in what is called the "life cycle of emergency management," which has identifiable stages. They are preparedness (which includes planning and prevention), response (which has several phases), and recovery and mitigation. Through the analysis of hundreds of various types of incidents, it has been found that our response to major events can progress through distinct phases. Each phase has unique characteristics, and each requires special management skills. In the next few chapters, we will discuss the distinct phases of the response stage: the crisis phase, the scene management phase, and the executive management phase.

It is important that you recognize the characteristics of each of the phases, the strategies you can use during each phase, and the outcomes you can expect from each phase. Table 3.1 provides an overview of the information that we will be covering in detail.

The Prevention and Preparedness Stage

The prevention of all critical incidents is impossible. This is especially true when we consider terrorist events involving individuals willing to commit suicide. Even countries without the freedoms and constitutional restraints we have in this country have been unable to stop all acts of terrorism. Obviously, tighter controls at border crossings and target hardening are initiatives that surely can reap benefits. Preparedness is a continuous process involving efforts at all levels of government and between government and private

Table 3.1 A Quick Overview of the Developments, Strategies, and Outcomes You Can Expect during Each Stage of a Critical Incident

PREVENTION PREPAREDNESS	CRISIS PHASE	RESPONSE STAGE		RECOVERY & MITIGATION
		SCENE MGT. PHASE	EXECUTIVE MGT. PHASE	
Duration — Pre-Planning Activities	**CRISIS PHASE** 0 to 60 Minutes	Several Hours/Week/More	Several Hours/Week/More	Several/ Days or Weeks/More
Characteristics • Pre-planning can be stressful if event is imminent • Usually a long-term Process • Ongoing Continuous Improvement	• Confusion • Panic • Rush to Scene • Gridlock	• Potential for Danger Continues • Continuation of Incident for Longer Duration • Arrival of Crowds, Resources, and Media • Requires Increased Management	• Size • Scope • Seriousness • Of the Event is Beyond the Ability of Scene/Field Command Post to Manage	• Incident Resolved • Order Restored
Goals • Meet NIMS requirements • Involve all Levels of Government • Reduce Potential for Casualties /Damage	• Stabilize Scene • Limit Acceleration & Growth/Incident • Insure Citizen & Responding Personnel Safety	• Establish an "Organized Decision Making Team" with ICS to bring about a safe and successful resolution of the event	• Establish a Fully-Expanded Incident Command System to Bring About a Safe and Successful Resolution of the Event	• Ensure Scene Integrity • To Bring About a Smooth Transition to Normal Operations • To Improve Agency Response to the Next Critical Incident • To Maintain Emotional and Physical Well-Being of the Organization • Reduce Risk for Next Occurrence

Response Strategy
• Intelligence Sharing
• Risk Assessments
• Tactical Operations to Disrupt a Threat
• Includes Monitoring, Testing, Isolation, Immunization Activities
• Plume Modeling and Air Monitoring
• Sandbagging and Diking Activities
• Joint Training
• Joint Exercising
	• Initiate "Tactical Management Style"
	• First Responding Supervisor Initiates "7 Critical Tasks"
	• Identify initial ICS* functions needed
	• Evaluate resource requirements
	• Evaluate Evacuation and/or Sheltering in Place Requirements
		• Select Site for Scene/Field Command Post
		• Staff Required ICS Functions
		• Develop & Implement Incident Action Plan
		• Evaluate Resource Requirements
		• Assess Communications Requirements
		• Initiate Evacuation Plan (if required)
		• Deploy "Specialists" to Bring About Incident Resolution
			• Establish EOC/Pre -designated Command Post
			• Unified Command Structure Established (if required)
			• In the EOC appointment of Ops Coordinator is determined by nature of incident. Resources required through policy and/or legal authority.
			• Area Command may be activated if required.
			• Evaluate Current Incident Action Plan
			• Support Field Operations
			• Executive Policy Group may formally convene.
				• Implement Plan for Returning to Normal Operations
				  -Account for all personnel
				  -Assess damage / injuries
				  -Reassign personnel
				• Re-establish evacuated Areas
				• Conduct Tactical Review
				• Conduct Stress Debriefing and Provide Counseling
				• Prepare After - Action Reports
				• Policy Review & Training Needs Assessment:
				  - What Happened?
				  - What Was our Response?
				  - What would we do differently- "The next time?"

Outcomes • Deter Threat • Agencies Prepared for any Eventuality • Compliance with NIMS Standards • Multi -Agency Coordination	• Safety of Citizens & Responding Personnel is provided • Scene Stabilized • Proactive Management of Scene to Move Ahead of Incident Acceleration	• A Unified Command Structure is Established (if required) • An Organized "Decision-Making Team" with ICS is Established	• A Fully Expanded Incident Command System Brings About an Organized Team Approach for the Safe & Successful Resolution of the Event	• Event Activity and Agency Response is Properly Documented • Provide Information That Will Benefit the Profession • Provide Opportunities for all Personnel to Receive Assistance with any Emotional and/or Physical Needs • Target Hardened Community

sector and nongovernmental organizations to identify threats, determine vulnerabilities, and identify required resources.

Preparedness and prevention involves all actions taken to avoid an incident or to intervene to stop an incident that threatens lives and property. It involves applying intelligence and other information to a range of activities such as: heightened inspections, improved surveillance and investigations to determine the full nature and source of a threat, public health testing processes, isolation and/or quarantines, as well as law enforcement activities aimed at interrupting and disrupting illegal activity.

Activities such as preplanning, training, and exercising will ensure our ability to respond in a coordinated effective manner. We must update all current response plans to ensure compliance with standards set by the National Incident Management System (NIMS), that is, utilization of ICS, unified command, and so forth. As we prepare, we must be mindful that any response to a major critical incident will involve our entire community and resources from other jurisdictions. Therefore our preparations should include representatives from those jurisdictions most likely to be involved in a response. This will allow for the building of relationships and role clarification in the calm environment of a classroom, as opposed to the sometimes-hectic environment of a command post.

The primary goal of this chapter is to provide you with a "response plan."

This plan will provide you with strategies and specific actions that will make a difference in immediately taking control of an incident as opposed to allowing it to "accelerate" out of control.

Developing a response plan for the response and management of a critical incident is similar to a coaching staff designing a game plan for an upcoming contest:

- An athletic team outlines a game plan for each opponent.
- A game plan is based on an analysis of the opposing team's strengths and weaknesses and on their own team's strengths and weaknesses.
- Assessing team characteristics and tendencies when faced with specific situations further develops the game plan.

The same philosophy holds true when developing a plan for the response to, and management of, a major incident.

Based on the analysis of different types of critical incidents—chemical spills, plane crashes, hostage situations, and even terrorist acts—it became apparent that regardless of the type of event, a common and specific set of scene management issues emerged. These issues were common to the onset of the event. It is essential that these issues be addressed when developing a plan for managing any type of critical incident.

In addition, this analysis determined that because there is a set of common management issues that occur at the onset of any type of major event, there should also be a similar set of response strategies that initiate control and management of the incident.

Most importantly, the analysis revealed that the actions taken or not taken by the Incident Commander could initiate control of the incident, or allow it to expand and grow out of control.

The Response Stage

As previously stated, the response stage of an incident *may* have three distinct phases depending on the incident (Figure 3.1). It will *always* have a crisis phase.

Crisis Phase

It's 0630 hours, the end of a quiet night shift. You're on your way back to the station when Dispatch notifies you of an MVA with confirmed injuries. Your first car on-scene advises that he has a school bus versus tanker truck. The tanker is leaking an unknown liquid that may be forming a gas cloud.

Several children appear to be trapped in the overturned bus. Three passersby, apparently not involved in the accident, are down and unmoving. Both the bus driver and tanker driver are dead or unconscious. Traffic is snarled in all directions.

You are in the crisis phase. What are you going to do to contain the situation? What questions do you need answered? What resources are you going to need?

All critical incidents share certain common characteristics at the outset. In the first 0–60 minutes or so of the crisis phase, you can expect confusion and panic on the part of the public. Criminal activity involving gunfire or explosions, for example, may create mass movement away from the incident. Motorists on the event fringes may slow down to see what's going on. At the same time, you and other responders will be rushing to the scene as quickly as possible.

The result is gridlock. The public acts blindly on little or no information until you, as the scene commander, can determine the nature of the situation

Figure 3.1 Uncontrolled emergency response can simply add to the gridlock at a critical incident scene.

and exert control. You must bring order to chaos. Confusion in the early moments can greatly hinder your ability to determine just what you're facing. Responding units and agencies may add to the confusion if you do not manage their response.

A critical incident compresses and accelerates all of your order, planning, and decision-making processes, especially when you are operating in a dangerous environment. The threat can come from a gas cloud or by gunfire. Others, such as the survivors of a bus or plane crash, may be in imminent danger. You don't have the luxury of conducting a meeting with other supervisors to discuss strategies—you must take action. Failure to act may lead the incident to accelerate out of control.

When you respond, you *must have a plan*. You can't rely on your ability to make it up as you go along. And as we pointed out previously, that plan must have been tested through training.

Initial Objectives and Strategies
Your initial goals are:

- To limit the growth of the incident,
- Ensure the safety of both civilians and responders, and
- Stabilize the scene. You have to take action to make sure the situation doesn't get worse before you can move toward resolution. Remember, the less time an incident has to develop in the crisis phase, the greater are your opportunities to stabilize it.

How do you achieve this? A critical first step is to adopt a tactical command presence at the scene. You must assume command and announce it over the available communication channel. (This simple practice has long been used by the fire service, but has not been embraced by law enforcement. A short radio communication establishing command clarifies on-scene authority for the dispatcher, your responding units, and other mutual aid resources directed to assist at the scene.)

In the parlance of the Incident Command System (ICS), you are the Incident Commander (IC). The IC collects the best available information and makes necessary decisions. Acting as an IC in the crisis phase of an incident requires a different management style from what you probably use day-to-day. This is referred to as the difference between "tactical" and "traditional" leadership styles.

Briefly, a tactical leader must be autocratic. You issue immediate and specific orders. Be aware that in a crisis, autocratic leadership rarely creates resentment. Rather, the reverse is true: Subordinates and civilians faced with a crisis situation rely on the direction only a confident IC can provide. If you act with confidence and decisiveness, your subordinates will too.

The first-responding supervisor or scene commander takes action to stabilize the situation and to preserve life and property. Because most critical incidents share common characteristics, it follows that you can use a set of common responses for bringing those incidents under control. These are known as the Seven Critical Tasks™.

The tasks are:

- Establish control and communications.
- Identify the "hot zone."
- Establish the inner perimeter.
- Establish the outer perimeter.
- Establish the command post.
- Establish a staging area.
- Identify and request additional resources.

Notice that the tasks are not numbered. You can perform them in whatever order is appropriate for your incident. Regardless of the order, these steps represent your game plan for managing the crisis phase of any type of critical incident. We will cover these crucial tasks in detail in Chapter 5.

Let's recap the functions of a first-responding supervisor in the crisis phase:

- Stabilize and limit the growth of the incident.
- Ensure the safety of citizens and responders.
- Take action to gain control of the scene, including preparing the scene for the entry of specialists (SWAT, bomb tech, HazMat, fire, urban search and rescue, and so on).

Outcomes

So what can happen at the conclusion of the crisis phase? As you might expect, events can go a couple of different ways. The incident may resolve itself at this stage. If your gunman surrenders, you would proceed to the recovery and mitigation stage of incident management.

This may happen, but it is *not a primary goal* for the crisis stage. *Not* seeking immediate resolution is a major departure from traditional incident response training. This is a key difference between the approach outlined in this book and traditional methodologies. In the past, we have been taught to go in and resolve a situation as quickly as possible. Years of hard experience have taught us that your *primary goals* need to be:

- Limiting incident growth
- Stabilizing the scene
- Ensuring the safety of responders and citizens

Early stabilization, rather than resolution, is a difficult concept for lay-people to grasp. In our opinion, the response to the Columbine High School tragedy in 1999 was unfairly criticized by nonresponders for this very reason. On-scene supervisors in that case acted with restraint and focused on incident control, stabilization, and intelligence gathering in the crisis phase. If responding agencies had acted without information and without control of the scene, that event could have been much, much worse.

You must beware of the "tunnel vision" that can lead you to focus on resolution in the crisis phase. You may be provoked to act impetuously and without information. This focus can allow a situation to escalate out of control. You *must* stabilize the scene first.

It is extremely unlikely your incident will be resolved in the crisis phase. But even if the incident is not resolved, you should at least have accomplished the three goals outlined in this section.

For example, you might still have a gunman barricaded in the house, but you have perimeters established and have taken other steps that allow you to progress to the next phase—scene management.

Scene Management Phase

Back at the intersection, you've accomplished the Seven Critical Tasks™ and stabilized the scene. The hardest decision you had to make was to leave the children in the bus for an extended period of time. Based on the placard on the truck, you determined that the fluid leaking from the tanker was acetone.

You have evacuated all houses and businesses within two blocks of the intersection. Your command post is in place, and you are coordinating with EMS to remove the wounded public and responders. Fire services and HazMat have begun to contain the spill. Concerned parents are arriving at the outer perimeter and clogging your communications center with inquiries about their children's welfare.

Now what do you do?

Once you've stabilized the situation but determined that the threat will continue for some time, you've entered the scene management phase. This phase can last anywhere from hours to several days depending on the nature and severity of the incident.

There is still a potential for danger to the public and responders, but the emphasis shifts to increased management. You are, for example, going to have crowds to manage—more spectators will gather and emergency responders will continue to roll up. The media will certainly arrive during this phase.

Initial Objectives and Strategies

This is where you shift gears from stabilization strategies to an extended and proactive management mode that will allow you to gain control of the situation.

You may have already begun the task of establishing a command post in the crisis phase, but scene management cannot take place without a safe location from which to coordinate your response. As you will learn when we get into the Seven Critical Tasks™ in Chapter 5, the command post should be between the inner and outer perimeters, in other words, outside the hot zone but in a controlled area well away from crowds.

It is not necessary for the command post to have an actual view of the incident scene. In fact, being that close can be both dangerous and a distraction from the larger issues you must address, such as coordinating incoming resources. As the Incident Commander, once you establish your command post, *stay there*. That way everyone knows where to find you.

It is possible that authority may shift at this point if a higher-ranking officer responds to the scene. If you have received a "traditional" ICS orientation, you probably learned that the command hand-off must be handled in a face-to-face briefing. This works for the fire service because of its integral team response strategy, which always places a team leader on-scene from the start.

Law enforcement is different. Officers, more often than not, respond alone and don't have the benefit of a supervisor on-scene from its inception. So it's important to keep in mind that a supervisor en route *can* assume authority over an incident. We've had students tell us they can accomplish several tasks from their vehicles while still minutes from the scene. They are thinking about their game plan, requesting support, and relaying commands to the officers currently on location.

That takes us to ICS, the other primary characteristic of the scene management phase. At this point in the incident, you have more resources and a new set of problems to handle. ICS is critical for creating a flexible command structure to adapt to these issues as they arise.

Your primary goal in the scene management stage is the establishment of an organized decision-making team. In the language of the ICS, this may be a unified command consisting of specialists and representatives from each responding agency with jurisdictional responsibility for the incident. This is where you let the men and women with hoses handle the hot stuff and those with the stretchers handle the injured. And by all means, let the responders in the "Level A" suits handle the glowing stuff!

In other words, deploy your specialists and let them do their jobs. Don't micromanage; allow the specialists to develop their plans. Remember, final approval of all operational plans is your responsibility as Incident Commander. Your command is growing, and you cannot make every decision or be everywhere at once. Don't try.

This phase requires that you drop the autocratic leadership style you used in the crisis phase. It would be counterproductive. During scene management, you will be working with more departments and specialists and need to revert to the collaborative, empowering management style you probably use day-to-day.

ICS consists of several functional areas such as operations, planning, investigation and intelligence, logistics, finance, and so on. We will go into more detail later, but the beauty of ICS is you need implement the functions only that apply to managing *your* scene. Do you need a Public Information Officer to handle the media? If the answer is yes, appoint one (don't do it yourself!). If not, don't worry about that function. It's a "toolbox" approach to incident management. Select the tools you need to accomplish the task at hand.

You need to be flexible in your thinking here. You will be constantly reevaluating the scene and integrating new ICS functions as necessary:

- If you find yourself managing a major incident, one of your first considerations should be appointment of a Safety Officer.
- You may need to appoint a Public Information Officer to handle the media. Trust us on this one.
- You will be required to keep a log of the events and decisions as they occur. This is critical for the evaluation that must follow all critical incident responses.
- There may be special considerations. For example, if children are involved, you are going to need a liaison to work with the concerned parents who will threaten to inundate and overwhelm your communications center and/or command post.

As the event unfolds, your communications requirements may change. Make sure all of your people have the resources they need to receive and act on orders as you issue them. If possible, establish dedicated frequencies for your agencies' responders and know the frequencies used by other agencies. You may need to pull people out in a hurry; you don't want to leave anyone behind because they didn't get the message.

There is one more ICS term we need to introduce here. Any actions you take at the scene management phase must be part of your overall **Incident Action Plan (IAP)**. Your IAP will cover an operational period and should include both the tactics and the long-range strategies you will use to bring the incident under control. For example, if your primary consideration is removing barricaded gunmen from a school, your IAP must include details about the goal and the techniques you are going to use to achieve it (i.e., waiting them out, negotiating, or performing an assault).

You develop the IAP in conjunction with the other members of your unified command. This approach ensures that the IAP meets the requirements of all participating agencies and/or disciplines. Make sure you receive input and analysis of the IAP from all main ICS functions.

Outcomes

Most incidents can be resolved at the scene management phase. In this case, you would proceed to the recovery and mitigation stage of incident management. But, resolved or not, at the conclusion of the scene management phase you should at least have:

- Organized a decision-making team using ICS
- Developed an Incident Action Plan
- Established a unified command structure (if required)

There certainly are cases in which a situation can no longer be dealt with effectively by the on-scene command post. Once the aforementioned elements are in place, an incident can more easily migrate to the next level of management: the executive management phase.

Executive Management Phase

The children are out, but technicians have been unable to control the release of the hazardous material.

HazMat responders determine that a larger area must be evacuated. The hot zone now includes a nursing home and the school to which the bus was headed. In addition to residents, you must now safely move 100 seniors and 250 elementary students.

Your evacuation area has spread into two other jurisdictions. Local and state officials as well as representatives from the local school district are responding to your command post. The large number of evacuees and the areas involved force you to recognize that you can no longer effectively manage the incident from the on-scene command post.

So how do you handle this escalation?

When the size, scope, and seriousness of an event exceed the capabilities of on-scene management, your incident has progressed to the executive management phase. This phase can last from several hours to several weeks or more.

These events are usually major incidents such as earthquakes, airline crashes, large-scale HazMat incidents, and civil disturbances. Remember that all critical incidents will move through the crisis phase. Most will make it to the scene management phase. You transition to the executive management phase when the size, scope, and seriousness of a major event requires a support system beyond the scope of the scene command and hence the activation of an Emergency Operations Center (EOC).

Because this chapter focuses on initial response and scene management, our discussion of the executive management phase will be brief. We will cover both the EOC and the Executive Policy Group in detail in Chapters 9 and 10. As an incident supervisor, you should simply be aware that an additional level of response is available when the community impact of an incident exceeds the ability of scene resources to manage. Your job is to resolve the incident; others will manage the consequences and impact of that incident on the organization or community.

Initial Objectives and Strategies

The primary objective of the executive management phase is the establishment of the EOC and an Executive Policy Group. Initiating an EOC represents a full expansion of the Incident Command System. An EOC is generally set up at a predesignated site that has been equipped and supplied for this purpose. As you will see later in Chapters 9 and 10, the EOC can vary from a highly sophisticated dedicated space found in large cities, counties, and states to a shared multipurpose facility in smaller governmental agencies and other nongovernmental organizations.

As the Incident Commander at the scene, you should have input into the decision to escalate a response to the executive management phase. It is your experience and firsthand knowledge of conditions on the ground that tell you that this incident is of sufficient size, scope, and seriousness to disrupt the normal operations of the community, organization, or institution, and your recommendation to activate the EOC is important.

It is critical that you realize that as Incident Commander, you are still in charge of incident resolution. The EOC mission focus is on "continuity of operations, community impact and support of the scene in terms of major logistical needs," not resolution of the scene. When you need additional field resources beyond your normal reach, request that the EOC provide those for you. The EOC is staffed by executives beyond your pay grade with contacts at state and national level; let them assist and keep them busy.

Keep the EOC honest. If it appears decisions are being made that do not correlate with your field observations, or you start to feel micromanaged, let them know. But be aware that the EOC operates with a focus on the "big picture"—outside the outer perimeter. It may well be that decisions that appear groundless to you may actually be sound. Don't be shy about asking for the logic behind the directives and/or requests that you receive. You are a commander and have a right to be fully informed.

Outcomes

The executive management phase provides a natural transition to the recovery and mitigation stage. Once you have resolved the initial event, the EOC will be taking over the transition to normal operations and operating long after you are home with your family.

Recovery and Mitigation Stage

As the vapor cloud dissipated and HazMat techs were able to contain liquids and drain the tanker, you maintained your perimeters. You made sure that all casualties were handled. With the threat controlled, you begin demobilizing resources and returning evacuees. Then you begin the assessment process.

Work with other departments to review your response. Check your timeline and log to make sure you have all the information you're going to need to face the inquiries that inevitably follow any critical incident.

Can you document the information upon which you based your various decisions? Can you show that you acted reasonably?

And don't forget about the well-being of your people. This was a traumatic event. Are you prepared to respond to their emotional needs? Should you pay special attention to the first-responding officer that you ordered away from the scene and who had to leave the children on the bus?

These are just a few of the hard questions that will need to be answered. You're still under pressure, but the nature of your stress shifts from incident crisis to the microscope of hindsight review. Will you be prepared for it? Once the threat has been resolved, everybody gets to go home, right? Well, eventually. The recovery and mitigation frequently gets less attention than it merits. While the EOC will handle much of the recovery, many crucial tasks may still need to be performed by the IC after an incident has been concluded.

Recovery and mitigation lasts as long as it lasts. It can take from a few hours, to several weeks, months, or in the case of major disasters even years. The primary characteristic is the restoration of order and the return to normal operations for the public and all responding agencies. Demobilizing an extensive response can take time. As a responsible IC you can't have people going back in service by simply driving away from the scene of a critical incident.

Objectives and Strategies

Your first task during termination is to continue to ensure scene integrity. Most scenes require cleanup and/or continued investigation. As first responders leave, new personnel, such as fire marshals or evidence techs, may need to perform duties at the scene.

This cannot be stressed enough. All too often perimeters collapse immediately following the resolution of an incident. After a gunman has been apprehended, for example, officers working crowd control may rush into the hot zone to offer support. This is when we find the media right in the middle of a scene interviewing traumatized victims and possibly destroying evidence. Give specific orders to maintain perimeters!

You need a plan for resuming normal operations. That includes accounting for all personnel, reporting injuries and damage, and reassigning responders to normal duties. Take your time. You now have the luxury of considered action.

You may have had the public evacuated from the hot zone. Provide for their orderly return to homes, schools, and businesses. This must be accomplished in a managed fashion. For example, before allowing residents to reoccupy evacuated homes in certain HazMat incidents, we must make sure pockets of gas have not become trapped in the homes. Hopefully you haven't released all of your fire or HazMat units with the appropriate detection equipment!

And not least of all: How are your people responding to the incident? Critical incident stress can undermine long-term health and operational efficiency. Make sure responders get the help they need to deal with exceptionally traumatic events. Depending on the severity of the incident, stress debriefings may be required for victims, bystanders, and responders. Your primary duty is to your people, but coordinate with other agencies to make sure all responders have access to the help and support they require.

How Did We Do?
Perhaps the most important task during the termination phase is your assessment of your response. There are three questions you should always ask:

- What happened?
- What was our response?
- What would we do differently next time?

Your report must clearly document the events that occurred and the actions you took. The log you initiate from the beginning of your response will be critical for your review of the incident management, and any external professional or legal review that may be ordered. You will *not* be able to reconstruct events from memory.

A review of your response must be completely honest. Were your actions the best options? Did you clearly communicate your orders to subordinates? Did you fairly weigh observations and suggestions from subordinates or co-commanders in your unified command?

All critical incident evaluations bring up the same issue: Had we been aware of certain facts at the time, we might have made different decisions. It's the hindsight effect. But more often than not, based on the information we had at the time, we made what we believed to be correct decisions. We must bear in mind that even when an incident did not go as planned, these decisions were *not* mistakes. They were simply decisions we made, based on the information we had at the time.

Don't be too hard on yourself. Remember that there are many factors that are out of our control. Did you focus on those you *could* control? Make careful note of the impediments to your response. We all face the same general issues. Did your radios function properly? Was crowd control effective? Did you encounter political opposition to your command decisions?

And lastly, you are not alone in this analysis. You must assess the efforts and decisions of everyone in your command. When debriefing responders, perhaps the most confrontational question you can ask is "What did you do wrong?" This immediately puts the responder on the defensive. We suggest you ask "What would you do differently next time?" This is a less judgmental, more constructive way to approach your assessment.

In the after-action review make sure you record the issues that are identified. Asking "What would you differently?" at this stage will produce ideas for improvement in any number of areas. The common ones would be: changes in policy or procedures, new or improved training, availability or suitability of equipment, availability or suitability of supplies, changes in team assignments, and so forth. One of your key goals in this recovery phase is to improve your organization's response to the "next incident." Failure to document and act on the output from these discussions puts the next failure, injury, or worse squarely on your shoulders.

Summary

We hope this chapter gave you a feel for the common stages and response strategies shared by all critical incidents. The stages and phases discussed in this chapter would have been similar for a severe transport accident, a botched bank robbery turned hostage situation, or a tornado. It's just a question of type and scope. Regardless of the nature of the emergency, it's up to you as the supervisor to recognize the requirements for each phase and respond accordingly.

Review Questions

- What are the stages in the life cycle of emergency management?
- What are the characteristics of an incident in the crisis phase?
- What is the primary goal of the first responder in the crisis phase?
- What are two strategies for the first responder in the crisis phase?
- What three questions should be asked during the assessment of an incident in the recovery and mitigation stage?

Tactical Leadership

4

Objectives

After completing this chapter, you should be able to:

- Identify the factors that determine leadership style.
- Describe the value of tactical leadership in the crisis phase.
- List the skills that must be mastered by the effective tactical leader.

As discussed in Chapter 1, the focus of the Incident Commander responding to any critical incident must center on *controllable* factors. We have long subscribed to the theory that the *most* controllable factor in a critical incident is the individual. That's you.

There are as many different leadership styles as there are leaders. Successful styles vary according to the task—what works for a hospital administrator might not work for a shift manager at an auto-assembly plant. This chapter will examine the consistent traits and style you need to successfully manage a critical incident in the early moments: the crisis phase.

Leadership Variables

First, you should recognize three common variables that affect management style. What we are talking about is "situational leadership." Your style will vary dependent upon:

- **The subordinate:** Some people simply require more supervision than others. This affects the tasks you assign and the manner in which you manage personnel.
- **The supervisor:** How comfortable are you with a situation, your subordinates, or command in general?
- **The criticality of the task:** In a life-or-death situation, you and your subordinates will respond differently from the way you would if you were discussing a matter of office policy. This is the primary factor that determines the management style needed at a critical incident. The more critical the task, the more directing you should be.

Of these three factors, which do *you* have the most control over—the task, your people, or you?

Leadership Style

If you are a police supervisor, ask yourself this simple question: "When is the last time I gave one of my subordinates a direct and specific order?" If you can't think of an instance, you're not alone. Giving orders in modern law enforcement has practically become a lost art. We have inundated our profession with trendy leadership styles from the private sector.

For years we have trained in the philosophies of democratic leadership, employee empowerment, and participatory management. The term "autocratic" tells us how *not* to supervise. The once-simple act of giving orders has become uncomfortable for today's law enforcement supervisors. And as for *following* orders…!

This is not to disparage the more empowering leadership styles. Nor do we advocate their abandonment. They are valuable in most day-to-day contacts with our team. And they are appropriate when an event evolves into the scene management phase. However, they simply do not work when the supervisor is attempting to manage the early minutes (the crisis phase) of a critical incident.

Are You a Coach or a Player?

Law enforcement personnel (with the exception of SWAT) are the only emergency responders who arrive at the scene as individuals. It is only *at the scene* that we form into teams. Think of our counterparts in the fire service. Firefighters arrive on a rig together, and each has specific assigned tasks. When did you last see several police officers pull up to an emergency scene in the same vehicle and immediately set about a series of predefined tasks?

Police departments expect initiative. We reward it. A common, positive note on employee performance reviews frequently reads something like "requires little supervision." In most cases, a police officer's independent style is necessary to do his or her job. In a critical incident, however, this characteristic is unacceptable. All responders must know the plan and stick to it. It's up to you to communicate the plan and make certain subordinates do exactly what they're told.

The police supervisor responds alone (usually) and creates his or her team from whatever resources are currently available. The supervisor assigns tasks and ensures the team interacts with other responders—all while the incident is unfolding. To accomplish this difficult task, the initial supervisor on an emergency scene must assume the non-politically correct "autocratic" style of leadership.

To relapse into sports analogy, you are the coach. You are not a player. A player does not have the big picture. A player performs a specific task assigned by the coach. You must step back from the action—no matter how hard it is!—and take in that big picture. Once you have assessed the situation and developed your game plan, you give your team members the play. As in sports, the higher the position of authority, the farther from the action the coach usually positions him or herself. Position coaches in football, such as defensive line coaches, are on the sidelines with their players, not on the field. As they are promoted to defensive coordinators, where do they usually position themselves? More often than not in a booth high above the action so they have a complete overview of the playing field. As basic as this sounds, it can be very difficult to step back from the "action." Good tactical leaders recognize that managing a scene is crucial to success. Experience shows that most critical incidents do not lack players, but often have failed to have a coach in charge.

A scene commander must issue clear and specific orders to responding units. That in itself may seem foreign. Now add the stress of operating in some of the most tragic and horrific circumstances imaginable. It is imperative that you demonstrate to responding personnel that you are in charge and have a clear plan to stabilize and ultimately resolve the crisis.

Crisis leadership forces you to make hard choices that must be respected by your subordinates. One of our students, for example, had to make a tough decision when an officer was shot during an incident. Because the gunman was still on the loose, the supervisor decided not to risk allowing other units into the area to care for the officer until the suspect's location and the potential hot zone could be better defined. He told us it was the toughest decision he has ever had to make—and not a popular one at the time. However, when the suspect was subsequently apprehended and interviewed, he told of his plan to ambush the first officers arriving on the scene, officers who never arrived due to the actions of that first-responding supervisor. This is the type of informed decision that will save responders' lives.

Practice Makes Perfect

Practicing critical incident management is key. This applies to personal as well as tactical skills. A supervisor who waits until a critical incident to assume an autocratic persona will probably cause confusion among subordinates.

"Who do they think they are? Why are they barking orders at me? They have never yelled at me before." Without practice, that supervisor may be unable to implement a credible autocratic style of leadership.

Take advantage of opportunities to assume this leadership style. Use minor incidents, such as a noninjury MVA, to demonstrate to subordinates the dynamics you'll expect on a critical incident scene. Issue those clear and specific orders.

There are two primary points to keep in mind when you practice:

- You should discuss the sudden change with your subordinates first so they can anticipate your command style. Don't blindside them with a drill sergeant personality when all along you've been the nurturing type. Make sure subordinates understand how you expect them to comply with specific orders.
- Subsequently, you should assess your effectiveness as well as the response of your personnel to this style—who followed orders and who didn't.

Through these situations, the supervisor can practice tactical leadership, and the subordinate can practice tactical compliance. The better the "coach" and "player" understand their roles during the crisis phase, the more organized the initial response will be. Organization brings about a quicker, safer stabilization and resolution to the incident.

Now that we've identified the kind of supervision a critical incident requires, let's turn to the specific functions the supervisor must perform. Across the board, successful autocratic leaders do the following:

- Assess problems by taking in and evaluating data.
- Decide on an appropriate course of action.
- Clearly relate that course of action to others.
- Maintain a command presence.

Seem like common sense? You'd expect these traits from managers on a day-to-day basis, right? Perhaps, but the point is that they are extremely difficult to carry out during the crisis phase of a critical incident. Now we'll take a closer look at each of these functions and how you can implement them successfully under stress.

Problem Assessment

Leadership in crisis requires the ability to take in data and process it under the most stressful conditions imaginable. You *must* do this, sometimes in a matter of seconds, or lives may be lost. The crisis phase of an incident is characterized by confusion, panic, rushing to the scene, and gridlock. All of these have a negative impact on information gathering.

In those critical first moments, you must ask the question "What and/or whom am I dealing with?" You must also assess the risk to your personnel. *Although this is a common practice in both fire and EMS training, it is seldom talked about in police training. The bottom line: A dead officer can't help anyone. Of course we perform unsafe acts. That's practically a definition of law enforcement! A proper risk assessment, however, ensures that we perform them as safely as possible.*

Risk Assessment

Risk assessment may involve the ability to determine if response personnel are properly equipped to respond to a scene. This may involve whether or not the police officer has the benefit of both a bullet-resistant vest and knowledge of the weapon a potential adversary is using. Will the vest stop that caliber or type of round?

At the scene of a bomb detonation, good risk assessment considers the presence of a secondary device. Therefore removal of the ambulatory injured in an expedient manner is advised ("load and go"). A further search for trapped or buried victims may have to be conducted by "suited-up" bomb squad personnel. This may also involve the subsequent search for evidence. Remember, at a bomb scene the victims and the entire scene may contain evidence.

In a chemical or WMD incident, the on-scene commander should determine if the responders are properly equipped to perform duties in the affected area. There are four levels of protection/protective clothing:

Level D: Level D is merely uniform or everyday clothing. This provides no protection for respiratory or skin contamination. Without additional protection, responders should avoid any exposure to chemical or biological agents.

Level C: Level C consists of chemical-resistant clothing, a hood, and an air-purifying respirator. This level of protection would be adequate for protection from airborne agents. It also provides protection against splash hazard. With a functioning respirator, this level provides adequate protection against airborne biological and radiological materials. Specialized training in the proper use of this level of protection is required to ensure that the responder understands its limitations when used to protect against specific chemicals, their concentration, and how long they will be effective in providing adequate protection.

Level B: Level B provides maximum respiratory protection, but less skin protection. It consists of a chemical splash-resistant suit with hood and SCBA (self-contained breathing apparatus). This level provides adequate protection in low-level oxygen situations. It is also effective in situations that pose no skin vapor hazard and/or have low-level splash potential.

Level A: Level A provides the maximum skin and respiratory protection and is effective in most HazMat situations, whether they have been intentionally or accidentally caused. Level A is attained when the responder is equipped with a chemical-resistant suit that is totally encapsulated with SCBA or supplied air with an escape device. This level of protection should be utilized when the exact chemical or threat has not been identified.

Responders should never enter a potential hot zone without benefit of at least Level B and preferably Level A protective clothing. This would include all law enforcement first responders, as well as first-response firefighters equipped in standard-issue turnout gear.

The responsibility for preventing entry into a potential hot zone lies squarely with the Incident Commander. The hardest decision one may ever be required to make is to not take a specific action at a scene.

Risk assessment is without question one of the most important responsibilities of any Incident Commander. The decision not to take an action may well be an acceptable tactic. It would not be uncommon at a fire scene that degenerates into a complete inferno for a fire commander to pull out his or her personnel, regardless of the potential for others to still be in the building. However, law enforcement is quick to criticize the decision to stand by or not to take an immediate action at a scene. The fire service has learned this lesson the hard way by losing personnel in past incidents.

The authors of this text cannot advise when or when not to take an action. Tactics cannot be dictated from an administrative office or off-scene. Only the on-scene commander can conduct a risk assessment and then determine the appropriate tactic to be deployed. We will discuss this further in subsequent chapters.

Quick assessment of the scope of the emergency and the risks posed by it can make all the difference between stabilizing a scene or allowing it to spiral out of control. Later we will discuss specific strategies you can use in this process. For now, we will focus on the skill of problem assessment as a whole.

Individuals with good problem assessment skills seldom overestimate or underestimate the seriousness of a situation. Two of the most common and inappropriate approaches a supervisor can take are:

- The "Chicken Little" approach, where every call is a critical incident
- The "One Riot, One Ranger" approach, where no call is a critical incident

Each misguided approach shares the same flaw: prejudging an incident. Instead, manage each incident on its own merits according to the information you have. Law enforcement is in a unique position here; if they don't do it, nobody will. They're usually the first ones there.

In one sense, managing critical incidents is similar to every call to which you respond. Prejudging a call before arriving and assessing the scene can get you into serious trouble. Surely you can think of examples of poor problem assessment skills you have encountered in *other* supervisors. When poor assessment does not result in death or injury, mishandled events become popular history and an opportunity for ribbing. Unfortunately, poor problem assessment skills can also cost responders and the public their lives.

To obtain information in a crisis, tactical leaders exploit any and all available resources. These sources may not be "official." A HazMat technician, for example, may not be on-scene or available during the crisis phase of a tanker spill. Good leaders use who or what may be available at the time. If one of your on-duty officers has a specialized skill area such as SWAT, volunteer fire, or HazMat, use that person's knowledge to perform the problem assessment. Keep that person near you as you handle a scene in his or her area of familiarity. Remember the old saying: "Good supervisors don't need to know all the answers, just where to find them."

And the time to look for those sources is not during a crisis. To the best of your ability, try to familiarize yourself with the special skills your people can bring to a scene *before* you need them.

Decision Making

Good problem assessment skills make for good information and thus result in good decisions. After a quick assessment of the situation at hand, the Incident Commander must decide on a course of action to stabilize the scene. As basic as this strategy sounds, it is not uncommon for supervisors to be so caught up in collecting information that they fail to make some basic decisions. You can *never* get all the information. You must act on what you have.

Back to sports. Think of the quarterback who is unable to decide on a receiver when under pressure. The inability to select a course of action usually results in an interception, sack, or incomplete pass.

Top quarterbacks make snap decisions and then follow through. They make the decision to throw based on the information they have at the time.

Yet even the best get intercepted. The same holds true for scene commanders. You make decisions based on what you know. You simply cannot wait for all the information.

Three things can cause a supervisor's inaction:

- Stress overload
- Personal indecisiveness
- Organizational culture

Whereas overload and indecisiveness are individual issues, organizational culture is not. It is something you can change through awareness and training.

As you will read repeatedly in these pages, it is imperative in crisis management to force decision making to the *lowest level possible*. The immediate need to stabilize a situation transcends any formal chain of command or daily standard operating procedure. Minutes of inaction during the crisis phase can translate into additional property damage, personal injuries, or loss of life.

We have mentioned the need for a game plan to address incidents. Well, if a supervisor has been rebuked or second-guessed for incident response decisions one too many times, his or her game plan when responding to an incident will be...to call the lieutenant! And if that lieutenant has been burned, their game plan will be...you can imagine.

The first responder cannot be reduced to inaction while awaiting a higher-level commander. That first responder must take immediate responsibility and assume command of the scene. This requires rapid decision making. A responder concerned with any priority beyond containment and control (such as politics) will not be decisive and will not take command.

Issuing Orders and Directions

Some say issuing orders and directions is a skill. Some say it's an art. The method you use to relate plans and strategies to others depends on your personal style. You have a lot of orders to issue, and success results when your team accomplishes all the little things correctly. Disaster can result when lots of little balls get dropped due to miscommunication.

Have you ever given an order or direction to a subordinate and then had that individual do something totally different? In these cases we usually fault the subordinate. In fact, one of two things actually happened. Either the receiver *did* misunderstand the order or he or she did *exactly* what we communicated to them. This is a clear, but subtle distinction: They didn't do what we wanted them to do; they did what they were told to do.

The ability to develop a picture in your mind and then relate it to others is not as easy as it sounds. This is especially difficult when the receiver is not present and we cannot supplement our words with gestures, illustrations, and other visual aids.

In the overwhelming majority of critical incidents, we give orders and directions to responding units via the radio. As discussed earlier, our radios introduce a number of inherent communication obstacles. Remember, the lowest bidder has provided most of your equipment. At times that's exactly the way it performs!

However, let's assume your equipment is functioning correctly. Now the burden is squarely on you to communicate orders clearly and concisely. No excuses—it's just you, your radio, and your subordinates.

During a barricaded-gunman incident, you give an order to seal off an intersection. You get on the radio and say, "Car 302. Proceed to the intersection of Main and Second and block traffic." What haven't you said?

- How can the officer get to the location safely? Do they know where your hot zone is?
- What specifically is expected of them when they arrive there? Should they stop traffic in all directions?

You must anticipate and answer these questions in the orders you give. You know what you want. Does your subordinate? Therefore the more appropriate order might be, "Proceed to the intersection of Main and Second. Approach from the South on Main and prevent traffic from proceeding northbound on Main from Second." If this is what you are envisioning, this is what must be related to your responders.

If there is any doubt as to whether your subordinate got the message, have them repeat to you what they will do based on your orders and directions. The ability to clearly communicate with other responders in a critical incident is essential to implementing any plan or operational tactic.

Think you can do that without practice?

Command Presence

This is, perhaps, the quintessential "you-know-it-when-you-see-it" leadership trait. Simply put, a crisis leader with command presence communicates confidence and control to subordinates through his or her actions. The mere tone of the supervisor's voice over the radio can incite anxiety or calm a situation. The ability to minimize confusion and panic in the initial minutes of a critical incident is essential to stabilization.

In the K-9 world there is a saying that "everything goes down lead." Translated, the dog becomes the handler. If the handler is excited, the dog will become excited. If the handler has a laid-back attitude, the dog will assume *that* trait. If you are fortunate enough to work with these teams, check this out the next time you call for canine assistance. You'll be amazed at how true it is.

In management, this concept means your subordinates take on your attitudes and characteristics. The hard-charging, aggressive units are usually headed by supervisors possessing these characteristics. In crisis management, this means your subordinates will mirror your controlled and confident response.

How do you achieve this presence? To some it comes naturally. For others it requires practice. One common technique is simply taking a moment to calm yourself before giving orders. This is very similar to the emotional gathering we perform before transmitting during a pursuit. Using this technique, a responder may be experiencing all of the adrenaline-fed physical reactions (accelerated heartbeat, time distortion, etc.), but still sound as if they were ordering breakfast at the local diner.

A supervisor must bring adrenaline reactions under control before giving orders, whether in person or on the radio. When you are overexcited, your communication is usually garbled and stresses your responders. Experienced responders force themselves to be clear and concise. A good crisis leader must be able to do the same. The ability to direct others in a calm, professional manner when the entire world seems to be coming apart is usually described as "command presence under fire." Command presence in a critical incident communicates confidence and control to your subordinates. They in turn will respond confidently and with control.

Civil Liability

One final point needs to be made about leadership and decision making. You will find that this book does not dwell much on civil liability. Frankly, as long as your agency does its job in a manner professional and consistent with SOPs (standard operating procedures), it is not an overwhelming concern. Critical incident management, however, is one major exception. If an event is major and controversial, you *will* come under a mountain of scrutiny once it is resolved. And you can certainly be the target of a civil suit if it appears your actions were unwarranted. But the news isn't all bad.

As a supervisor, you should realize a fairly consistent standard exists for determining the appropriateness of your actions in any critical incident. That standard states in substance: "Based upon the information available to you at the time a decision was made, did the supervisor act as a reasonable person would have?"

Note that the standard does not allow the reviewing body—be it a federal court, civilian review panel, or other inquiry—to consider information learned *subsequent* to the moment of the decision. This greatly limits "second-guessing" decisions made in the heat of crisis.

This standard has probably been applied during the review of incidents in which you have been involved. But remember, you must be able to prove what you knew and when you knew it. Your incident log is critical!

Summary

Analysis of hundreds of critical incidents has shown that the traits discussed in this chapter are mandatory for leaders in critical incidents. Failure to master skills in these areas will almost certainly have a direct negative impact on your ability to stabilize and resolve an incident in the crisis phase.

Remember, *you* are the most controllable factor on your scene. When you have yourself in hand, your subordinates will better fall into line. After that, all you have to do is manage the incident!

Review Questions

- What are three factors that can determine management style?
- How are team members and the public likely to respond to tactical leadership in the crisis phase?
- How can you hone your tactical command presence?
- List four skills that must be mastered by the effective tactical leader.

Seven Critical Tasks™ 5

Objectives

After completing this chapter, you should be able to:

- State the value of a "universal game plan" for crisis phase response.
- Establish a control-oriented response to the crisis phase.
- Describe each of the Seven Critical Tasks™.
- List resources you can bring to bear on a critical incident.

The first moments of an incident's development are crucial. This is where you control the situation or it controls you. You *can* contain a scene in the early stages and make decisions that will help ensure long-term resolution. But to do so, you must take actions we refer to as *critical tasks*.

The decisions you make to accomplish the tasks will vary depending upon the specifics of the incident you are attempting to stabilize. As this text has emphasized, similar problems or obstacles exist in the crisis phase of almost every critical incident. Experience shows us, therefore, that a game plan that minimizes their negative impact will apply in all situations, regardless of the type of incident or the location where it occurs.

The critical tasks in this chapter give you that universal game plan. The final paragraphs of this chapter will relate the Seven Critical Tasks™ to the first-first responder. Initiating the tasks prior to the arrival of the first official responders may well be the difference in ensuring a safe and appropriate response.

This approach to the early phases of critical incidents differs markedly from both the training you may have received in the academy and the actions you take daily when responding to calls. The emphasis in the crisis phase must be on stabilization, *not* resolution. If you try to look too far into the future, events developing in the present may spiral out of control. We refer to this as "tunnel vision." It leads to all kinds of problems.

The Seven Critical Tasks™ are:

- Establish control and communications.
- Identify the hot zone.
- Establish the inner perimeter.
- Establish the outer perimeter.

- Establish the command post.
- Establish a staging area.
- Identify and request additional resources.

Although we present the tasks in this sequence, you should not consider them to be a one-two-three approach. Instead, think of the critical tasks as pieces of a puzzle. Accomplish all of the tasks, regardless of order of completion, and you will enhance your chances of success. Omit any specific task, and you make your job of containment and stabilization that much more difficult.

These critical tasks have been validated by the thousands of police supervisors and other responders we have trained since 1990. If you ever need to use them, we'd like to hear about *your* experience.

Establish Control and Communications

Assuming control of an incident means more than just driving up on-scene. We frequently hear supervisors say, "If I go, people know I'm in charge." This cavalier attitude simply doesn't work when new officers aren't familiar with your voice or there are multiple agencies responding. Announce your command both at the scene and to Dispatch.

Our counterparts in the fire service are unambiguous about command assumption. "Engine 132 will be Main Street command." We hear this all the time. Why is it so difficult for police supervisors to do the same?

Frequently, the responding law enforcement supervisor may be the only supervisor on duty for that shift. He or she may consider announcements of command to be pompous or egotistical. *They are not!* Announcing your response to and command of the scene removes any question as to who is in charge. On-scene personnel know to whom they should direct their requests, questions, and information. Dispatch knows to whom it should direct external communications.

For example, a first-responding supervisor with call number "Car 20" would issue a brief and simple radio transmission, such as "Car 20 to Dispatch. I am responding to 250 Main Street. I am assuming command of the scene. Keep all units responding to the incident on this frequency, and take all other traffic to a secondary frequency." If no secondary frequency is available, then give the order to hold all nonemergency communications. We'll discuss frequencies in more detail shortly.

Problem Assessment

Once you've assumed control of the scene, your next step is to size up the situation. Good sources of information include first-first responders, initial emergency responders, and bystanders, if they are available. Ask initial responders the following questions:

- What is the nature of the incident?
- What is the exact location of the incident?
- How many suspects am I dealing with?
- What is the number and type of weapons involved?
- What type of chemical is involved?
- Is this a possible terrorist threat?

As basic as this may sound, determining the exact nature and location of the threat may be one of the most difficult tasks you must perform in the crisis phase of an incident. This task is further complicated by the confusion that characterizes the crisis phase of an incident. Determining the exact location of an incident is an early priority. As you seek this information, bear in mind that the severity of the incident and resultant stress factors, such as the number of dead or injured, has a direct impact on the communication abilities of those reporting to and those involved in the incident.

For example, a commercial airline crash in San Diego, California, showed that a downed commercial airliner in a highly populated area could be difficult to pinpoint. During the crisis phase, Dispatch sent units to both Falcon Street and similar-sounding Felton Street, even though the streets were several blocks apart. In this case, the sheer magnitude of the incident crippled the ability of both Dispatch and responders to communicate clearly.

To pinpoint the exact location of an incident, you may need to calm both communications personnel and/or first units on the scene. Maintain your composure, and others will do the same.

Remain calm in the face of different kinds of threats. For example, most law enforcement personnel recognize gunfire as life threatening. Therefore it tends to restrain officers from taking unsafe actions at a scene. Unfortunately, the same cannot be said for chemical releases, whether accidental or intentional.

Depending on the nature of the threat, your hardest decision may be to not take an action. Stories of police officers being seriously injured or killed in chemical releases are all too common. When you see an officer down, your first instinct is to rush to assist. We go in. That's what we do! But in HazMat situations, as we'll discuss later, the fire services usually have the appropriate tools and the primary scene responsibility. Your job may be to restrain your own resources from charging in and becoming part of the problem.

Communications

In any crisis situation, establishing communications must be a priority. You are going to need to talk to possibly dozens of people to obtain and share intelligence about the incident. Make sure the communication lines are open and that they stay open.

As law enforcement supervisors, we have become conditioned to keeping the main frequency available for normal traffic and therefore usually take any unusual occurrence to a secondary frequency. In the crisis phase of a critical incident we must break this habit. During the crisis phase, keep your radio communications on the original frequency used when the incident began. Tell Dispatch to send all other traffic to a secondary frequency, if available.

This simple but critical act not only clarifies lines of communications but also informs communications personnel that a supervisor is assuming command of the scene. Any attempt to change the main communication format only enhances the possibility of communications failures.

If you have access to alternate radio frequencies, use them later in the scene management phase when you have more time and resources. If you are working with one frequency, restrict traffic to incident-specific communications as much as possible.

When using phone lines, make sure they stay open and available. Don't rely on cell phones. Everyone even remotely associated with the incident will be trying to make calls, and cell relays will become overloaded. Try to get dedicated landlines.

You may need runners. You may need hand signals! Regardless of the communication mode, secure it so you'll always have access to it.

Of course, communications extend beyond the incident scene. If you cannot control the situation in the early phases, you may also need to establish lines to an extended ICS team operating remotely. Make sure you have the landlines, cellular, or radio capacity to work with remote groups. Generally, this level of communication is a characteristic of the scene management incident phase.

Identify the Hot Zone

"Hot zone" is a descriptive term for the area immediately surrounding an incident—the area of imminent danger to responders and citizens. This is the field of fire for gunmen barricaded in a house. This is the location of a ruptured tanker and the vapor cloud of the chlorine gas leaking from it.

Why "hot zone"? The reason for this is to establish common terminology with other first responders. The term emanates from the military as identifying an area such as a landing zone that is under fire. It was adopted by the fire service and has been used by them for years. Originally this text and our course advocated the term "kill zone" in hopes it would clearly define the life-threatening status of any given area. In an attempt to standardize response terms with other first responders, we have incorporated the term

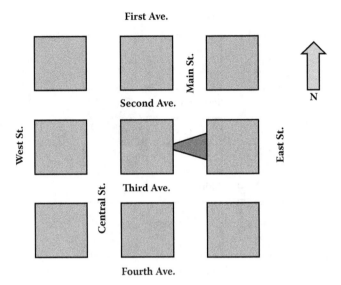

Figure 5.1 The shaded area shows the hot zone for a barricaded gunman in a first-floor apartment with a small-caliber handgun. In this case, the hot zone is the suspect's field of fire as limited by nearby buildings.

"hot zone." Make no mistake, it still designates an area that presents a clear and present danger to the life and safety of anyone within that area, including responders. Figure 5.1 shows a potential hot zone for a barricaded gunman with a small-caliber handgun in the first-floor apartment at 250 Main Street.

In this scenario, the correct initial radio transmission by the supervisor should be, "All cars responding to the incident at 250 Main Street. *I want no cars on Main Street between Second Avenue and Third Avenue.*" This simple transmission identifies the hot zone to all responding units, prevents inadvertent response into the area, and may well save officers' lives. The hot zone may be as small as a portion of a city block, as depicted in Figure 5.1, or (as we'll see later) may involve multiple city blocks or entire towns, in the case of a chemical spill or civil disorder.

Critical incidents can happen anywhere. For an incident on an interstate highway, responders may define the hot zone on the radio like this: "No cars on Interstate 90 between mile marker 128 and mile marker 129." The physical identification of the hot zone will vary from incident to incident, but the need to clearly identify that area will not.

Once you've identified this zone, deploy personnel to ensure no one moves in or out of the area (public *and* responders). The two exceptions are evacuations and controlled movement. And as we'll see later when we get into more hazardous-materials responses, it can frequently make more sense for civilians to "shelter in place." On a windy day, a HazMat hot zone can be deceptively large, making evacuation impractical.

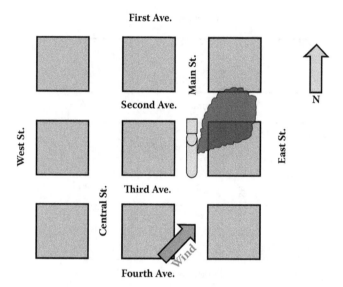

Figure 5.2 Numerous factors, such as wind, terrain, and nature of the release, can affect a HazMat hot zone. It can also change rapidly, forcing you to be extra conservative in your threat estimates.

Controlled movement refers to getting the public clear of the hot zone. You do not, however, simply let them run screaming into the surrounding neighborhood. Chances are you might lose suspects and witnesses that way. If you have any reason to believe suspects may try to mingle with the crowd, pat down and interview all persons leaving a criminal scene. At a minimum, take names and check IDs. You may need these people later.

As Figure 5.2 shows, the hot zones for a barricaded gunman and a HazMat spill would be very different. The first is determined by the caliber of the gunman's weapon and the surrounding buildings. The second is determined by the size and nature of the spill and then by wind and terrain.

There are no hard-and-fast rules for the size of a hot zone. Your own observations of the terrain, the surrounding buildings, the nature of the threat, and weather conditions will dictate how large it will be.

The size and shape of the hot zone determines the size and shape of the area we will discuss next: the inner perimeter.

Establish the Inner Perimeter

The inner perimeter defines the area just beyond the hot zone and within which responders operate to directly control the situation. One of your primary jobs is to strictly limit inner-perimeter access to responding emergency agencies.

The inner perimeter is *not the hot zone*. It's the line immediately behind which you and other responders are working. The boundary of the inner perimeter must completely surround the hot zone and be tightly controlled to keep the incident from expanding. You control access to the hot zone, directing who goes in (such as a coordinated assault team) and who goes out (such as fleeing suspects trying to blend in with a crowd). This is the boundary beyond which you conduct all operations. Although the inner perimeter can be an offensive position, it must afford cover, concealment, and/or proper safe distance for responders working behind it.

Remember, your objective at this point is containment. The boundary must be stable, and your people should have assigned posts that they do not leave. *No independent actions* should be taken. This is one of those times when personnel should do only what you tell them to do. Independent action from an inner-perimeter position can make things worse. By nature, officers constantly reevaluate and try to improve their strategic locations. This usually translates to getting closer to the scene. Left uncontrolled, this tendency has on numerous occasions led to officers exposing themselves unnecessarily to gunfire within the hot zone and further complicating an already deadly situation.

Figure 5.3 shows a typical inner perimeter set up in response to the barricaded gunman at 250 Main Street. The next several paragraphs will refer to this illustration.

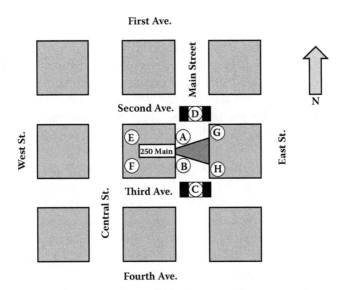

Figure 5.3 The inner perimeter defines the boundary within which responders work to contain and resolve the incident. This illustration shows a possible inner perimeter for a barricaded gunman with a small-caliber weapon.

A and B represent the first-responding officers. They answered the initial call and got pinned down by gunfire at the scene. You, as the first-responding supervisor, have announced response to and command of the scene. You conducted a brief problem assessment, identified the hot zone, and communicated that information to additional responding units. Although this zone may change as the situation evolves, such as suspects opening up with longer-range weapons or gaining access to higher ground, the area posing the known danger to first responders has been identified.

You must now deploy resources to contain and control the situation. Marked units C and D are positioned to block off all vehicular and pedestrian traffic from entering the area. This includes emergency vehicles and personnel responding to the scene.

You must deploy resources with clear and concise radio communications. Orders must contain not only duties but also the route for safe arrival at the desired location. You may be the only one who has this information. Share it! For example, a command given to marked unit C might sound something like this: "Respond the intersection of Main Street and Third Avenue. Avoid Main Street between Second and Third. Approach the intersection from the south on Main or the west on Third. Stop all vehicular and pedestrian traffic from proceeding northbound on Main Street."

A similar direction, complete with safe access route and duties upon arriving, would be given to marked unit D. These types of detailed communications may seem cumbersome, but they are exactly what the phrase *clear, concise order giving* means. Don't assume your people know something that you take for granted. Keep it brief, but spell it out.

Positions E, F, G, and H represent other officers that may be deployed in safe cover around the incident scene to ensure containment. As you would expect, their orders should also include safe routes and detailed directions as to their duties and responsibilities. These positions may be temporary. Specially trained personnel, such as SWAT, may relieve most, if not all, of their positions.

Some supervisors might attempt to remove officers A and B from the hot zone immediately. That may be a good strategy if it can be accomplished safely and without compromising the containment of the suspect. However, it may be impossible to achieve without undue risk. Also, officers pinned down may refuse to move for fear of exposure. If you decide to attempt an extraction, make sure you take the affected officers' input into account! The procedure will require their cooperation. If the officers have adequate cover and are in a position of relative safety, they should be left in place until they can be moved safely with the assistance of specialized personnel and equipment.

A few other points need to be made about the inner perimeter. As just stated, the inner perimeter must afford cover, concealment, and/or proper safe distance for responders working behind it. Good cover is often defined as the position we put ourselves in immediately *after* the first shot is fired in our direction. Your job as supervisor is to make sure responders have proper cover *before* they draw the attention of a gunman.

Assess the cover requirements of the assigned units before sending them into harm's way. Keep in mind that this is extremely difficult to do if you have positioned yourself as a player instead of a coach.

As an active participant, you can develop a kind of tunnel vision that severely limits your ability to see the big picture. Place yourself in a position that allows you to conduct ongoing assessments of the scene (and all of its elements) in relative safety. You can't do that if you're crouching behind a trash bin to avoid hostile fire. Of course it's possible you may start out as a player at a scene, but pull back as soon as you can. We know you would probably rather be right in there on the front lines. Don't worry about what anyone might think! You have multiple responsibilities, and cover assessment is just one of them.

Of course, cover from a gunman is not the same as cover from a cloud of poisonous gas. When you're faced with a ruptured chlorine tanker, for example, your people need to be a minimum of 900 feet away and upwind. This figure comes not from a visual assessment of the scene and your own street smarts, but from an invaluable reference book, the U.S. Department of Transportation *Emergency Response Guidebook* (ERG). We go into the ERG in more detail in Appendix B.

The inner perimeter may not be as dangerous as the hot zone, but it still requires significant safety measures. Cover in the case of HazMat means either distance from a scene or protective clothing, which law enforcement responders won't have. Therefore they must rely on training and experience to avoid contact with a released substance.

Uniformed Personnel

Our next two points pertain to people within the inner perimeter. The first concerns plainclothes personnel. It may seem obvious to limit inner-perimeter access to emergency responders. Now we'll take that a step further and argue that, particularly in criminal-activity scenes, responders should be limited to *uniformed* personnel. If plainclothes are initially deployed, remove them and replace them with uniforms as soon as possible. The wide success of plainclothes units has been due in part to their ability to blend into the general population. They are indistinguishable. You don't want to put your detectives at undue risk from members of other departments or overzealous homeowners.

Of course, removing plainclothes personnel from an inner perimeter isn't always an option. If the only officers available to contain a suspect are plainclothes personnel, then use them. However, you as the supervisor must make their presence *very clear* to all responding units. Use positions and descriptions, if necessary. Failure to do so may have tragic results.

Public within the Inner Perimeter

We introduced dealing with the public in our hot-zone discussion. During the crisis phase of a critical incident, there may well be innocent people trapped within the inner perimeter. In the scenario depicted in Figure 5.3, the area identified as the hot zone and encompassed by the inner perimeter could contain numerous civilians.

Usually, the best strategy in the crisis phase is to keep individuals who are in relatively safe locations, such as their homes, in those locations until they can be moved in a safe and orderly manner. This strategy is known as *shelter-in-place*. It is a strategy often used in chemical spills that involve no threat of fire or explosion.

The alternative to shelter-in-place is evacuation. However, evacuation is seldom a good option in the crisis phase of an incident. Evacuation is almost always better accomplished in the scene management phase when sufficient resources are available to carry out this tactic.

Although crisis containment and responder safety are paramount, you should not let the public be an afterthought. As part of the problem assessment process during the crisis phase, determine who or what might be endangered within the perimeters you've established. Accept that you may not be able to adequately handle the public as well as you might like to at this point. That may have to wait until the scene management phase.

Lastly, take areas of critical vulnerability into account when you create your inner perimeter. Such areas can include hospitals, schools, gun shops, and power plants. Anything that could significantly add to the seriousness of the incident if it were to become involved must be locked down as quickly as possible. For example, if you don't want your hostage situation to involve a nearby school, it's up to you to recognize the threat and make sure the building is locked down or evacuated, depending on the specific situation.

The bottom line is that during the crisis phase you must identify and secure the public and at-risk locations to the best of your ability. That gives you the breathing room you need to develop and implement more detailed response strategies in the scene management phase.

Establish the Outer Perimeter

While the inner perimeter controls the incident, the outer perimeter controls the *response* to the incident. You will have crowds, specifically, three types of crowds:

- Civilian bystanders, which vary by location and time of day
- The media, which vary by location as well as the nature and severity of the incident
- Emergency responders, which also vary with the type of incident

(Prepare, however, for a major media and emergency response even in remote areas with small civilian populations.)

The area between the inner and outer perimeters is where responders get their work done. It is essential that you tightly control access to this area. Even other responders can cause confusion if they have unrestrained access to a scene. The appropriate deployment of arriving units is one of your essential scene command tasks. That frequently means establishing a staging area, an area to which resources can respond and from which you can deploy them as required. (We will discuss staging later in this chapter.)

The typical management problem transitions from too few resources in the crisis phase to possibly too many resources in the scene management phase. Those large numbers of resources require careful management to make sure they are used to their maximum efficiency.

Time and again the initial response of emergency responders to a scene has caused gridlock and inhibited successful operations. This forces you to disconnect from scene management and concentrate on undoing the gridlock. Valuable time and energy is focused on a problem *caused* by those who are attempting to help. The early establishment of an outer perimeter provides an open area in which to stage and operate and an additional safety zone for nonemergency workers.

Figure 5.4 depicts with police units a typical outer perimeter responders might establish for the 250 Main Street gunman incident. The outer perimeter shown in Figure 5.4 has been established far enough away from the incident location to guarantee public safety outside its limits, yet close enough to keep the area between the inner and outer perimeters a manageable size.

The outer perimeter is not an offensive position. If it becomes so, then it's too close to the actual incident. Its primary function is to control movement to and from the scene, not deal directly with developments in the hot zone. As with the inner perimeter, personnel assigned to outer-perimeter posts should be sent to specific locations and instructed to stay there.

A good field test to apply to an outer perimeter is whether nonpolice personnel can staff it safely. If personnel on the outer perimeter need to wear breathing apparatus and protective equipment, then it is not an outer perimeter. If you feel the need for armed officers on your outer perimeter, then you have not positioned the boundary correctly. No weapons should be unholstered or displayed at any point on the outer perimeter. The inner perimeter is the business end; *that's* where your offensive resources should be deployed.

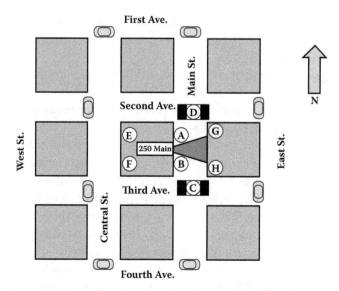

Figure 5.4 The outer perimeter (represented by the black-and-white units) for a barricaded gunman with a small-caliber weapon. The region between the inner and outer perimeters provides a safe work area for responders.

The mere presence and readiness of firearms on the outer perimeter opens the door to inappropriate response. Officers beyond effective range might fire toward a central location surrounded by other responders. Your job is to minimize this possibility by making sure there are no weapons at the ready position on the outer perimeter. Unless there is potential for serious civil unrest, officers at outer stations need be armed only with the tools essential for traffic and crowd control. They need also be aware of relevant incident information that they can pass on to responding units, such as command post and staging area locations.

To be effective, the outer perimeter must completely enclose the inner perimeter. The actual size of the perimeter depends entirely on the scale and nature of the event. For example, if you expect four entire fire companies and two HazMat response teams on-scene, your outer boundary had better expand to allow for those vehicles to stage securely.

The outer-perimeter example we've used so far has been based on criminal activity. But recall the cloud of chlorine gas in Figure 5.2. With a variable hot zone comes a variable inner perimeter and a variable outer perimeter. In this case, where are you going to be comfortable allowing crowds to gather? Depending on weather conditions, you may be looking at an outer perimeter of possibly dozens of city blocks. Play it safe!

When a rail tanker explosion demolished 90 percent of the business district of Crescent City, Illinois, there were no fatalities. Responders recognized the threat in time and evacuated the entire town. The lesson? Even your inner perimeter can quickly look like the borders of a midsize township. It's unlikely you would have the resources to completely enclose an area that size with an outer perimeter. In that case, you would simply blockade incoming traffic and set up a working area on one edge of the evacuated area. It would be big enough to hold staging and command functions, but small enough for you to control access.

Now that you have established the incident scene layout and created a place to work, it's time to turn to the tasks you must accomplish to coordinate your resources. The final three critical tasks also happen to be important components of the Incident Command System and, by extension, the National Incident Management System.

Establish the Command Post

At just about any scene, the supervisor's vehicle will serve as the initial command post. Therefore where you park your vehicle upon arriving on-scene is critical to your ability to command the incident. The mere location selected may make the difference in whether you will be a participant/player or a manager/coach.

Any command post, whether it's a mobile or fixed site, must be located outside of the hot zone and between the inner and outer perimeters. This gives your people (and you!) safe access to the command post in a controlled area. The initial placement of your vehicle should also meet these criteria: not so close that you come under threat, and not so far away that you'll have to move closer once you establish the outer perimeter.

This assumes that other responders get to the scene before you. This may not always be the case. If you are one of the initial responders to arrive on-scene, you may choose to position your vehicle to deny access to the hot zone. In this case, you stay there until you can get another unit to replace you. Only then can you back off the front line to a safe and controlled location.

As discussed earlier, if you remain on the inner perimeter, your focus will be on event particulars and not on the overall operation. Only by removing yourself from the immediacy of the action can you develop that broad overview of the situation you need to be an effective supervisor. There is a common management principle that tells us we tend to manage what we can see. If we put ourselves on the inner perimeter of an incident, we will tend to manage from that perspective and possibly fail to handle issues not in our immediate line of sight.

*Any command post involving armed individuals, either fixed or mobile, should **not** be located within line of site of an incident.*

If you can see them, they can see you. The last thing you want to give suspects is a bird's-eye view of the activities at your command post. By locating a command post out of sight of an incident, you not only enhance the security and safety of command post personnel but also force the management of the scene to a different perspective. And what is that perspective? The big picture.

Figure 5.5 indicates one possible location for the initial supervisor to park his or her vehicle for our gunman scenario. This spot would also be a good choice for the establishment of a fixed-site command post. Keep in mind this is only one of several potential sites.

We know our command post should not be in or near the hot zone because of line-of-sight and command perspective issues. But there's another factor to consider: wind direction. While we always take wind into account during chemical or hazardous-material incidents, we tend to neglect it when addressing barricaded or armed suspects—that is, until the deployment of tear gas by a SWAT team incapacitates our command post, which we have located downwind from an incident. Employing chemical weapons to extricate or temporarily incapacitate armed suspects is standard operating procedure for SWAT teams. You can't manage a scene if you're suffering as much as your suspects are.

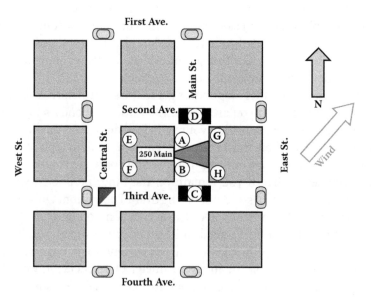

Figure 5.5 A command post (▨) should be in a safe, controlled location. This illustration shows the first-responding supervisor's unit within the outer perimeter and out of line of sight of the hot zone.

Be Flexible

Wind direction may not be a major factor in the initial placement of the supervisor's vehicle. This is by definition a *mobile* command post. As the initial supervisor, you may park your vehicle only to realize you are downwind from the suspect location. You move. However, wind must definitely be considered when you select a fixed-site location. And even then, keep in mind that the command post location may change several times during the course of the incident as requirements dictate.

As the incident progresses, any number of variables (weather, requirements of your responding resource, length of operation, etc.) may require additional changes of location. It is your responsibility as the first-responding supervisor to identify a safe and appropriate command post location. Whether the location remains static for the entire incident is immaterial. It may well change. You should not feel that your authority or decision-making ability is being questioned.

Few critical incidents can be stabilized and resolved using only a police vehicle as a command post. Two more likely alternatives are a transfer of authority to a fixed site or to a mobile command post vehicle. Of course, the location of either should meet the same criteria outlined for the initial placement of the supervisor's vehicle.

Fixed-Site Command Post

The transition from a single-vehicle command post to a fixed-site command post usually occurs when your requested resources arrive at the emergency scene. These resources may be additional supervisory law personnel, fire personnel, emergency medical service personnel, or specialists requested for scene resolution. If you do not have ready access to a mobile command vehicle, establish a fixed-site location.

To be effective, your fixed command post must have the following:

- Electricity
- Drinking water
- Restroom facilities
- Access to telephone lines
- Ability to monitor television broadcasts

Remember, although cellular phones may be of great assistance in the crisis phase and early on in the scene management, you still need telephone landlines. Cellular systems are prone to overload and are less secure even than the radio frequencies we use daily.

The command post should have heat in the winter and air conditioning in the summer. If such options are unavailable, the command post should at least provide shelter from the elements and an atmosphere conducive to communication and decision-making processes. Avoid open-air command posts. Even if weather is not a factor, the noise and activity of an open-air command post can be a major distraction.

The availability of television and video equipment, once thought a luxury, is now a necessity. This equipment may well provide intelligence that can be vital to decision making. The same can be said of computers, fax machines, copiers, and other equipment that has become part of our daily administrative lives. Chances are that if you find yourself setting up a fixed-site location, the incident may last for quite a while. Make sure the command post supports the command functions and provides for all conceivable needs.

Mobile Command Post Vehicles

The other likely option is to transition to a mobile command post vehicle. Mobile command posts can, by nature, be redeployed easily. For example, a mobile command post is required in a hazardous-material incident due to the possibility of wind change and the subsequent need to fall back to a safer area.

All of the elements required for a fixed site should be available in a mobile command post. In the last several years, numerous companies have begun producing vehicles that meet these requirements. Such vehicles, we feel, are truly worth the investment.

Unfortunately, jurisdictions frequently misuse mobile command posts as nothing more than mobile communications centers. Filled with additional radios, telephones, and assorted other equipment, they often lack the critical, basic requirements of an adequate command post. If in fact the mobile command post available to you *is* nothing more than a communication vehicle, use it in conjunction with a fixed site.

Regardless of which option you choose, there is always one common requirement for any adequate command post: It must provide an atmosphere conducive to the communication and decision-making processes that will take place. The command post must have the ability to minimize stress factors, such as noise, confusion, and panic, and the distracting effects they can have on those in charge.

Establish a Staging Area

The staging area is a specific location to which additional resources respond and await deployment to the scene. Do not confuse the staging area and the command post. These two terms have often been interchanged, and many times the two functions end up as a combined area. Keep them separate, if possible.

In smaller incidents, such as a minor chemical spill, it *may* be appropriate to combine command and staging. However, in a barricaded-gunman or armed hostage situation, the two should always be separate. Combined command post/staging areas tend to be crowded, difficult to access, and noisy. This does not make for the calm, quiet decision-making atmosphere we look for in a proper command post!

The area designated for staging should be well out of the hot zone, but between the inner and outer perimeters. It must be large enough to accommodate all of the responding resources, and close enough to allow for quick transfer to and from the scene. Parking lots and blocked-off streets are optimum locations. Figure 5.6 gives a possible location for our incident at 250 Main Street.

The staging area is an absolute requirement. Create it and use it appropriately. Too often a supervisor phrases a request to Dispatch as, "Send me a fire company and ambulance support down here." This directive results in the requested resource responding to the incident location—in other words, into the hot zone. The establishment of a staging area prevents this from occurring.

The designation of a staging area in mass-casualty incidents is extremely important. Failure to do so will result in all responding EMS units going directly to the scene, usually resulting in gridlock of critical resources by other resources. Response to a staging area, and then deployment to the

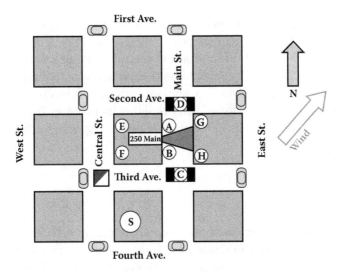

Figure 5.6 The staging area (Ⓢ) for additional resources must be in a controlled area and have good access to the scene.

scene, allows for not only access to the scene but egress as well. There have been numerous incidents where this overresponse and gridlock directly to the scene have resulted in the need to hand carry victims long distances before reaching a unit capable of getting them to a medical facility.

As when ordering in your initial resources, a sample transmission for the scenario depicted in Figure 5.6 might be: "I need fire and ambulance units standing by in the parking lot on West Street at Fourth Street. They must avoid travel on Main Street between Second and Third."

When you establish a staging area, don't forget to appoint a Staging Area Supervisor. Resources directed to a staging area have a reasonable expectation to be met and briefed by a command representative. If you neglect to assign a Staging Area Supervisor, you lose contact with and control over incoming resources. Responders will not stand by indefinitely without being briefed on the situation and tactics. Also, without the appointment of a Staging Area Supervisor, the Incident Commander has a harder time finding out that requested resources have arrived and are available for deployment.

Identify and Request Additional Resources

Our final critical task is the identification of and call for additional resources. Although we treat it here at the end, keep in mind this doesn't necessarily mean it is the last task performed. You may determine the need for a SWAT or HazMat team response in the early moments of a critical incident. If so, make the call immediately.

Resources take time to mobilize and arrive at the scene. Therefore the sooner you identify and request them, the sooner they will be ready for deployment. If the initial responding supervisor is not of a rank or position capable of authorizing the mobilization, then someone of that rank should be notified as soon as possible so he or she can authorize the requests. Resources available within the law enforcement discipline include specialty teams with training and expertise in specified areas of police response, such as:

- SWAT teams
- Hostage negotiators
- Bomb squads

Identify and request additional resources proactively. Do not simply request what you know you already need—brainstorm to predict what *might* be needed. The following sections include some examples and issues particular to nonpolice resources that you may activate for a critical incident.

Emergency Medical Services (EMS)

A crucial part of your job is anticipating and requesting EMS support, whether it is public or private, professional or volunteer. Waiting until someone is injured at a scene is too late. Surprisingly, time and again emergency responders fail to proactively order these resources to stand by. This is especially true where the agency may be charged for the stand-by service. The result may be a bomb squad moving a suspicious device without a medical team on-scene. We think it's probably worth a few dollars to save the life of one or more of your bomb techs.

Critical incidents by their very nature pose a threat to the general public and to the emergency responders. Request EMS to stand by at the staging area for every critical incident regardless of initial need.

The Fire Service

Although you are surely quick to recognize the need for fire response at a scene involving flames or hazardous material, you may overlook that need in what are generally considered "police scenes." Incidents involving barricaded gunmen, armed hostage scenes, and high-risk warrant executions are some examples of scenes where fire resources may not be routinely requested to stand by.

Again, think proactively. Most of the police scenes described previously will be resolved with the deployment of a SWAT team. Specialized teams bring specialized equipment such as tear gas, "flash bang" diversionary devices, and/or explosive entry devices. Any or all of these gadgets are capable of starting fires, regardless of whatever nonflammable characteristics they may claim. If you know that one or more of these tactics are being considered, have a fire company standing by in the staging area.

Additionally, fire companies bring tools and equipment law enforcement officers do not normally have available in their police vehicles. Ladders, supplemental lighting, SCBA, ropes, pry bars, axes, and tarpaulins are just a few of the items that may prove exceedingly useful.

The Media

There is one resource that responds to the scene whether we request it or not—the media. Of course most supervisors don't exactly see journalists as an asset. But think about it: Today's media can establish instantaneous communication with our jurisdictions. They can provide the public with directions and instructions regarding your incident. Just a few examples include areas to avoid, recommended evacuation areas, and public refuge locations.

Don't think of reporters and photographers as adversaries. That stale old prejudice simply forces them to find whatever story they can. They *will* get their story, with or without your input. Why not give them the story you want them to have, the actual story? Hopefully you have a well-equipped command post that will allow you to monitor what the media is reporting about your event. If you work with them correctly, the media can be invaluable for controlling rumor that can inflame your situation.

For purposes of the critical tasks, the main responsibility for the first-responding supervisor is to direct all media representatives to the staging area. Situating the media there has several excellent advantages. Note this is within your outer perimeter. It may seem self-evident, but keeping the media in a controlled area gives you at least some ability to manage that media.

- Maintaining the media in the staging area gives your Public Information Officer (an ICS function that will be covered in Chapter 6) a good location for conducting timely, periodic news briefings.
- Reporters like to be where the decision makers are. But you don't want them at your command post. The staging area provides a good backdrop for on-camera talent. They are safe yet they will not feel isolated from events.
- In general, the media has the same right of access as the general public. Granting the media staging area access gives them a privileged vantage point from which to broadcast. Use this privilege to ensure their cooperation. If a certain crew fails to comply with reasonable requests from commanders or fails to control their personnel, restrict that crew to beyond the outer perimeter. They will no longer have access to your briefings and will therefore be at a particular disadvantage in trying to cover your incident.

We walk a fine line between press access and scene security. Never allow live television broadcasting from the hot zone of any type of ongoing criminal activity. Such reports may endanger the lives of citizens and/or officers involved in the incident. For example, a "live eye" helicopter camera broadcasting deployment positions, arrival of additional resources, and or other strategic information poses a definite and direct threat to both officers involved and citizens. One tragic example occurred during the coverage of a hostage incident in Berkeley, California. The suspect saw live broadcasts of SWAT teams deploying against his location and began to shoot his hostages.

At Columbine High School, numerous students in the school reported hiding in classrooms and watching the police response outside of the school on television sets in the classroom. There is no evidence the suspects did the same, as they were never debriefed, but the danger to responders is obvious when such real-time broadcasts are permitted.

As a side note, most bomb squads prefer not to be photographed while addressing a potential device. The equipment and strategies thus shown may aid a potential bomber to defeat their efforts the next time.

The "live eye" ban is a basic ground rule of critical incident management that your department should discuss with media representatives in your area before a critical incident occurs. The heat of an incident is not the time to try and establish ground rules for a good relationship. This is something you must work toward long before an incident arises.

Utility Companies

Power companies (gas and electric), telephone, television, water, and sewer are all examples of utility companies you may call on to assist in resolution a critical incident. Let's examine a few situations in which their services might be required:

- **Power Companies:** Where a threat of fire or explosion exists, the need to terminate electric or gas service is readily apparent. Some supervisors believe terminating power to barricaded or armed hostage scenes is also standard operating procedure. This is not always the case. SWAT teams often prefer the power left on, especially at night. Power may also be a bargaining chip for negotiators. Therefore although you might call power authorities to the staging area, don't make the decision to terminate power to a scene without consulting the responding specialist.
- **Telephone Company:** Notify the local phone carrier, especially in hostage situations, as quickly as possible. The ability to limit the incoming and outgoing calls to a specific phone is crucial. Unfortunately, to control cell phone calls we must have the specific number assigned to a phone.
- **Cable/Satellite Television:** The popularity of nonbroadcast television gives us an additional option in critical incident management. Historically, one of the reasons given for cutting power to a location was to limit a suspect's ability to monitor television reports of the incident. Many older-model televisions are not capable of receiving a clear signal without benefit of a cable connection or external satellite dish. A single call to the service provider can result in termination. Providers frequently can do this right from the broadcast location and might not need to come on-scene.

These strategies are just a few of the many possibilities. Only the innovative thinking of the crisis manager limits the services utility companies can provide. Identify these resources as you begin to stabilize the crisis phase. Their response time will vary from location to location.

Official Resources versus Realistic Resources

Most of the resources discussed to this point have been *official* resources. They are usually listed in resource manuals. The development and implementation of a quality resource manual is definitely worthwhile. But creating the manual is only the first step. Keeping it up to date and accurate is an ongoing responsibility. If your agency has such a document, do two things:

- Take it out and verify whether it has been updated recently. If not, call the numbers and check the names of the officials listed. You may be surprised to find how inaccurate your information is!
- Check on actual response times. Sure, a resource may be listed, but how much good is it going to do you if it can't get to your scene for eight hours? The availability (or nonavailability) of a resource has a direct impact on your strategy planning.

Realistic resources are those that are available in your jurisdiction when you need them. These can be official or unofficial. Responders working in rural or isolated areas tend to be skilled at utilizing unofficial realistic resources. These responders learn to improvise simply because they don't have the resources available to urban responders. Conversely, urban officers frequently lack this skill because specialized backup is usually just a call away.

Ask yourself this question: "You are responding to an in-progress crime scene where an officer has been wounded and extraction is imperative for survival. What could you use as a cover vehicle to rescue the victim?" If this question is not addressed in the calm of preincident planning, someone in the emotion and confusion of a crisis will probably try to make the rescue without proper equipment or cover vehicle.

An official resource manual may list a state National Guard armored vehicle you could activate through official channels. This process will probably be time consuming in the best of conditions. If your incident occurs on New Year's Eve, it may be impossible. The armored vehicle becomes a non-resource for your incident.

On the other hand, your jurisdiction may contain a private armored car company. If so, *before a crisis*, contact the manager and find out how you might be able to activate one of their armored cars in the event of an incident. (You'll also want to make sure it truly is armored!) Get home and/or pager numbers for the person with the keys. A little planning on your part may make available a *realistic* resource that can make the difference between life and death. The more we plan in advance, the less we will have to rely on reactive, spur-of-the-moment decisions when managing a critical incident.

The Seven Critical Tasks™ and the First-First Responder

Although the Seven Critical Tasks™ are clearly designed for implementation by trained emergency responders, the first-first responder, as previously described in this text, may be in the best position to initiate them prior to the arrival of the first responding units. Although establishing an outer perimeter most likely won't occur in the first few minutes of an incident, several of the critical tasks should be accomplished as soon as possible.

If the first-first responder is the person calling 911, or another emergency number requesting help, there are several tasks that should be initiated. By giving their name and exact location, they have established themselves as the person with knowledge on-scene, or the Incident Commander. Their exact location designates the initial command post. Following the criteria established earlier in this chapter, it should be out of the hot zone and accessible by others.

A simple direction such as "Tell responding officers to avoid the south side of the building" or "Tell responders not to enter the third floor of the building as that is where the chemical spill has occurred and there are strong fumes there" may be used to designate the hot zone to responders. By initiating these two tasks, the responders now know where to find the person with the most information and what areas pose the greatest danger to them.

Positioning students, other teachers, or coworkers to prevent access to the hot zone is also an action that may be taken in the first few minutes of an incident. When a gunman was on a rampage at Dawson College, in Montreal, Canada, an unarmed campus security officer was credited with saving lives by positioning himself to prevent students and faculty from accessing a hallway that led to the gunman's location.

Active Shooter

In this section, we will address facing an active-shooter situation from two perspectives—first, as a first (law enforcement) responder, and then as an individual faced with the presence of an active shooter in his or her workplace, school, or other environment. To do this you need to be able to distinguish between a "hostage" situation and an "active-shooter" situation.

In a hostage situation, there may or may not have been shots fired, but you have been made aware that someone with a gun is in your area. A hostage taker will take control of one or more persons by force and then make demands of other people to achieve a goal. That goal can vary: assistance with an escape, demands for money, publicity for a political statement, personal attention, and/or dozens of other reasons. The key criterion here is that there is no current evidence of an ongoing taking of lives.

In an active-shooter situation, there is a continuance of gunfire in areas where you know people are or should be. Your initial assessment needs to be that lives, yours and others, are in imminent danger, and you must take action. The question is, what action should you take?

As a potential first-first responder, you may have been trained to stabilize and isolate threats through setting up perimeters, calling for other resources, and so on. This strategy applies to almost all situations and types of emergency events. In an active-shooter situation, you will return to this strategy after you assess your options and take some initial actions to protect lives, including your own. If you have studied these situations, you know that they typically last a very short time. Most are over in 20 minutes or less. This tells you that quick and decisive action must be taken.

Active shooters do not seem to be concerned with escape like many hostage takers. They are bent on destruction and, while they may have some focused targets, will randomly kill or wound anyone in their path. The most common outcome for these events is suicide by their own hand or "suicide by cop."

In the aftermath of the school shootings at Columbine, police departments across the country began to access their response to these tragic events even to the point of holding national symposiums on response and training options. From a law enforcement standpoint, the response has shifted in most jurisdictions from a "secure the scene and call up the SWAT team" approach to an organized four-person "active-shooter response team" approach using the first officers that arrive on scene. While the training, supervision, equipment, and tactics may vary, the mission is focused on moving toward the sound of the shots and eliminating the threat. Although it may be apparent, immediate action must be taken; selecting the proper action is critically important. The decision to employ this tactic should not be taken lightly. If your department has properly trained and equipped officers in active-shooter response, then deployment may be the exact tactic required.

However, when it comes to tactics, each situation requires an assessment and tactic selection that fits the scene. Tactics cannot be dictated from an administrative office. As we have advocated throughout this text, we believe the first-responding supervisor is the individual in the best position to determine the specific tactic to be utilized in any situation. The following will clarify our position on proper training, equipment, and deployment:

- **Proper training:** The proper training of active-shooter tactics should include classroom instruction *and* simulation exercises. The use of "simunitions" and role-play exercises is critically important. To ensure officer proficiency with these tactics, follow-up training should occur. As with any skills, training the ability to actually perform a physical task may diminish if it isn't reinforced through follow-up training.
- **Proper equipment:** Specialized equipment for active-shooter response varies greatly from department to department. Some departments have purchased items such as patrol rifles, protective vests with greater ballistic-stopping capabilities than the personal vests that officers are issued, Kevlar helmets, and the like. However, departments where vests are not mandatory are also training this tactic. Therefore the possibility exists that the first four officers on a scene may attempt this tactic with none of the officers having benefit of a bullet-resistant vest or other critical equipment.
- **Proper deployment:** Clear guidelines need to be established for the proper deployment of active-shooter response. Two situations where this would not be utilized are hostage situations and barricaded-shooter situations. However, we have observed that officers in training continue the tactic even when an active-shooter scenario transitions to one of the prohibited situations. A clear understanding of when to use the tactic is paramount to proper deployment of this strategy.

Any officer who has experienced walk-through training will also relate that in the overwhelming majority of training situations at least one member of the team would have become a victim. This often becomes the source of posttraining humor. The authors of this text have observed firsthand the effect that an officer being shot has on his or her coworkers. Not only from an officer safety viewpoint but also from a pure management standpoint, we must take every precaution to prevent this from occurring. A lesson learned from our brother and sister responders in the emergency medical service and the fire service is a simple one: A dead responder helps no one. To those who state it is our job to do dangerous things, we totally agree. It is also our responsibility to our officers to do dangerous things as safely as possible. A dead cop helps no one!

When the HR Director in our scenario returned to the office, he found himself confronted with an active-shooter event. He knew from recent training that distinguishing between an active-shooter situation and the more common hostage situation was a critical first step. Should you ever find yourself in the HR Director's shoes, it will be critically important for you to assess what is going on very quickly. Even though people feel that being involved in a situation like this is "something that happens to other people," we strongly advise you to set up training for yourself and others in the organization. We have mentioned "mental preparation" and have asked you to imagine what you would do in the situations we have presented throughout this book. The secret to proper mental preparation is having the correct information and strategies presented in a powerful way so that you and others can internally rehearse your response. Some will panic or freeze up, especially if they have never anticipated being in such a situation. But those who have been trained will respond quickly and with purpose.

One of the options you might consider to train individuals in your organization comes from the Center for Personal Protection & Safety. They have an excellent CD-based program entitled "Shots Fired," which is complete with lesson plans and student materials. Historically, we have been very skeptical of programs and "experts" that always seem to pop up after incidents like Columbine and/or the shootings at Virginia Tech. Is it useful or just opportunistic? What are the credentials of the authors and developers? When introduced to this program, we expected a historical recap of events with old video feeds showing shooting scenes filled with innocent victims. Instead, this program delivers a prescriptive strategy that individuals can apply whether they are at work, dinner, or the mall should an active-shooter situation present itself.

The "Shots Fired" program encourages individuals to adopt a "survival mind-set," to use their intuitive skills, and to trust that "gut" feeling or what they call "knowing without knowing why." Police officers will tell you that one of the most frustrating parts of their job happens when people who were suspicious of a person or an event fail to call because they didn't want to bother anyone. If you think a person is out of place or acting strangely, you need to act on that feeling. If you think those sounds might be gunshots, then act as if they were. Individuals who have prepared mentally *act*, while others are lost in denial or fear.

The "Shots Fired" program uses a mnemonic centered on the word "out," which aids in recall:

- **Figure Out:** Is what I'm hearing really gunshots? Where are the shots coming from? How are you going to survive? Which of the following options are best?
- **Get Out:** Is there a path of escape? Alert others and make your escape; leave your belongings.
- **Hide Out:** Find an area where you can conceal yourself; stay quiet and make a plan.
- **Keep Out:** Lock or barricade yourself in a room; turn out the lights and stay quiet; silence cell phones.

- **Call Out:** As soon as it is safe, whether you have gotten out or are hiding out, you need to call out to authorities with specific information on who, what, and where the incident is happening.
- **Spread Out:** If with others, do not huddle together, making an easy target.
- **Take Out:** As a last resort if discovered, make a plan to take out the shooter and commit everyone to action.

People in your organization should be informed and trained as to what to expect and how to respond to the initial officers. They are not going to be diverted from their mission to assist in escape or render aid, as every minute lost could result in another potential injury or death to a new victim.

This straightforward strategy is presented with convincing clarity and video examples of how each step can be accomplished. Having this presented to your organization by a competent law enforcement trainer can go a long way toward mitigating the impact of, or even preventing, this type of occurrence.

A case in point is our Human Resources Director who had received this training a few months before that fateful day when he returned to his office from lunch only to hear what sounded like gunshots being fired within his area. It has been demonstrated repeatedly that good training will trigger automatic responses when you are faced with circumstances similar to those in which you were trained.

Upon hearing the sounds, the HR Director flashed back to the video and the techniques presented by the officer from the local police department who had conducted the sessions. He knew he had to **figure out** what was occurring and assume that the noises he heard where in fact shots. He also knew they were continuing and were fairly close, so quick action was called for. Luckily the building had multiple exits, and they were on the first floor. His mental preparation after the initial training kicked in and:

- He decided he could **get out** going in the opposite direction from where the shots were being fired (a conference area at the end of the hall).
- He was able to alert and create action together with others between his office and the exit to get out. Many had expressions of fear and confusion and looked to him for leadership.
- He escorted the group into an adjacent building and secured himself in a locked room with the others, once they were out of the building.
- He then **called out** to 911 and gave an accurate description of the event.
- He calmed the group, after which he was also able to shout to others from the window and direct them to avoid entering the HR building, setting up a type of "verbal" perimeter.
- He phoned the organization's emergency manager, alerting him to the event.

- He could hear the responding officers approaching, and once the officers had made their entrance he made contact with the police sergeant, who assigned an investigator to debrief him and the group.
- He was allowed to leave after his debriefing and proceeded to the organization's predesignated emergency operations center.

Let's examine the impact of these actions he took as a first-first responder:

- First of all, his training and mental preparation led to action rather than the fear that gripped others at the scene.
- While he could not save everyone, he did evacuate any number of persons who were confused and may have fallen prey to the shooter when he started down the hall from the conference area.
- Had he gone toward the conference room to investigate, stopped to gather important belongings, failed to instruct others, hesitated to call, or the like, he and many others could have died.
- Once safe, he calmed and kept the "witnesses" together in a safe environment so they could be debriefed. Had they randomly dispersed, some may have attempted to return for property, and valuable information would certainly have been delayed for responders.
- While he was not the only person to call 911, he did not assume others would. The redundancy and additional information allowed the responders to make better decisions knowing this was a "real" event.

Remembering earlier training on the critical tasks, he did his best to identify the hot zone to police in his call. He was even able to set up a partial inner perimeter, preventing several persons from walking into a death trap by warning them from his safe position.

And, he was able to alert his own organization's Emergency Manager before moving on to his natural position in the EOC.

Because of the training provided and his subsequent mental preparation, he was able to assess and select an action from a number of options that ultimately saved lives.

Summary

It probably took us longer to explain these tasks than it would take you to actually implement them in the field. This is the crisis phase; things happen quickly. Your radio is blaring; your heart's pounding.

Remember, you have a universal game plan that calls for you to:

- Establish control and communications.
- Identify the hot zone.

- Establish the inner perimeter.
- Establish the outer perimeter.
- Establish the command post.
- Establish a staging area.
- Identify and request additional resources.

Take a deep breath and assume your tactical leadership persona. Focus on incident containment and perform your critical tasks.

Review Questions

- If incidents share common characteristics, then you should be able to apply...what?
- What are your primary goals in the crisis phase?
- Can you think of how the Seven Critical Tasks™ would have applied to an incident in which you have participated?
- What are the criteria for the appropriate placement of the command post and staging areas?
- Can you think of some realistic resources you can call on in your jurisdiction?

NIMS and ICS

6

Objectives

After completing this chapter, you should be able to:

- Recall the major components of the National Incident Management System.
- Describe the role and duties of the Incident Commander.
- Recognize the functional areas of the Incident Command System.
- Apply the Incident Command System to both planned events and unplanned critical incidents.

The information in this chapter will summarize the National Incident Management System and the Incident Command System in their current format, as of this publication. Keep in mind that any worthwhile system will always be changing and improving as it is implemented. Changes in functional names, where they report, symbol designations and/or colors, and the like may well change over time. However, the basic concepts and information discussed in this chapter have remained consistent for the last 30 years and will do so in the future.

National Incident Management System: Organizing a "Decision-Making Team" for the Effective Management of a Major Incident

Homeland Security Presidential Directive 5 called for the creation of a National Response Plan (NRP). Now called the National Response Framework, a National Incident Management System (NIMS) was developed. The system ensures a consistent nationwide framework for local, state, and federal agencies to work effectively. An integral part of the framework is the use of the Incident Command System (ICS).

The National Incident Management System (NIMS) is a comprehensive, national approach to incident management that is applicable at all jurisdictional levels across functional disciplines.

The key components are:
1. Preparedness
2. Communication and information management
3. Resource management
4. Command and management
5. Ongoing management and maintenance
6. Reliance on Incident Action Plan
7. Manageable span of control
8. Incident locations and facilities
9. Comprehensive resource management
10. Establishment and transfer of command
11. Chain of command and unity of command
12. Dispatch and deployment
13. Information and intelligence management
14. Accountability

Preparedness

Effective incident management begins with a number of preparedness activities. They include a combination of:

- Planning, training, and exercises
- Defining the roles of elected and appointed officials, as well as non-governmental organizations and private sector participants
- Continuity of business and/or government functions
- Equipment acquisition and certification standards
- Links to national preparedness guidelines, national strategy documents, and the National Response Framework
- Mutual aid agreements and Emergency Management Assistance Compacts (EMACs)

Communication and Information Management

Concepts and Principles

NIMS identifies the requirements for a common operating picture for information management and information-sharing support at all levels of incident management.

Incident management organizations must ensure that effective interoperable communication processes, procedures, and systems exist across all agencies and jurisdictions. These systems must be reliable, scalable, and portable. They should also possess resiliency and redundancy.

Management Characteristics Section

Information management systems help ensure that information flows through standardized communication types. This requires policy and planning issues that address standardized systems and platforms. These must be agreed upon by all parties identified in response plans. This requires equipment and standards training.

Organizations and Operations

The necessity for accurate information in the decision-making process is crucial. This will require consistent communication standards and formats.

Resource Management

When fully implemented, NIMS will define standardized mechanisms and establish requirements for describing, listing, mobilizing, dispatching, tracking, and recovering resources over the life cycle of an incident. To ensure preparedness, two components are required. The first component should be a continual process. The second involves the response stage, the management during an incident.

Command and Management

The *Incident Command System* defines operating characteristics, management components, and the structure of incident management organizations throughout the incident.

Area command is used for multiscene incidents.

The *Multiagency Coordination System* defines the operating characteristics, management components, and organizational structure of supporting entities.

The *Public Information System* defines the processes, procedures, and systems for communicating timely and accurate information to the stakeholders during emergency situations.

Ongoing Management and Maintenance

The National Integration Center: The Department of Homeland Security (DHS) established the National Integration Center to provide strategic direction and oversight support of routine and continual refinement of NIMS and it is components over the long run. This includes administration and compliance, standards and credentialing, training and exercising support, and publications management.

Supporting Technologies involves principles necessary to leverage science and technology to improve capabilities and lower costs.

Since its inception there have been changes to the National Incident Management System. This is a good thing! For the system to remain effective, it must adapt its requirements and mandates based on lessons learned. The ongoing efforts of the National Integration Center will ensure that this doesn't become an antiquated system so bogged down in theory that it cannot be effectively changed and updated to meet current needs. In simple terms, it will not become "flavor of the week management."

There is no legal mandate to utilize the National Incident Management System. An agency or organization can choose not to conform. However, failure to conform will result in no federal support financially or otherwise. Obviously, conforming to the National Incident Management System not only makes operational sense but also is crucial to a unified response and attaining all of the support, financial and otherwise, that will be needed.

The establishment of training guidelines is one area that was welcomed by the authors of this text. We have submitted, and have had approved, three separate training courses. A first responder course, a command post course, and a telecommunicator course have all undergone rigorous scrutiny during the approval process. In the aftermath of disasters, unfortunately the rush to address issues sometimes leads to hastily developed training programs. The standardized approval process was thorough and ensures all training is compatible with a consistent response approach. As with all NIMS requirements, if not followed, federal dollars would not be spent on the programs because they would not be approved. The three aforementioned programs are eligible for federal reimbursement, as they have undergone the approval process.

Incident Command System

The Incident Command System (ICS) has been the subject of numerous hours of mandated training sessions in recent years. Many of those sessions involved extensive focus on the administrative requirements of the system (utilizing the proper form). Other ICS training efforts involve examining a fully operationalized, multiagency, multijurisdiction event. There are approximately 140 functional areas, which may require staffing in incidents requiring this level of response.

As with many of the individual subject matter areas addressed in this text, we will provide an overview of the subject. However, keep in mind that the real need is to start to build an ICS team correctly. The ability to form a solid foundation is critical to success no matter how large the event may become. We will provide a solid base of information for the initial response to a scene. This response will require the familiarity with and establishment of a basic incident command system team. This knowledge and ability will allow for expansion to that fully operationalized team, should it be necessary to do so, without dismantling the team in place and having to rebuild from scratch.

To this point in the text, we have referred to the Seven Critical Tasks™ as your game plan. In keeping with the sports analogy theme, the Incident Command System is your "playbook." If you consider the purpose of a playbook, it defines the individual roles of team members. ICS serves the same purpose for its individual functional areas, as well as the duties and responsibilities of all participants.

History and Development of the Incident Command System

ICS was developed through a cooperative interagency (local, state, and federal) effort. The organizational structure of the ICS is based upon a multiagency response to a multijurisdiction fire emergency, which has been developed over time by local, state, and federal fire protection agencies.

ICS can be used to manage the five categories of critical incidents already discussed:

- Terrorist attacks/weapons of mass destruction (WMD) incidents
- Natural disasters
- Transportation accidents
- Criminal-activity scenes
- Chemical spills and fires

Additionally, ICS can be used to organize an agency's response to a planned event. It is applicable for events such as parades and Fourth of July celebrations, or it may be used to organize a response to a one-time event, such as a planned demonstration or large concert.

Because of the "functional unit" management structure, the ICS is equally applicable to small incidents in normal operations, as well as major incidents involving the highest levels of public safety command and private sector interaction. The system structure will develop naturally based upon incident size, scope, and seriousness.

Every public safety agency and most private industrial firms can make use of the ICS. In some cases, all may be working together during an incident or they may work in various combinations.

The types of agencies involved include fire, law enforcement, health, public works, emergency medical services, and the like, working either together or in various combinations, depending upon the type of incident.

ICS provides the flexibility needed to rapidly activate and establish an organizational "modular" structure around the functions that need to be performed.

The specific ICS organization that will be formed is dependent upon:

- The size, scope, and seriousness of the incident
- The agencies involved
- The objectives and strategies selected

In this chapter, we'll look at how you can actually use ICS in your responses, the structure and functions of ICS, and a variety of optional system elements you can bring to bear on your particular incidents. As mentioned before, a chapter in a book is no substitute for training. However, it will give you a good overview and some ideas about how you can realistically apply ICS.

ICS Operating Requirements

The following are basic system design and operating requirements for the Incident Command System:

- The system will provide for the following types of operations:
  - Single-jurisdiction/single-agency
  - Single-jurisdiction/multiagency involvement
  - Multijurisdiction/multiagency involvement
- The system's organizational structure must be able to adapt to any emergency or incident in which public safety agencies would be expected to respond.
- The system is applicable, acceptable, and understandable to users throughout the country.
- The system must be able to expand in a rapid manner from crisis phase to scene management phase and, if necessary, to the executive management phase (EOC). It must be able to reduce its size just as readily as the organizational needs of the situation decrease.
- The system is able to expand in a logical manner as the incident grows and accelerates.
- The system has basic common elements in organization, terminology, and procedures that allow for the maximum application and use of already developed plans and policies.
- The system must be effective in fulfilling all of the preceding requirements and be simple enough to ensure ease of understanding and application.

ICS was designed to be adaptable and easy to understand, and it is. But it's of no use to anyone if you don't practice it and use it on your scenes.

ICS Components

The Incident Command System has a number of components. These components working together interactively provide the basis for an effective ICS operation:

1. Common terminology
2. Modular organization
3. Management by objectives
4. Integrated communications
5. Unified command structure
6. Reliance on Incident Action Plans
7. Manageable span of control
8. Incident locations and facilities
9. Comprehensive resource management
10. Establishment and transfer of command
11. Chain of command and unity of command
12. Dispatch and deployment
13. Information and intelligence management
14. Accountability

Common Terminology

It is essential for any management system, and especially one that will be used in joint operations by many diverse users, that common terminology be established for the following elements:

- Organizational functions
- Organizational resources
- Facilities

Organizational Functions   A standard set of major functions and functional units has been predesignated and named for the ICS. Terminology for the organizational elements is standard and consistent. For example, if an individual is designated as Logistics Officer, most experienced responders have an idea what that person would be responsible for accomplishing. However, each person on the team may have a different idea of those duties. By utilizing the Incident Command System, everyone on the team knows exactly what the Logistics Officer is responsible for accomplishing, and perhaps most important, the duties and responsibilities are clear to the person appointed to this function.

Organizational Resources   Resources refer to the combination of personnel and equipment used in tactical operations. Common names have been

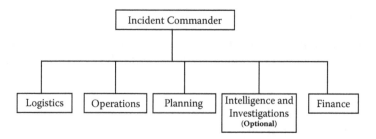

Figure 6.1 The basic Incident Command System structure.

established for all resources used within ICS. Any resource that varies in capability because of size and power (e.g., helicopter) is clearly designated as to capability.

Facilities   Common identifiers are used for those facilities in and around the incident area that will be used during the course of the incident. These facilities include the command post, staging areas, and the like.

Modular Organization

The ICS organizational structure develops in a modular fashion based upon the type and size of an incident. The organization's staff builds from the top down with responsibility and performance placed initially with the Incident Commander. As the need exists, four separate sections can be developed, each with several units, branches, and groups that may be established as required.

The specific organizational structure established for any given incident would be based upon the management needs of the incident. If one individual can simultaneously manage all major functional areas, no further organizational expansion is required. If one or more of the areas requires independent management, an individual is named to be responsible for that area.

Within the ICS, the first management assignments will be made by the Incident Commander and will normally be the appointment of one or more section chiefs. Their purpose is to manage the specific functional areas.

Section chiefs will further delegate management authority for their areas as required. If the section chief determines the need, functional branches, supervisors, or units may be established within the section. The section chief may appoint a deputy section chief, if the need arises.

The **sections** are:

- Operations Section
- Planning Section
- Logistics Section
- Finance and Administration Section
- Intelligence and Investigations Section (optional)

The fifth section, Information and Intelligence, may be established if the incident requires. This function may also be located within the command staff, as a unit in the Planning Section, or as a branch within the Operations Section.

The Incident Commander will activate specific command staff positions based on the nature and type of incident. The following **command staff positions** report directly to the IC:

- Deputy Incident Commander
- Public Information Officer
- Safety Officer
- Liaison Officer
- Agency Representative(s)

Incident Commander   Let's start at the top with the Incident Commander (IC). The IC sets objectives and priorities. This person has the overall responsibility at the incident, including development of the Incident Action Plan, and the approval and release of all resources.

The IC is the first responder. Of course in the case of more serious incidents, a higher-ranking officer may relieve that person. If the original IC is relieved, he or she will likely be reassigned to another position, such as Operations Section Chief. It's nothing personal!

This book has spent a good many pages discussing the leadership characteristics essential for the crisis phase of a critical incident. Those techniques apply "pre-ICS." Once you move into the scene management or possibly executive management stages, you will find that the autocratic style required in the crisis phase is no longer effective.

We will abandon sports analogies for the moment. Now that you have a larger group to coordinate, we'll liken the IC to a symphony conductor. A conductor doesn't try to play every instrument. A conductor simply makes sure everyone is on the same page of the score (the Incident Action Plan) and ensures everyone starts, stays in tempo, and stops together.

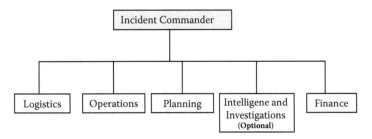

Figure 6.2 It all begins with the Incident Commander.

If you do your job correctly, you should feel completely "underwhelmed." Everyone may seem busy but you. It will be an odd feeling, but this is the only way you can be sure to concentrate fully on the command function. If you are frantically trying to develop a tactical plan to dislodge a barricaded gunman, how much attention do you have to spare for the other 50 incident developments that require your attention?

Your co-commanders and section officers must be competent or you would not have appointed them. An IC is not a dictator or micromanager. An IC empowers subordinates. Let them do what they are paid to do. You wouldn't try to tell the bomb squad how to do their job, would you?

Operations Section   Operations is the section where most emergency first responders tend to be most comfortable. It's where most of us have worked for the bulk of our careers. Whenever you find yourself setting up an ICS response, expect supervisors to gravitate to this area.

This section runs the units that are directly responsible for tactical incident stabilization and resolution. Operations and the **Operations Section Chief** are charged with short-term, tactical thinking and related input on the IAP.

The nature of the incident determines the makeup of the Operations Section. If your incident is a criminal activity, Operations will be composed of law enforcement personnel. If it is a fire or HazMat scene, this section will be made up of fire or HazMat personnel. If it is a water main break, it will be facilities or public works personnel. For a pandemic, it will be health-related personnel, and so on.

Reporting to the Operations Section Chief are the **Mission Unit Leaders**. These individuals lead the frontline response specialists (SWAT, immunization teams, Canine Unit, Mounted Unit, Hazardous Materials Response Unit, etc.). They coordinate with other Mission Unit Leaders to implement the IAP.

One resource that should be used regularly is the **Operations Dispatcher**. The Operations Dispatcher reports to the Operations Section Chief and serves as communications coordinator for all radio traffic to and from the command post.

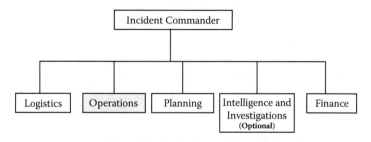

Figure 6.3 Operations rolls up its sleeves and directly controls the incident.

The Operations Dispatcher is crucial for making sure all commands by the Operations Section Chief are verbalized at the command post. The Operations Section Chief does not deliver orders over the radio personally, but directs the dispatcher to relay them. This allows others, such as the Safety Officer (SO), to monitor operational orders and provide input before orders get to the field.

An example of an Operations Section Chief delivering orders directly on the radio might be:

> Operations Section Chief into radio: "Car 20, perform task A-B-C."
> SO to Operations Section Chief: "Hold it, you can't do that."
> Operations Section Chief into radio: "Car 20 standby."
> Operations Section Chief to SO: "Why not? ... Oh, I see."
> Operations Section Chief into radio: "Car 20 disregard previous order. Perform task D-E-F."

If the Operations Section Chief verbalizes the order before going to the radio, the Safety Officer has a chance to intervene if necessary. Funnel all commands and directives from the command post through the Operations Dispatcher.

One of the key Operations responsibilities is maintaining the staging area. You may recall that establishing a staging area is one of your Seven Critical Tasks™. The Operations Section Chief appoints a **Staging Area Supervisor** to manage the location to which personnel and equipment are sent before being put into service. This supervisor briefs incoming resources and maintains a status log of all available and deployed resources.

Planning Section   The Planning Section is responsible for the collection, evaluation, and dissemination of information to measure the size, scope, and seriousness of the incident. It also assists with development, implementation, and updating of the Incident Action Plan.

This section will be responsible for identifying technical specialists to assist in planning "incident resolution" strategies. Examples of specialists

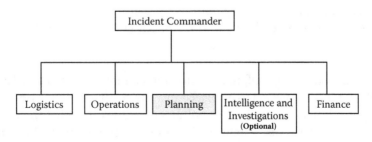

Figure 6.4 Planning anticipates the little surprises that can trip up a response.

would be psychologists, environmental scientists, structural engineers, industrial chemists, and so on.

The Planning Section may also activate the following units when appropriate: Situation Unit, Documentation Unit, Resource Unit, Medical Unit, and Demobilization Unit.

Planning also asks "what if" questions. For example, during the tragedy at Columbine in 1999, the Planning Section Chief might have asked, "What if this school *isn't* the primary target?" What if the school attack had been a diversionary tactic, and the actual target had been a raid on the U.S. Mint or the federal courthouse? It can be very useful to have someone thinking that way when all other resources are tightly focused on a specific event. Another term for this process would be "contingency planning." The Planning Section consists of a person or group of people responsible for examining all of the potential outcomes of an incident and then planning to address those outcomes. Bottom line, there should be "no surprises" with a quality Planning function operationalized.

"What if" questions needn't be that seemingly far-out. They could be as mundane as asking, "What if this incident lasts into the night?" When a unit calls in to the command post at dusk and requests lights, you don't want to have to tell them it will take two hours. You want to be able to say that the lights are standing by in the staging area. Your teams will appreciate it! Planning should develop a wish list of resources and work closely with Logistics, which we'll discuss next.

The Planning Section uses the information it gathers to help the IC develop the Incident Action Plan and at least one backup plan. It also prepares a plan for both responders and the public to return to normal operations.

Intelligence and Investigation Section Intelligence and Investigation ensures that all investigative and intelligence operations, functions, and activities within the incident are properly managed, coordinated, and directed. This function may be located:

- Within the command staff
- As a unit within the Planning Section
- As a branch within the Operations Section
- As a separate general staff section. If activated as a section, the intelligence section chief will head it.

The importance of staffing this function cannot be overstated. The system allows for the function to be placed in a variety of locations as evidenced by the preceding information. The authors of this text feel that the function is so critical that it is best established as an individual section when operating in the Incident Command System during a major event. In examining

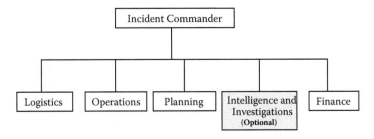

Figure 6.5 Optional Intelligence and Investigations function.

numerous preplanned events that resulted in critical incidents, the one common element was poor intelligence. Intelligence that is dated, inaccurate, or not identified leads to poor planning.

Logistics Section The Logistics Section makes sure you have what you need when you need it. It is a proactive function. Logistics should work with other sections to determine early on what facilities, services, and resources might be required to support incident resolution. Logistics encompasses several critical areas and ICS concepts.

Logistics is responsible for a couple of additional areas as well. The Logistics Section Chief oversees the following:

- **Security Unit Supervisor:** Coordinates the activities of the security unit and supervises assigned personnel. You'll need someone to secure the command post, staging area, and other areas.
- **Personnel Group Supervisor:** Evaluates personnel requirements, maintains a master listing of personnel assignments, and performs time-keeping functions.

As one Army general is credited with saying, "Operations is for amateurs; *logistics* is for professionals." Even the best plan cannot be successfully executed if it is not supported logistically.

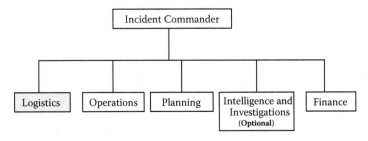

Figure 6.6 Logistics holds the whole show together with infrastructure and services.

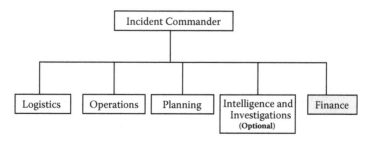

Figure 6.7 Finance foots the bills (or at least sees to it that everyone gets paid!).

Finance Section   Somebody has to pay for all of this! A large-scale incident can present you with dozens of financial considerations you don't want to have to think about. You want to focus on your scene. The Finance Section provides emergency purchase orders to pay for any resources ordered.

The **Finance Section Chief** reports to the IC and performs all financial and cost analysis of the incident. Finance also performs record-keeping and administrative duties. Subordinate finance functions may include the Time Unit, Procurement Unit, Compensation Claims Unit, and Cost Unit.

Staff Positions   In addition to the four to five functional sections, ICS provides for a number of additional staff positions to support a response. These staff positions are:

- Deputy Incident Commander
- Safety Officer
- Public information Officer
- Liaison Officer
  - Agency Representatives

As before, the IC activates only those positions that are needed. One person can hold down multiple positions as long as that person is not overwhelmed.

Deputy Incident Commander   The Deputy Incident Commander is the second in command. In smaller incidents, this function certainly may not be required. In larger incidents though, a Deputy IC is a must. If the IC needs to leave the scene to meet with the mayor, the Deputy IC assumes control. Therefore a Deputy IC needs to be aware of all the leadership issues associated with the IC position.

The Deputy IC acts as "systems manager" for the command post, making sure things run smoothly. Activities include coordinating section heads, reviewing status reports, and making sure all unit logs get submitted to the IC on time.

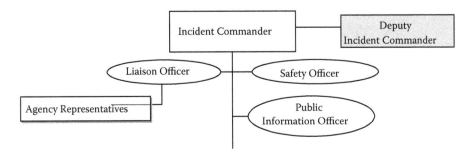

Figure 6.8 The Deputy IC manages the command post and steps in whenever the IC is unavailable.

Safety Officer   The Safety Officer (SO) role is integral to fire response, but it has to be one of the most frequently overlooked positions in law enforcement. The Safety Officer is *not* interested in the safety of the general public. The SO focuses exclusively on responders. He or she assesses the Incident Action Plan and proposed tactics with *nothing* in mind but the safety of responders. This is the person who checks the wind before a tear gas assault and makes sure all officers have proper cover.

When this officer finds an unsafe condition or planned action on the scene, it is his or her duty to bring the problem to the IC's attention. If time or other developments do not permit that, the SO has the authority under ICS to unilaterally stop all activity. We mean *everything*. If the SO says "*No,*" that particular task does not go forward.

It is important to note that the Safety Officer should present his or her observations in terms of "safety issues" not solutions. This is a subtle distinction but an important one. On a hot day with long durations on an outer perimeter point, the Safety Officer should raise an issue of hydration for the officers, not present a plan to get them water. It is up to the Operations Chief or Planning Section to determine the proper method to address the hydration issue which will then be reexamined by the Safety Officer. We have a tendency to fall in love with our own plans. If the Safety Officer is presenting solutions the question becomes, Who is checking those solutions for safety issues?

When a plan or activity is stopped by the Safety Officer the Incident Commander needs to evaluate the issues he or she has presented and make a decision. That decision could be to reassess and request changes to the plan or action, *or* continue with the plan or action acknowledging the safety issues but determining that not taking action presents an even greater risk. In either case the Incident Commander needs to acknowledge that the Safety Officer is acting appropriately and thank him or her for the input.

As you can imagine, you don't want a shrinking violet or "yes man" in this position. You need an officer with an assertive but nonabrasive personality.

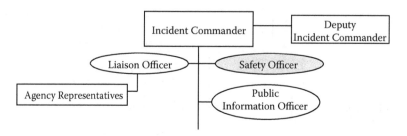

Figure 6.9 The Safety Officer can yell "Stop!" if responders are in unnecessary danger.

We frequently use a good SO as an example of a round peg for that round hole. It's wonderful when there's a fit. (On larger incidents, the SO function can be filled jointly by representatives from law, fire, EMS, etc. Each will have primary responsibility for his or her own department personnel.)

It is our opinion that you should *never* run a critical incident scene without an SO. And when you create the position, don't make that person multitask. Let the SO focus exclusively on what he or she is there for—to save lives. This is so important we will say it again: *The Safety Officer is* not *interested in the safety of the general public. The SO focuses exclusively on the safety of responders.*

A good example of command failing to take this function into account comes from the Bureau of Alcohol, Tobacco and Firearms (ATF) 1993 raid on the Branch Davidian Compound. (The source for this analysis is the Treasury Department report of September 1993.)

The two requirements for the raid to go forward were:

1. The ATF must have the element of surprise.
2. Upon ATF arrival, the men of the compound must be outside the buildings.

As we all found out afterward, the raid occurred despite the fact that *both* of these requirements were not met.

The ATF raid plan, from what we could determine, did not include a Safety Officer. Therefore no one had the authority under ICS to say "Stop! They know we're coming!" Tragically, gunfire from the compound killed four ATF agents.

Public Information Officer   The Public Information Officer (PIO) is responsible for formulating and releasing (with IC approval) all information regarding the incident to the media and other personnel.

The PIO is your primary and only media point of contact. This person provides press releases and news conferences as necessary. If appropriate, the PIO coordinates interviews between the media and other responders on-scene. You want this type of access as tightly controlled as possible.

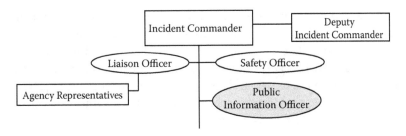

Figure 6.10 The Public Information Officer keeps the media informed and off the IC's back.

We've mentioned that an individual can handle multiple ICS functions, but there is one important exception: *The IC should not be the Public Information Officer.* In the first place, you don't want to take time away from managing the situation to talk to the press. Second, the PIO can always plead ignorance when faced with tough questions. That is not an option for a commander. The IC should address the press only when the incident is concluded.

The PIO doesn't necessarily have to be a member of the police department. It helps, but it's not a requirement.

Liaison Officer and Agency Representatives   The Liaison Officer helps initiate mutual aid agreements and serves as the point of contact between the IC and assisting agencies. This is the person on your staff who knows everyone and has the best people skills.

The Liaison Officer works closely with representatives from each responding agency. These Agency Representatives are (or should be) empowered to provide the IC with whatever resources may be required. If you need a fire company, the fire service rep can activate the engines from staging and can relay orders. If you need ambulances, the EMS rep will get them. In fact, Agency Representatives should be able to make any and all decisions regarding their departmental resources. Agency Representatives who must go back to their individual agency leaders to verify decisions create an unacceptable waste of time.

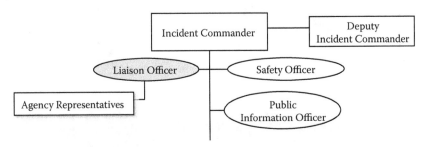

Figure 6.11 The Liaison Officer helps ensure all agencies and jurisdictions seamlessly work together.

Agency Representatives can make invaluable contributions, from the formulation of the Incident Action Plan to the efficient demobilization of resources. However, there should be only one representative from each involved agency at the command post. This keeps down the head count at the command post and eliminates confusion as to whom the IC should go to for support requests.

The Agency Representatives report to the Liaison Officer or directly to the IC if the Liaison Officer is not available.

Weapons of Mass Destruction Incidents   The Operations and Planning Sections will appoint deputy section chiefs in any weapons of mass destruction (WMD) incident. Agents from the FBI will staff these functions. This will allow for full integration of federal resources to address the incident at hand. Additionally, the FBI will participate in the unified command function.

Management by Objectives

The ICS is managed by objectives that are communicated throughout the entire organization. Both the establishment of specific measurable objectives for various incident management functional activities and directing efforts to attain them are essential to a successful operation.

Integrated Communications

Communications at the incident are managed using a common communications plan and an incident-based communications center established solely for the use of tactical and support resources assigned to the incident. All communications between organizational elements at an incident should be in "plain text."

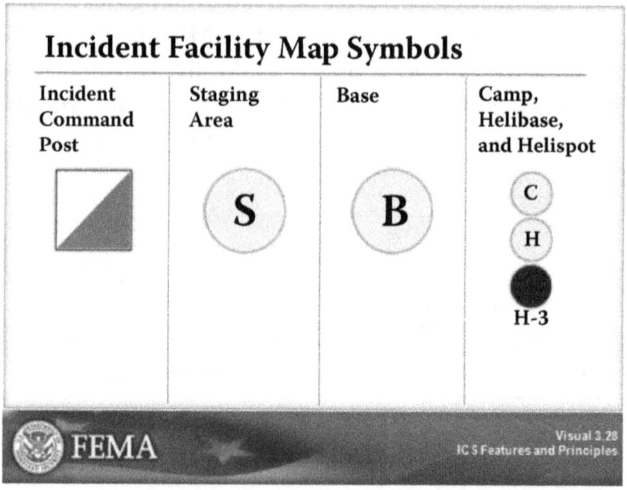

Figure 6.12 Each symbol is currently used to designate the facility listed above the symbol.

All communications should be confined only to essential messages. The Communications Unit is responsible for all communications planning for the incident.

This will include incident-established radio networks, on-site telephones, public address systems, and off-site incident telephone/microwave/radio systems. This area includes:

- Hardware systems that transfer information
- Planning for use of all available communications
- Frequencies, such as:
  - *Command frequency:* This frequency should link together incident command, key command staff members, section officers, and key supervisors.
  - *Tactical frequency:* There may be several tactical frequencies. They may be established around agencies, departments, geographical areas, or even specific functions. The determination of how frequencies are set up should be determined between the Planning and Operations Sections.
- *Support frequency:* A support frequency will be established primarily to direct resources, as well as for support requests and certain other nontactical or command functions.

The procedures and processes are used for transferring information internally and externally.

Unified Command Structure
The need for a unified command is brought about because:

- Incidents have no regard for jurisdictional boundaries. HazMat spills, floods, hurricanes, as well as many types of criminal activities can develop into multijurisdiction events.
- Individual agency responsibility and authority is normally legally confined to a single jurisdiction.
- It is required under HSPD-5 and NIMS.

The concept of unified command simply means that all agencies that have a jurisdictional responsibility for a multijurisdiction incident will contribute to the process of:

- Determining overall Incident Action Plan with objectives
- Selection of strategies
- Ensuring that joint planning for tactical activities is accomplished
- Ensuring that integrated tactical operations are conducted
- Making maximum use of all assigned resources

The proper selection of participants to work within a unified command structure will depend upon:

- The location of the incident—which political or geographical jurisdictions are involved
- The kind of incident—which functional agencies of the involved jurisdiction(s) are required

A unified command structure would consist of a key responsible official from each jurisdiction involved, or it could consist of several functional department managers within a single political jurisdiction. Common objectives and strategies for major multijurisdiction incidents should be written.

For example, a major incident or WMD incident may require numerous levels of response. The need to coordinate various responding jurisdictions, disciplines, and resources from the local, state, and federal levels is paramount in guaranteeing an adequate response. This coordination can be achieved by operating in a unified command structure. Each level of response will have roles and responsibilities in a major incident or a WMD incident. Following are examples of a local, state, and federal response.

Local Response   As the initial responders to any critical incident, local authorities will be primarily responsible for the following in the initial stages of an incident:

- Law enforcement response
- Fire response
- Emergency medical response
- Emergency management/preparedness response
- Medical Examiner/Coroner
- Community team
- Elected officials
- Department heads, such as public works, communications, and so on
- Legal team

All of these may have authority and jurisdictional responsibility for the affected area.

Although the assistance of numerous other assets may be required for resolution, keep in mind that in the crucial first few hours or possibly days of an incident, it is the local response that will be responsible for managing the scene. Our planning and training must prepare local responders to assume that responsibility.

State Response   In some cases, state agencies may act as first responders—for instance, when local authorities lack the resources and capabilities to effectively respond to an incident, or when state control has been established by law and/or statute, or when local authorities relinquish control. If there has been a separate and distinct local response, the state response may involve:

- Providing support resources (personnel and/or equipment)
- Providing specialized resources (HazMat team, SWAT team, bomb disposal unit, etc.)
- National Guard support
- Issuing state declarations
- Requesting federal assistance

Federal Response   The utilization of federal assets has been of great value in past incidents, such as the 1993 attack on the World Trade Center, the Murrah Building Bombing, and the World Trade Center attacks of 1993 and 2001. Presidential Directive 5 mandates the use of ICS and unified command to respond to any WMD or terrorist attack in this country. Federal authorities will be responsible for the following:

- Lead criminal investigation: The initial response to any WMD incident scene will have to establish containment and initiate rescue/evacuation measures. While rescue efforts are primary, recovery efforts may be delayed until the scene can be properly processed for evidence. The FBI WMD Coordinator should be consulted prior to the evidence collection process. Since responsibility for the investigation of WMD incidents has been assigned to the FBI, all issues relating to evidence collection and preservation should be addressed by unified command involving the FBI WMD Coordinator. He or she may authorize the collection of noncontaminated evidence by local or state evidence technicians.

    WMD response teams from the FBI are properly equipped to handle both contaminated and noncontaminated evidence. Should they not be available, potentially contaminated evidence should be handled and preserved only by hazardous materials response personnel.
- Federal recovery assistance (FEMA) consequence management plan: This branch of government found itself the subject of criticism subsequent to Hurricane Katrina. Think back to Chapter 1 in this text when we stated that you never want to be the responder to address the first-of-its-kind incident. Everyone will learn from your response—a response you probably had to create as you went along, because no one had ever had to respond to this type of incident before. Such was the case of the FEMA response to Hurricane Katrina—an incident that required the evacuation of a major American city for the first

time, but also impacted numerous other states and major population centers. The lessons learned during this incident were put into place in subsequent incidents. Make no mistake about it, FEMA is an asset you definitely want involved in major incident.

- Providing federal assets, such as specialized resources
- Military support: This area, although restricted by federal statute, may become utilized more frequently in the future. In the aftermath of Hurricane Katrina, the need to build an entire residential area for misplaced citizens became evident. The U.S. military is best equipped to do so. Who else has the experience and ability to go into an unpopulated area and build a facility that is complete with all the required human necessities?

All state and local response plans need to be reviewed and brought into compliance with NIMS standards. This will ensure smooth integration with federal responders.

The objectives and strategies (Incident Action Plan) then guide the mission of the ICS. The implementation of the IAP will be accomplished under the direction of a single individual—the Operations Section Chief.

The Operations Section Chief will normally be selected from the agency that has the greatest jurisdictional involvement. Deputies to the Operations Section Chief may represent other jurisdictional agencies in all WMD incidents; members of the FBI will be assigned as the Operations Section and Planning Section Deputy Chiefs.

When operating in unified command, the following five rules should always apply:

- No agency's authority is compromised or neglected.
- There is one Incident Action Plan.
- Participants speak for their agency.
- Unified command must speak with a single voice.
- All facilities will be shared.

An excellent example of unified command was the response to the BP Oil spill in the Gulf of Mexico. The team addressing the issue was comprised of local, state, and federal officials, as well as experts from the BP Company. As an outcry arose to eliminate BP officials from the team, the Incident Commander explained their value as team members due to their expertise and resources. Although this was a complex problem and not easily resolved (a first-of-its-kind disaster), by working together in unified command the spill was eventually stopped.

Reliance on Incident Action Plan

Every incident requires some form of an Incident Action Plan (IAP). For small Type 4 or 5 incidents of short duration, the plan may be verbal. For larger incidents (Types 1–3) written IAPs are required.

The following are examples of when written action plans should be used:

- When resources from multiple agencies are being used
- When several jurisdictions are involved
- When the incident will require change in shifts of personnel and/or equipment

The Incident Commander will establish goals and determine strategies for the incident based upon the size, seriousness, and scope of the incident.

When a unified command structure has been implemented, incident objectives must adequately reflect the policy and requirements of all jurisdictional agencies involved. The action plan must be a consensus of all involved.

The action plan for the incident should cover tactical and support activities for the operational period. Multiple ICS forms will be utilized, such as ICS 202, and submitted with the IAP Cover Sheet.

Manageable Span of Control

Safety factors as well as sound management planning will both influence and dictate span-of-control considerations. In general, within the ICS the span of control of any individual with emergency management responsibility should range from three to seven with span of control of five being established as a rule.

Of course, there will always be exceptions (i.e., an individual Mission Unit Leader will normally have more than five personnel under supervision.)

The type of incident, nature of the task, hazards and safety factors, and distances between elements will influence span-of-control considerations. An important consideration in span of control is to anticipate change and prepare for it.

This is especially true during rapid buildup of the organization when the management is made difficult because of too many reporting elements. Planning is critical at this point, to avoid runaway ordering of resources and thereby overloading effective span of control.

Incident Locations and Facilities

There are several kinds of facilities that can be established in and around the incident area. The determination of these facilities and their locations will be based upon the requirements of the incident and at the direction of the Incident Commander. These facilities can be used as:

- The incident command post
- One or more staging areas
- A base
- One or more camps (when needed)
- A helibase
- One or more helispots

Some incidents may require facilities not included on the standard list such as mass care centers, evacuation centers, and so on.

Weapons of Mass Destruction (WMD) Incidents   In the event of a WMD incident or terrorist attack, the federal government will activate certain facilities. Federal authorities will activate a Joint Operations Center (JOC) and a Joint Information Center (JIC). As in all unified command structures, these facilities will be shared with all participants of the unified command. The main function of the JOC and JIC will be the coordination of federal resources committed to the incident.

Comprehensive Resource Management
Resource management includes processes for categorizing, ordering, dispatching, tracking, and recovering resources. Resources are defined as personnel teams, equipment, supplies, and facilities.

Establishment and Transfer of Command
The command function must be clearly established from the beginning of incident operations. The agency with primary jurisdictional responsibility designates the individual at the scene responsible for establishing command. Procedures must be in place to allow for a smooth transfer of command when applicable.

Chain of Command and Unity of Command
Chain of command refers to the orderly line of authority over incident operations. Unity of command means that every individual has a designated supervisor.

Dispatch and Deployment
Personnel and equipment should respond only when requested or when dispatched by an appropriate authority.

Information and Intelligence Management
The incident management organization must establish a process for gathering, sharing, and managing incident-related information and intelligence.

Accountability

Strict accountability for all resources is essential and can be accomplished by:

- An orderly chain of command—the line of authority within the ranks of the incident organization
- A mandatory check-in procedure
- Assigning a current status condition to all resources
- Ensuring that all changes in resource locations and status conditions are promptly reported to the appropriate functional unit

As we have stressed, ICS provides a "toolbox" approach to managing critical events. You activate only the functions you need for a particular incident. Bear in mind that ICS is about functions being performed, not people manning positions. If one individual (you!) can simultaneously manage all major functional areas, then you don't need to bring other people onboard.

Should you ever start to feel overwhelmed, however, get some help. As you add to the structure, one person may still manage more than one function. But should that person become overwhelmed, add additional command personnel to relieve the pressure.

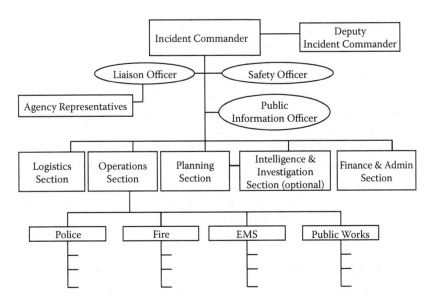

Figure 6.13 A fully-expanded Incident Command System structure. Usually only large-scale incidents, such as natural disasters and major terrorist strikes, would require activation of every management function.

Using ICS for Planned Events

Beyond giving you a powerful tool for managing the unexpected, ICS can aid you in preparing for and executing planned events. As we've mentioned before, we constantly review and evaluate critical incidents that have occurred across the United States and abroad. Repeatedly we find that police agencies in most cases do not follow ICS guidelines when planning for major events in their communities. Many of those planned events turned into critical incidents, catching responsible agencies totally and completely unprepared.

ICS makes your life so much easier! But you have to implement it. Here are some examples of the types of events for which ICS can provide your agency with a planning and operations framework:

- Major drug raids or high-risk warrant service operations
- Annual community events that attract large crowds
- Demonstrations or planned civil disobediences at which you expect large crowds
- Major concerts or sporting events

Why reinvent the wheel or run the risk of missed assignments each time you have one of these occasions?

As you now know, ICS gives you a blueprint for placing agency personnel in key planning and management functions. You also have a command and response structure in place that you can expand rapidly to deal with whatever happens. We will discuss several essential functions you must activate when planning a major event, such as Incident Commander, Safety Officer, Operations Section Chief, and so on. The size of the planning team will depend on the type of event for which you are organizing.

This team planning method also helps prevent your organization from being dependent upon one officer knowing how to handle, say, the traffic patterns you might expect at a festival. If only one person understands a certain "detail," that knowledge can leave your organization with that person. Get this critical knowledge in writing!

We'll use the example of a major, multiact rock festival to highlight functions you should activate and the tasks and potential developments you must address:

- **Incident Commander:** As in a spontaneous incident, the IC assembles a team to ensure the Incident Action Plan. This is not only operationally sound but also considers all alternatives, is supported logistically, and is as safe as possible for those charged with implementing the plan. The IC makes sure all functions are filled and that everyone is comfortable with their duties.

- **Safety Officer:** The SO lays down basic requirements or prohibits certain activities that affect responder safety. These safety characteristics certainly apply to our rock festival. The SO might look at issues such as EMS support and how officers could be backed up for crowd control, if necessary.
- **Public Information Officer:** The PIO manages vital information that must be released to the public before an event. For example, we would probably work with concert organizers to restrict what people can and cannot bring into the concert for security reasons. If large backpacks or glass bottles will be prohibited, the PIO should get this information to the media well beforehand. Restricted parking, access routes, or public gathering areas will be easier to manage if those attending the festival have the information before the event. Having one point of contact also ensures security for confidential information that you may not want made public.
- **Operations Officer:** This individual is responsible for making the plan happen on the street. Historically in non-ICS managed responses, this person was forced to perform all of the functions we have described, from media contact to logistics. By utilizing ICS, you can allow this individual to concentrate on plan execution, such as crowd and traffic control.
- **Planning Section:** In addition to assisting in developing the operational plan for the event, the Planning Section will be responsible for contingency planning. For example, what if inclement weather forces the movement of an outdoor event to an indoor site? The identification of an adequate alternate site would be the responsibility of the Planning Section.
- **Intelligence and Investigations Officer:** Bottom line...you don't want any surprises. To help avoid the unexpected, the intelligence and investigations officer might examine past music festival events. If you find out that a certain act attracts rowdier fans, you can plan for it. You will be prepared to respond or perhaps restrict activities to prevent a reoccurrence of a critical incident that occurred during a previous festival. The possibility that you will have to deal with an unexpected situation can never be totally eliminated, but it is greatly reduced when you staff this function.
- **Logistics:** Staffing this function ensures you will have all of the people, equipment, and other assets needed to successfully implement your plan. Preplanning logistics eliminates the need to scramble for resources in a hurried or panic mode. Also, nonemergency purchasing is usually more cost-effective. Just a few requirements of our festival might include barricades, overtime personnel, portable lights, and commissary facilities.

Implementing ICS for planned events allows you to develop a *comprehensive* plan rather than simply focusing on reactive tactics or operations. The various command staff and sections work independently to develop their own plan segments. These independent segments combine to produce one final all-inclusive plan for the event that no one commander or section head could come up with on his or her own.

As you begin to use the ICS to prepare for major events in your community, you will quickly find that it is the only way to develop a comprehensive and defensible response.

Summary

That's it for our quick tour of the personnel, structure, and application of the Incident Command System. These are functions our experience has shown us to be critical to initial responders. You may not need all of it for each incident, but you should at least know what ICS can bring to bear on your incidents. In Appendix A of this text, we have provided detailed checklists for each of the functional areas described herein. They can serve as a playbook for those participating in the Incident Command System as they define each individual's role on the "team."

The bottom line for you as the IC is to understand how ICS can help *you* and to plan, plan, plan. Then act swiftly and sensibly. Your response should follow the old carpenter's maxim: Measure twice and cut once.

Let's pick up on the roof collapse involving our Maintenance/Facilities supervisor who was present when the roof of a workout area in an educational facility collapsed, trapping numerous faculty, staff, and students. As you remember, he was the first-first responder and took action at the scene to **assess, notify, and isolate**, saving any number of further injuries.

He was at the scene for approximately two hours assisting the fire department's urban search and rescue team with information on shutoffs for gas and electric and other critical information such as chemical storage in that facility. In that capacity, he was an Agency Representative from the campus to the unified command post at the scene and was assigned by the Incident Commander to the Operations Section.

The fire department was able to rescue about 15 people from the scene who were then triaged by EMS, with 9 people being transported to area hospitals and 6 treated and released from the scene.

One of his early communications resulted in the campus activating its EOC and Executive Policy Group, who had been operating for about an hour when the rescue was completed and fire, police, and EMS responders left the scene.

The traditional unified command post was then transitioned into a command post for campus personnel tasked with damage assessment, cleanup, and repair. In accordance with state and NIMS requirements, this command post was set up using ICS principles and functions. This is not only appropriate but logical, as this situation has safety issues, has logistical needs, has long- and short-term planning issues, needs to be properly supervised, and so forth. This command operation lasted for several weeks and focused upon resolving the issues at the scene, while the campus EOC focused initially on replacing the educational/business capacity that was lost while that building was out of service and then on the reopening or return to service of that facility and the one that had been put into service temporarily.

Let's examine the "walk" this maintenance supervisor took in three short hours:

- First, he was on scene as a first-first responder and put his training to work, potentially saving lives and preventing further victims from entering the scene.
- He was able to notify 911 with the information they needed to get appropriate resources on the way quickly.
- He then put the campus's emergency management system into gear with a notification to the Emergency Manager.
- Once the fire department arrived, he was officially part of their unified command because he had resources to assist the operation, the building was under the jurisdiction of the campus (as well as the fire department), and he personally had a needed skill set.
- Once the life/safety issues were resolved, he was transitioned into the campus ICS in the Operations Section where he continued to function until the building was brought back online.

This shows the flexibility of the Incident Command System. In three hours this nontraditional responder was placed in the position of an IC as first supervisor on-scene and then transitioned through two command posts.

Review Questions

- Can you recall the major components of the National Interagency Management System?
- Can you describe the management style of an ICS Incident Commander?
- Can you describe the four primary functional ICS areas and at least three staff positions?
- Can you recall the benefits of using ICS to prepare for planned events?

Hazardous Materials and Weapons of Mass Destruction

7

Objectives

After completing this chapter, you should be able to:

- Identify unique threats presented by various hazardous materials.
- Describe the differences between accidental and intentional releases.
- Apply the Seven Critical Tasks™ to a HazMat scene.
- List response strategies specific to HazMat threats.

It may seem unusual, but we'll start this chapter by telling you what we're *not* going to do. The goal here is *not* to replicate traditional HazMat training. No single chapter can do that. While the following pages will touch on much of the same material that you might expect at an awareness-level class, the presentation restricts itself to information required by an initial responding law enforcement supervisor, one who is forced to make critical decisions in the early stages of an event.

We've filtered this information over the years, distilled it, if you will, into those factors that most directly affect your area of interest.

As we are all too aware, HazMat incidents can be accidental or intentional. In either case your response in the crisis phase will be exactly the same. Therefore by improving your response to *all* critical incidents, you automatically improve your response to terrorist attacks. Although this chapter will focus on accidental releases, keep in mind that the crisis phase strategies discussed apply to weapons of mass destruction (WMD) attacks as well.

The primary differences between accidental and intentional releases are in the details. With an intentional release, you may have criminal activity to control while you worry about the HazMat aspects. You may have criminal investigations to conduct afterward. Regardless, in the crisis phase you always use the same basic game plan.

Our hope is that this chapter will have something for everybody. Even if you already have advanced HazMat certifications, you may still find our emphasis on practical, layperson's response strategies useful.

The Method to Our Madness

A police officer is the first responder on-scene in the overwhelming majority of HazMat incidents. Yet HazMat response training traditionally gets second-class treatment in many departments. Law enforcement tends to think of it as a fire responsibility. It certainly can be, but what you as the first-responding police supervisor need to realize is that the decisions *you* make during the crisis phase of a HazMat incident can determine the course of the event and the eventual toll it takes.

This chapter will focus on absolutely must-know information. You've probably been through at least HazMat awareness-level training. You've probably sat in front of an authority from the fire service and been presented with hours of perfectly true and excellent information. Your eyes probably glazed over at some point. Listening to a HazMat expert can be a lot like listening to a neurosurgeon. It can be overwhelming.

We are not HazMat technicians. Our expertise and experience lie in the initial response as law enforcement supervisors. We focus on what you need to do in the first moments of any critical incident, be it criminal or chemical.

Our goal is to change your perceptions of HazMat incidents, to make you paranoid. Our goal is to help you protect yourself, the people who work for you, and the citizens you have sworn to serve.

Fire and Law and Enforcement

Before we get into the nuts and bolts of our discussion, we would like to address one of our pet issues: fire/law enforcement coordination. Our classes frequently include both fire and law responders with ranks ranging from firefighters and police officers to chiefs. We always conduct the same exercise. We ask the police officers (sitting on their side of the room), "How many of you train with fire?" Maybe one chief that attended a joint ICS class raises a hand. We then ask the same question of the fire service representatives. Same response.

Then we ask, "How many of you respond with the other department on critical incidents?" Every hand goes up.

Fire and law enforcement must work together on *all* critical incidents, but HazMat in particular dictates a multidisciplinary response. There must be improved communications and tactical coordination between these two most vital community services. As the world becomes a more dangerous place, anything less than a perfect working relationship is unacceptable.

We strongly recommend joint training programs. Don't wait to be told to do it. Be proactive. In recent years, we have seen this trend beginning to change as more and more we are training together. If you do not do so in your jurisdiction, please become an advocate for such training.

Classes of Hazardous Materials

Here we go. A hazardous material is defined as any product, chemical, or substance that can cause damage or injury to life, the environment, or property when inappropriately released from its container. Our society runs on hazardous materials. They are in our stores, rolling down our streets, and in our homes.

We'll start this discussion with a quick overview of the kinds of materials you are likely to encounter. These materials are divided into nine classes, which you probably had to memorize for your awareness certification. For our purposes, it is not critical that you be able to recall them in order. What you *should* be able to do is recognize the particular threat that each represents.

Unfortunately, just about any of these materials has the potential to become a weapon of mass destruction in the wrong hands. An explosion at a water treatment plant might result in a chlorine cloud smothering an entire neighborhood. This could be just as terrifying as an anthrax release at a busy airport terminal. Many of our most common hazardous materials are readily accessible and represent the basis for low-tech weapons.

Essentially, the primary threats from these materials fall into three types: fire, explosion, and health. It is enormously important that you understand the nature of the threat so you can take appropriate action.

Most of the classes are further divided into divisions. We've thrown in sample materials for each class and division. As we'll discuss later, one or more unique placards with dedicated colors and numbers represent each of the classes. These are the intimidating skull-and-crossbones type of signs you see on the trucks that pass you doing 90 mph on the highway.

- **Class 1: Explosives**—There are six divisions that range from a mass explosion hazard (1.1–black powder) to low (1.6–fertilizer).
- **Class 2: Gases**—Three divisions include flammable (2.1–propane), nonflammable (2.2–anhydrous ammonia), and poisonous (2.3–phosgene). Flammable or nonflammable? This information is critical for state troopers in the habit of dropping flares at accident scenes.
- **Class 3: Flammable Liquids**—Examples include gasoline, kerosene, and diesel fuel. These are some of the most commonly transported hazardous materials.
- **Class 4: Flammable Solids, Spontaneously Combustible Materials, and Materials Dangerous When Wet**—These are solids that burn (4.1–magnesium), ignite when brought into contact with air (4.2–phosphorous), or react badly to water (4.3–calcium carbonate).

That last division is an odd one. Some materials actually combust or give off toxic gases when wet. Think the fire department would be grateful for that information before they start spraying?

- **Class 5: Oxidizers and Organic Peroxides**—Some materials create their own oxygen and therefore burn more actively (5.1–ammonium nitrate) or contain oxygen in a certain chemical combination (5.2–ethyl ketone peroxide). What *is* ethyl ketone peroxide, you ask? A good reason to have an *Emergency Response Guidebook* in your unit! (See Appendix C.)
- **Class 6: Poisons and Etiologic Materials**—The chemical industry uses a number of poisons to make up common compounds (6.1–arsenic). These substances are more prevalent than most of us care to know. *Etiologic* refers to infectious agents (6.2–hepatitis). Perhaps more than any other class, this last is most closely associated with terrorism. If you're dealing with a biological attack, you can guess it won't be placarded! Look for clues in bystanders, such as difficulty breathing. You will need to rely on your wits and training to assess the situation from a distance to avoid succumbing yourself.
- **Class 7: Radioactive Material**—Transport hazards range from small amounts of medical radioactive materials to depleted uranium reactor rods. Any of these could be used to produce radiological weapons or so-called "dirty bombs." We're guessing you don't keep a Geiger counter in the trunk of your squad car. If you even suspect a radiological hazard, back off and call for help.
- **Class 8: Corrosives**—A corrosive is defined as any liquid or solid that eats away at human skin or a liquid that severely corrodes steel or aluminum. Sulfuric acid is a commonly transported corrosive.
- **Class 9: Miscellaneous Hazardous Materials**—A label with this on it isn't terribly informative. At least you'll know what a load *isn't* (flammable liquid, explosive, etc.). The definition of class 9 is fairly technical and includes substances like PCBs and asbestos.

Identifying Hazardous Materials

The placards for these classes are just one means of identifying materials. They cannot always be relied upon, however. For one thing, you won't find them on buildings that you may *know* contain hazardous materials. For another, transports may be improperly placarded. (This is a serious offense, and many states have units dedicated to enforcing placard laws.) Some placards are of the "flip" type, and an accident may cause them to flip to another ID number, leading to misidentification and inappropriate action.

First, how do you *not* identify materials? There is some well-known footage of a major-city battalion chief walking right up to a railway tanker

Figure 7.1 These are just a few samples of DOT placards. Note that in the real world all have distinctive colors, such as orange for explosives and red for flammable liquids and gasses.

leaking an unknown substance. After swiping his finger through the ooze and sniffing it, he *tastes* it! That just about covers every technique of how *not* to identify hazardous materials.

In law enforcement, we frequently hear the terms "copometer" and "blue canary." This is the officer that rushes into a scene or stands in a cloud directing traffic with eyes streaming and throat burning. Up clumps a HazMat technician in full level A containment and asks the officer to describe his or her symptoms. Don't let this happen!

These illustrations aren't meant to be derogatory, but they do show a failure to realize that in most cases we are not dispatched to a HazMat scene, but rather to an MVA or industrial accident. It is usually only after the "blue canary" discovers the hazard that fire and HazMat specialists are notified. Without proper notification, *they* may well drive unprotected into a scene. Regardless, law enforcement must learn to react quicker and smarter once we have any indication of a HazMat situation. Traditionally we stay too close for too long. Our initial response should be best described using the EMS expression "load and go." Exit the scene as soon as possible, and take anyone that you can safely grab with you.

There are six acceptable methods for recognizing hazardous materials. Note that HazMat teams require at least three of these before initiating an action based on the material type:

- **Department of Transportation (DOT) Placards or Labels:** These placards are required by law and must meet certain size, shape, color, and position requirements. They are your first and best option for identifying transported materials.
- **Markings, Symbols, or Colors:** Beyond placarding, also look for common symbols and colors, such as orange for explosions, red for flammable, and skull and crossbones for poisons. Beware of military vehicles, which will probably have no markings of any kind. If you see a military transport on its side and the driver hot-footing away at top speed, that's a bad thing.

- **Bills of Lading or Shipping Papers:** All modes of transport must carry papers detailing the nature of hazardous materials. (For whatever reason, these papers have a different title depending on whether you find them on a ship, truck, plane, or train.) Bills of lading, for example, should be kept in the cabs of all trucks carrying hazardous materials. Of course, you can't run up and grab them if the tank contents are pouring out!
- **Occupancy or Destination:** You can make some educated guesses about the contents of a building based on the nature of the business. Similarly, you can guess that a tank truck heading into a refinery might be carrying crude oil or petroleum additives.
- **Type or Shape of Container or Carrier:** Is the trailer you see on the highway designed for solids, liquids, or gases? Are the containers spewed across the interstate cardboard boxes, 55-gallon drums, or steel-reinforced concrete casks?
- **Environmental Detection Equipment:** This is the surest way to determine exactly what you might be facing. Of course equipment sophisticated enough to determine material natures and concentrations is usually found only with HazMat specialists. If you're lucky enough to have some of this equipment in the trunk of your car, get in the habit of using it!

The caution exhibited by a HazMat team is similar to the intelligence gathering conducted by a SWAT team prior to taking action. In both cases, the "specialists" will not act unless they have sufficient information to maximize their chances for success. They make informed decisions.

Where We Find Hazardous Materials

Simply put, HazMat threats are just about everywhere. You find them in both fixed locations and moving down our roadways, waterways, and airways—commercially and privately. Each location presents its own particular risks and challenges to the first responder.

The number of chemicals and materials used in daily life has increased many-fold during the last generation. Common objects that used to be made of natural materials, such as your sofa cushions and your kids' toys, are now made from synthetics. These materials have complex components that start at plants, change chemical and physical form, get transported, and end up in your homes.

Our society runs on hazardous materials. Let's look at some of the common places you might encounter HazMat incidents and some first-responder considerations.

Commercial Locations

Do you know what goes on in your jurisdiction? Do you have chemical plants and industrial parks in your area? Frequently, you're not even allowed on commercial industrial property. Processes and components are often proprietary. Nevertheless, you had better educate yourself quickly if you're faced with a fire or other incident at any kind of production facility. Locate a plant manager or safety manager and get a list of the materials that may be involved.

One particularly handy piece of paper is the Material Safety Data Sheet (MSDS). Each chemical that rolls out of a production facility has such a sheet listing the material's full name, reactivity, hazards, and other useful information. If you're lucky, the plant manager will be able to tell you the primary hazards and then produce a book of these sheets. You can then hand it off to the specialist.

But dangerous substances are not limited to plants and industrial parks. As you know if you've ever gone shopping, many stores (particularly large discount stores) can have a huge range of potentially hazardous materials. They carry everything from nail polish to brake fluid. Just a few other places with specialty materials include photography shops, hobby shops, garden shops, dry cleaners, and agricultural supply stores.

Colleges, particularly research universities, also represent a wide range of possible threats. A few campuses have nuclear reactors, many have biological research programs, and most have chemical facilities. And what kind of security do you think most of these campuses have? Would it compare to military or even industrial security? Probably not.

Transportation Vehicles

Airplanes, trucks, railroad cars, and ships: Each jurisdiction has its own transport hazards. If you're lucky, the load laying in the middle of the highway will be placarded and the placard will be visible. You can then make the correct decisions to control the incident and preserve life.

Question: What is perhaps the most dangerous vehicle to find involved in a bad accident? *Answer:* a parcel delivery semitrailer or aircraft. These vehicles carry mixed loads of small quantities of substances ranging from radiological to infectious. And because the shipped quantities are frequently *just* below federal minimums, no placarding is required!

There is an unfortunate effect known in chemistry as "synergy." Normally we think of synergy as a good thing, but in this case the term refers to the fact that there is no way to predict the behavior or characteristics of randomly mixed chemicals.

Tank Cars with Flat Ends have been insulated to control
product temperature

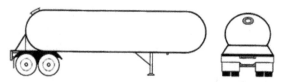

Rounded Ends suggested pressurized contents

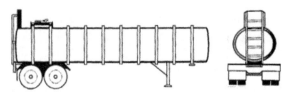

External Ring Stiffeners are used for Corrosives or Poisons

Figure 7.2 It pays to be able to recognize the types of vehicles that routinely transport hazardous materials. These samples show corrosive liquid and high-pressure tanks.

The danger of synergy applies not only to parcel transport but also to delivery trucks associated with large discount stores. These semis could contain paints, thinners, ammunition, bulk photo-developing chemicals, pool chemicals, beauty aids, and automotive fluids, just to name a few. Mix them all together and what have you got? Now, just to add some additional realism, imagine them on fire. You probably don't want your people walking through *that* cloud.

Illegal Drug Labs

Drug labs fall into both fixed and mobile categories. They can show up anywhere, from a rundown motel by the railroad tracks, to a million-dollar home in a ritzy neighborhood, to a fancy camper rolling down your interstate.

Methamphetamine production in particular is widespread and generates enormous profits. Although produced from over-the-counter ingredients, when combined and cooked these processes yield a laundry list of highly toxic substances.

You cannot run into a suspected drug lab without SCBA and some sort of protection suit. You've heard about the booby traps, but more likely than not it's the atmosphere that will put you in the hospital. Get trained and be careful.

Miscellaneous

How many other locations can you think of for hazardous materials? How about public and private swimming pools? Chlorine gas can be a problem if a cloud of it rolls over your neighborhood. And what about water treatment plants? Lots of chemicals there. And how about hospitals? There you're looking at a huge range of substances, from infectious to corrosive to radiological.

And last, but not least, *your house.* Think about all the chemicals we keep in our garages, sheds, basements, and under our sinks. A fire in any of these locations can create a toxic cloud of completely unknown properties. You shouldn't have to wonder why firefighters always wear SCBAs to even the smallest fires.

The point of this discussion is to instill the mild paranoia that will keep you alive. Any critical incident can turn into a HazMat scene. Be aware of the potential and be ready with strategies to mitigate the event.

Responding to Scenes

As we've been emphasizing, when you respond to a HazMat scene, chances are good you won't realize you are responding to a Hazmat Scene. You may receive a report of an MVA, a person down or incoherent, or an explosion or fire.

Although you may have heard of it and scoffed, the rule of thumb is an excellent technique for ensuring safe distance from a suspected HazMat scene involving a trailer or tanker. You stop at the point where your thumb, held up at arm's length, can just cover the scene. Obviously, this rule applies only when you've got good line of sight. Use it when you can.

You should have binoculars in your unit, and you'd better have a copy of the DOT's *Emergency Response Guidebook*, which we cover in some detail in Appendix C. For now, we'll simply say that we believe this book to be as important as your gun and your radio. It can save your life. If you have *any* doubt as to why law enforcement should use this resource, be sure to read the focused discussion in the appendices.

Law enforcement responders frequently fall prey to a machismo that forces them to drive right into unreasonable danger. What kind of cop would stop 500 yards away from an accident scene when people are obviously hurt and in danger? A smart one. A live one. You can't help anyone if you're incapacitated or dead.

We probably won't change these long-standing attitudes in one book, but we can at least make a start. Our goal, we repeat, is to simply keep you alive and give you the game plan you need to make correct decisions in the first few minutes of a HazMat incident. You have the hard job; you have to make those decisions.

Experience Is the Best Teacher

It is frequently hard to get law enforcement officers to take HazMat seriously until they have been directly impacted. In the worst case, a colleague dies immediately. Only slightly less tragic is a slow death that takes days, weeks, or years to occur. Nobody wants to spend one's last years on disability.

When you are exposed, even briefly, to a hazardous agent, the long-term effects can be both insidious and horrible. Although it would be a good attention getter, detailing the nature of such effects is beyond the scope of this book. We will instead mention just a few of the immediate logistical implications of exposure.

One of the first things that happens when you even *think* you or one of your team members has been exposed is that you fill out an exposure report. You must, must take this seriously. Many substances create no immediate symptoms. If, down the road, one of your officers begins complaining about chronic headaches or fatigue, you must be able to pinpoint the date of exposure and have an established medical baseline.

Part of the exposure report process is a trip to the hospital, possibly several trips over the course of a year or more. And of course many responders simply don't want to go. Excuses abound: "I just got a whiff." "I held my breath." "I showered and washed my uniform as soon as I got off shift." These excuses don't work. Just a few parts per million of some meth lab chemicals on your shoes could contaminate your home and endanger your family.

One of the surest ways to impress an officer with the importance of avoiding contact is for the responder to have been subjected to a complete decontamination on a scene. This is an extremely unpleasant experience. Off comes the entire uniform. On comes a little smock. Then you get a lovely and often public trip through a series of children's wading pools getting *every* inch sprayed and scrubbed.

Most officers need to go through this only once to get the message!

Who's in Charge?

In general, law enforcement wants to quickly hand over control of HazMat scenes to the first-responding fire units. This may not be the most appropriate action. Before relinquishing command of a scene, determine the competency level of the fire responder. If they are no more experienced than you are, retain command and wait for a specialist to show up. Even then, you may remain IC and give the operations position to the HazMat specialist. You may be the better choice to retain overall control of the scene and allow the specialists to focus on containment, evacuation, and/or decontamination. Some states, such as New Mexico, require that a state police officer assume incident command at HazMat scenes. Frequently it is not so clear. Do a little research to find out what state or local rules may dictate your command response.

So whom can you count on at a HazMat incident? There are several levels of HazMat certification. Each ensures the individual is capable of performing certain duties in any HazMat incident. We'll just quickly review these so you'll know who the players are:

- **Level 1: First Responder**—Also referred to as "HazMat Awareness," this is the most basic level, usually a two-day course. First responders can recognize the presence of hazardous materials, protect themselves, secure the affected area, and call for specialist response.
- **Level 2: Operations**—A more intense 40-hour program, commonly for fire and law enforcement supervisors. A person with this certification can act to protect nearby persons, environment, and property from materials release. This person responds defensively to control the release from a safe distance.
- **Level 3: Technician**—These responders can directly control hazardous materials using specialized protective equipment and instruments.
- **Level 4: Specialist**—These are very similar to technicians, except that they have specialized knowledge of response plans, personal protective equipment, and instruments.
- **Level 5: Scene Commander**—This person is responsible for the overall command of a HazMat scene.

Unified Command

We have stressed that fire and law need to work together. Well, there are two federal regulations (OSHA 29 code of federal regulations 1910.120 and EPA code 40 of federal regulations 311) that *require* HazMat responders to initiate ICS and manage through a unified command structure.

Over time, many scenes change in nature. These changes require different commanders to take charge of different phases. A typical HazMat scene will start out with just a police response and therefore police command. It may later require triage or removal of injured. In that phase, EMS will be in control. Ultimately, an event may well end up a fire scene. Once the release is mitigated, the security of the scene and any investigative tasks may fall back on law enforcement officials. This would be especially true in an intentional-release situation. Establishing a unified command with representatives from each agency (under one incident commander) ensures a smooth transition through these various stages.

Both the OSHA and EPA regulations have three strict requirements for HazMat response:

1. **Use of the "buddy system":** This is a common fire service tactic in which for every two responders directly involved with a hazardous material, two additional responders are fully suited and prepared to go in to perform any required rescue (also called "two in/two out").
2. **Use of the Incident Command System:** Covered in detail in Chapter 6, ICS provides a flexible set of command staff and operational area functions. HazMat scenes by their very nature always demand a multidisciplinary approach!
3. **Appointment of a Safety Officer:** Although technically part of ICS, the Safety Officer is a particularly critical role in HazMat incidents and deserves special attention. This is the person who does nothing but make sure responders are never put in unreasonable danger.

One tragic example of interdepartmental miscommunication comes from the McKinsey Report on 9/11. A police helicopter hovering over the World Trade Center North Tower reported that it could *see* the exposed beams of the building glowing red. It advised the immediate evacuation of the tower. Police and fire maintained separate command posts, and that word never got to the fire command, with results we know all too well.

If you find yourself in a situation with two command posts, make sure a police representative with a radio is at the fire command post and vice versa. This is not an optimal solution by any means, but if it is the best you can manage, do it!

"Unified command" and "interoperable communications" are two terms we will define in detail in our Incident Command System chapter. Although the operating criteria and requirements may become lengthy, accomplishing both begins with one simple step. Bring the commanders of the participating agencies together at a single location. It is the first step and the most crucial. If they remain separated at different command posts, it will be almost impossible to achieve either. Never overlook the simple solutions to complex problems! As a former police commander, one of the authors of this text made it a practice when responding to HazMat scenes to always determine where the fire department or responding HazMat team had established their command post. It was almost always at a safer location than any initial police responders were located. That is where the technical experts would be, so that was where he wanted to be to get any information needed to make crucial decisions during an incident.

Seven Critical Tasks™ for HazMat Response

All of the issues raised in Chapter 5 on the Seven Critical Tasks™ apply to HazMat scenes. You can't go far wrong if you focus on your critical tasks.

Establish Communications and Control

If possible, clear the current frequency of all routine traffic. Assume and announce your command of the scene. This is critical so that responding HazMat units know to whom to report. Provide dispatch with as exact a location for the incident as possible. Report the nature of the incident, wind direction, and relevant topography.

Wind and topography are primary determinants for the extent and path of a release. Wind obviously determines the direction and speed of a plume spread. Topography is obviously important for determining which way a liquid will head. It also affects certain gases. If a gas is heavier than air, it will drift down to low-lying areas, such as valley highways and sewers.

Let's make a quick note about wind direction. Some officers may not understand terms like "upwind," "downwind," "windward," or "leeward." When giving orders relating to wind direction, be explicit. For example, "Wind is blowing *from* the northwest *into* the southeast. Stay north of the intersection of Main and Second." Define "upwind" and "downwind" as simply: "Upwind" means you remain standing up; "downwind" means you're going down.

Identify the Hot Zone

Based on what you know about the nature of the spill, the wind, and topography, establish a conservative hot zone. Let no one in or out. Somewhere adjacent to the hot zone, establish a decontamination area and an area of safe refuge for dislocated public, if necessary.

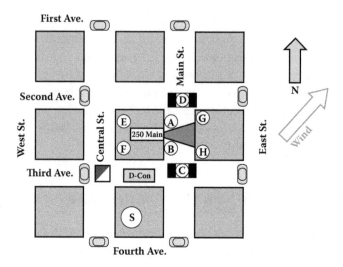

Figure 7.3 The hot zone, and therefore the inner and outer perimeters, of a HazMat scene can change suddenly. Be conservative! In traditional HazMat response training, you may have seen these areas referred to as the "hot," "warm," and "cold" zones.

Establish the Inner Perimeter

Once you establish an inner perimeter, your working area may encompass more civilians. Now you really need to develop a plan for evacuation or sheltering in place. We will deal with these issues in more detail later in this chapter.

Also, take into consideration the safety of the personnel assigned to perimeter duty. If there is substantial danger of inhalation or other contamination, replace them as soon as possible with properly equipped HazMat or fire personnel.

Establish the Outer Perimeter

Your primary concern here is that the outer perimeter puts the public at a safe distance from the incident. There have been many examples of releases that forced the evacuation of entire towns. That's a huge perimeter for which you are responsible. It is best to staff this perimeter with law enforcement personnel, but use nonsworn personnel if necessary. You are probably going to have a large response, so make sure your outer perimeter gives your people room to stage and to maneuver.

Also, continually monitor the outer perimeter to ensure it is a safe distance from the incident. While this perimeter may have been safe when first deployed, factors such as wind conditions and the amount of release can force changes as the incident progresses.

Establish the Command Post

As in all incidents, the initial command post will be the first-responding supervisor's vehicle. The primary advantage of this is that it is mobile. As we discussed earlier, the advantage of a mobile command post when dealing with a HazMat incident should be fairly obvious. When the wind shifts, you want to be able to close the doors, roll up the windows, and put it in drive. Most HazMat teams have sophisticated mobile command posts.

Establish the Staging Area

For the same reasons that you need to establish a large outer perimeter, you need to establish a good-size staging area. HazMat units can be double semi-trailers, and the staging area may also be used as a decontamination area. A decontamination area can consist of anything from one or two inflatable wading pools to sectioned, portable tents capable of processing hundreds of people at a time.

Victims should be moved from the hot zone to the ambulatory patient assembly area where triage will be conducted. From this area, patients will be moved to a decontamination area. Subsequent to decontamination, patients will be prepared for transport to further medical attention, if needed. This procedure is in compliance with the Emergency Decontamination Corridor System.

Decontamination is usually performed before the patient reaches a hospital environment by trained EMS, fire, or health personnel. When clothing is removed, a "roll down" method is used to prevent inhalation of airborne particles and the like. Gross decontamination removes more than 95 percent of external contamination and renders the patient safe for access by care providers.

Weapons of mass destruction incidents involving CBRNE (chemical, biological, radiological, nuclear, high-yield explosives) agents may result in a mass-casualty incident or person-to-person exposure. The person-to-person exposure may be limited by the use of prophylaxis procedures. Prophylaxis of these agents can often occur during this incubation period from exposure to the agent until the onset of symptoms, thus reducing the spread of disease. Widespread public exposure to a terrorist agent, particularly a biological agent, would therefore require large-scale mass prophylaxis of the public. Mass prophylaxis will be directed and coordinated by the public health system on a local, regional, or statewide level.

The procedures from the Emergency Decontamination Corridor System just outlined must be followed with potential suspects prior to their transport to secure locations. Additionally, clothing items removed during the gross decontamination process should be retained for evidentiary purposes.

Types of Decontamination Procedures

- **Spot Decontamination:** Used when the contaminants are bodily fluids. Follow blood-borne pathogens procedures.
- **Basic Decontamination:** Used to decontaminate large numbers of potential victims. Water is the only solution used in this process. In some cases, runoff may be captured.
- **Field Decontamination:** Employed to safely extricate personnel from protective clothing. This is a more thorough form of basic decontamination due to the potential of direct contact with contaminants. A formal decontamination site must be established and runoff captured.

    In a WMD incident, this may be crucial, due to the potential for evidentiary value.
- **Personal Decontamination:** Performed for the purpose of maintaining personal hygiene and may be used in lieu of basic decontamination procedures. This involves water, soap, and possibly another solution.
- **Equipment Decontamination:** Removes contaminants from vehicles, tools, and equipment.

Identify and Request Additional Resources

The sooner you recognize that you have a HazMat incident, the sooner you can get the appropriate resources rolling. Question bystanders and victims, if necessary. Use any and all of the techniques we discussed earlier in the chapter to identify the substance. Try to tell the specialists as soon as possible what they're getting into, and, as always, direct these resources to the staging area.

Evacuation and Sheltering in Place

You have two primary methods for dealing with the public impacted by an incident: Get them out or protect them in place. Each has advantages and disadvantages. The choice you make depends on your ability to accurately assess the nature of the threat. The essential question is: Will the public be safer where they are or will they be safer somewhere else?

There are also numerous legal ramifications associated with each method. Let us be clear that there are few clear-cut laws or precedents associated with public evacuation. These are evolving issues that we as responders have to deal with as they present themselves. All you can do is act professionally and base your decisions on the best intelligence possible.

Evacuation

Evacuation is seldom a first choice. It is obviously disruptive to society and creates numerous logistical problems for police. Evacuation is an option only when you can accomplish it in a *safe* and *orderly* manner. The image of the police unit rolling down Main Street and telling people to simply leave immediately is largely a myth. Such an uncontrolled exodus would be characterized by panic and gridlock. Of course you can use a bullhorn or PA system if you provide people with the information they need to head calmly in the desired direction.

There are actually two kinds of evacuation:

- **Primary evacuation** is the initial movement of people out of the hot zone. The first-responding supervisor normally carries out this type of evacuation.
- **Secondary evacuation** is the movement of people from the affected area to a specific location, such as a decontamination site. This type of evacuation is normally based on the analysis and recommendations of a HazMat specialist.

There are some clear guidelines for a controlled evacuation. Police and other first responders from around the country have developed these over many years of trial and error:

- **Always evacuate from a location to a location.** Have a *destination* in mind for evacuees. Don't just drive people from their homes and let them spread across the countryside. If possible, identify a safety zone, such as a high school or other designated shelter, well upwind of the event.
- **Keep a log of those individuals evacuated.** Where's my mother? How can I find my son? Expect these types of questions as soon as word of the evacuation gets out. Make as complete a list as possible including name, contact information, and the location to which an individual was evacuated. Give this list to Dispatch, as they will be the first line of defense fielding this sort of call.

- **Clearly mark evacuated locations.** This is critical to ensure officers don't duplicate efforts. You can use colored tape to indicate the status of a particular residence or business—for example, blue for evacuated, red for unable to contact, yellow for in-progress, and so on. This technique leads, unfortunately, to the next tip.
- **Provide security for evacuated locations, if possible.** That colored tape can also serve as a road map for looters. As you mark a mailbox with blue tape and move on, a van may pull into the driveway behind you and clean the place out. Restrict evacuated area access to emergency workers. Check ID of civilians in the area.
- **Remember purses, pills, and pets.** Always remind evacuees, if time permits, to bring critical documents, wallets, prescriptions, and pets.

Take advantage of available resources, such as your state or local emergency management agencies. They're waiting for your call! They have personnel and connections that will greatly facilitate your evacuation. They will coordinate with the Red Cross to set up shelters. What's more, they will not try to tell you how to do your job. They are there to help. There is an 800 number available to you. Use it!

The decision to evacuate is usually a tough call, but there is one case in which it's an easy one. In the case of fire or explosion threat, evacuation is mandatory. If there is *any* chance that a person left in the hot zone could provide a point of ignition, he or she has to go. Imagine a neighborhood sewer filled with gasoline from a tanker spill. Do you really want to leave a bunch of locals smoking in a corner tavern?

Evacuation Techniques

We are unaware of any laws that empower law enforcement to evacuate the public from their homes or businesses. Most legislative authority along these lines lies with elected officials and fire chiefs. That means that, in the absence of a state of emergency, we frequently have to be creative.

Getting people to leave requires us to occasionally "dazzle them with footwork." We heard of one enterprising sergeant in Florida who came up with a unique approach. This sergeant was dealing with trailer park residents who wouldn't leave in the face of Hurricane Andrew. He went back to the office and made up "next of kin" notification forms and required holdouts to fill them in. That got their attention. This strategy has been employed numerous times since. During a hurricane, the mayor of a major American city, in a televised statement, told people, "If you choose to remain behind, please write your Social Security number on your forearm in indelible ink so we can identify your remains."

Another technique utilized by a Florida department during a HazMat incident was the use of gasmasks as they attempted to evacuate an apartment complex. The complex could have been in the hot zone with a slight shift of wind, so deputies were sent to evacuate the complex. As they went door to door dressed in their normal police uniforms, few people wanted to leave. Subsequently, those same deputies wearing gas masks went door to door to evacuate the area, and the results were much different.

Sheltering in Place

The decision to shelter-in-place is usually made by a HazMat specialist based on an assessment of the type of release. Three criteria determine the value of sheltering-in-place:

- **Is it safer?** If the public will be safer in their homes than out on the road or in an evacuation center, leave them there.
- **Can structures be sealed?** Newer building construction is quite tight, so in the event of a chemical or biological release, occupants might be better off staying inside, turning off HVAC systems, and taping off doors and windows (if possible).
- **Does sheltering pose a danger to others?** As we pointed out earlier, if the release involves the threat of fire or explosion, sheltering-in-place is not an option.

There is serious discussion under way throughout our discipline about the use of force in evacuation and sheltering-in-place scenarios. There is no clear consensus. Many informal class discussions have addressed the issue, specifically in the context of bioterrorism.

Put yourself in this position: You are forced to lock down a large office building because of a confirmed smallpox exposure in the mailroom. Nobody goes in; nobody goes out. Suddenly the president of the company shows up at the front door and insists that he be allowed to leave the building. You can't go near him, so physical restraint isn't an option. You definitely can't shoot him. What do you do?

The best solution we can suggest is that you attempt to reason with him. Make it clear that he poses a threat to his family, friends, and community. Also, try to educate him about the course of the disease to which he is suspected of having been exposed. This highlights the need to have a specialist (HazMat or medical) on hand to help you make decisions. Does his leaving pose an immediate threat of death or serious injury to others? If so, you may need to use appropriate force to keep him inside, such as less-than-lethal weapons.

This is just one example of the type of issues we as responders will be called upon to deal with. We will be exploring many such gray areas in the coming years.

Summary

That's it for our five-cent tour of a 20-dollar topic. Although brief, this extremely focused approach has real value for first-responding law enforcement supervisors. If you don't need detail, don't clutter your mind with it. Focus on what you need to know. Apply the Seven Critical Tasks™. Familiarize yourself with the *Emergency Response Guidebook* (don't miss Appendix C!). Let the specialists do what they do. Work well with others.

Review Questions

- How would your response differ for an accidental versus an intentional release?
- Can you name the nine hazardous materials classes?
- Could you apply the Seven Critical Tasks™ to a HazMat scene?
- Can you recall the criteria for evacuation versus sheltering-in-place?
- Can you describe how law enforcement works with other agencies on HazMat scenes?

Critical Incident Stress

8

Objectives

After completing this chapter, you should be able to:

- Define critical incident stress.
- Recognize acute and delayed stress symptoms in responders.
- Identify stress-mitigating techniques for use before, during, and after an incident.

The preceding chapters have covered just about every element of critical incident response...except the one that maybe takes the highest toll among emergency responders. We have asserted that all incidents share common characteristics. Here is the common result: critical incident stress. Our main goal in developing numerous critical incident training courses, and in writing this text, was to save lives—the lives of innocent bystanders and emergency responders, both during and after a critical incident.

There is no way of knowing the total number of losses emergency responders have suffered due to stress. In the law enforcement profession, it is estimated that two to three times the number of officers killed in the line of duty fall victim to suicide every year. Many of these suicides, of both active-duty and retired officers, can be traced back to unresolved critical incident stress. There are numerous cases of firefighters and emergency medical technicians also falling victim to suicide every year. Another result of unresolved stress is "professional suicide." The responder leaves the profession and moves on to another career path. Emergency responders are adept at masking their emotions. What is known for sure is that *every* responder to a critical incident experiences stress. All handle it in their own unique ways—some by processing, others by suppressing.

As with other topics addressed in this book, critical incident stress is a subject worthy of semesters of college-level work. This discussion will be brief because we restrict our focus to stress as it directly relates to law enforcement, fire, EMS, and first-first responder supervisors. We'll look at types of stress, how to identify it in your responders, and some guidelines for addressing it. Although attitudes toward stress are changing, there is certainly room for improvement in our profession's awareness and handling of the problem. Just as it is time, we feel, to bring a new response to critical incidents themselves, it is well past time for an enlightened response to critical incident stress.

Sources of Stress

Stress occurs when we are forced to endure an emotionally tragic or physically threatening event. That just about exactly defines the type of incidents discussed in these pages. Gunfire, fatal accidents, and HazMat releases all contribute to stress that can scar the strongest of us.

Some typical events that can create critical incident stress for emergency personnel include:

- The death of someone you tried to save
- A personal threat, such as an attack by gunfire
- A fire or explosion that results in death or serious injuries
- Investigating a fatal vehicle accident
- Handling a child abuse incident that results in death or serious injury to the child

Also keep in mind that success may have no impact on the amount of stress a responder experiences. Many "successful" responders have participated in critical incidents and saved lives only to fall victim to suicide in the aftermath due to unresolved stress issues.

Robert O'Donnell was a paramedic for the Midland Texas Fire Department. In 1987 he was the individual who carried "Baby Jessica" McClure from a water well that she had fallen into and been trapped in for three days. He was hailed as a hero. He later became addicted to painkillers, and lost his marriage and his job. Eight years after his heroic rescue, Robert O'Donnell committed suicide.

Terry Yeakey was a sergeant with the Oklahoma City Police Department, and a first responder to the Murrah Building bombing. He is credited with at least four rescues during his response to the scene. He was injured at the scene when he fell two stories and seriously injured his back. In the aftermath he constantly second-guessed his actions, feeling that if he hadn't fallen he may have been able to save additional victims at the scene. Thirteen months after the incident he committed suicide. A book commemorating the bombing was found near his body.

Robert Long was a nontraditional responder. As an engineering firm surveyor, he was called upon to operate a global positioning system in the rescue efforts at a coal mine in Somerset, Pennsylvania. As a direct result of his efforts, the miners were located and then rescued. Subsequently there were tensions among rescuers and the miners over book and movie rights. According to his mother he received death threats. Eleven months after the rescue in which he had played a critical role he committed suicide.

These are just three examples of critical incidents where the responders played positive roles and contributed to successful outcomes during the incident but ultimately fell victim to the incident. It has been predicted that in any terrorist event, the second wave of victims would be the first emergency responders on the scene. A tragic example of this was the attack on the World Trade Center. The first wave of victims were those in the towers when the planes struck. The second wave were the responders killed when the buildings collapsed. The preceding examples and the countless others that have occurred create what we refer to as the "third wave" of victims, those who succumb to the stress of response, sometimes years after the incident.

The list is virtually endless. It is important to remember that what might be brushed off by one responder could be crippling for another. We're human and we each bring unique experiences, strengths, and limitations to our profession. There is absolutely no shame in experiencing critical incident stress. The only shame is allowing it to go undetected and untreated. It's a shame if you lose a valued friend or colleague to it.

Many factors affect the intensity of critical incident stress. For example, if there is any physical contact with a person you've tried to save, the post-traumatic stress can be greatly magnified. While it is commonly cited as a problem for EMS and fire responders, law enforcement runs the same risk. Attempting a rescue at a traffic accident or dragging a wounded officer out of the line of fire can affect us just as greatly.

There is one stressor particular to law enforcement: the use of deadly force. Next to taking a round ourselves or watching a colleague die, this is perhaps the most stressful event that can happen to an officer. Just about every officer you talk to who has used deadly force regrets it. They say they simply had no other choice. They wish it had never happened.

Time and again, members of our profession convey their feelings of concern to such officers inappropriately. When a subordinate or colleague uses deadly force, you may think you're helping by saying "great shot" or "you should have shot him again." You're doing the officer a serious disservice. The officer needs counseling, not locker-room backslapping. Perhaps no personal incident involving the police is more misunderstood by individuals both outside *and within* our profession. Only those directly involved can truly appreciate the impact it has had on their lives.

Stress Types

When one of your responders endures a horrific experience, stress can manifest itself in two ways: acute and delayed. Each has specific warning signs that you as a supervisor must be keyed in to.

Acute Stress

Acute stress reaction occurs during or shortly after an incident. You can often recognize immediate acute stress in what we call the "thousand-yard stare." You could be standing directly in front of a person and they will not see you.

As Table 8.1 shows, symptoms manifested from acute critical incident stress can be grouped into three broad categories: physical, mental, and emotional. These are things to look for during and immediately after an incident.

We'll touch on a few of these in more detail shortly. Watch your responders for these symptoms at your scene debriefing. If you as a supervisor become aware of stress effects in your people, you must take action. Discuss these warning signs with your responders. Be frank and open. And of course, you can't be everywhere at once; ask them to look out for each other.

Crying at a critical incident scene is not unusual. Tears may be of remorse, joy at having accomplished a rescue, or sheer relief at having survived. Unfortunately, there is one particular group that is simply not allowed this option: female responders. While women are no more or less likely to experience critical incident stress, they *are* more likely to suppress the symptoms. No female wants to reinforce the attitudes of "dinosaurs" who believe professions such as policing and firefighting should be male-only occupations. There are individuals who would exploit tears as evidence that women simply can't handle the job. Therefore your female responders are more likely to suppress any and all symptoms of critical incident stress, especially crying. Just one more thing to be aware of.

You *must* discuss flashbacks; they can lead responders to think they are going insane. Flashbacks are a normal cognitive response to stress. But the first time it happens, you can bet they aren't going to volunteer the information. They'll expect to be taken off the streets if they do!

One symptom, to which supervisors must pay particular attention, is withdrawal from family and friends. Something that can't be talked about can't be resolved. It really doesn't matter if the discussion takes place with a counselor or informally with the officer's support system of friends, relatives,

Table 8.1 Acute Critical Stress Symptoms

Physical	Mental (Cognitive)	Emotional
Nausea	Impaired thinking process	Fear of event repetition
Sweating or tremors	Inability to concentrate	Depression and grief
Disorientation	Confusion	Withdrawal from friends and family
Increased heart rate	Poor attention span	
Hyperventilation	Forgetfulness	Resentment of others who appear to be handling the incident effectively
Crying	Flashbacks of incident	
Difficulty sleeping		

and colleagues. In the days before formal counseling was made available to our responders, many handled their stress though their support systems such as family, brother and sister responders, friends, and so on. This is where the withdrawal from friends and family can be so debilitating. If a responder is not receiving formal counseling and is withdrawn from his or her support system, you should see a big red flag. And lastly, resentment can grow when a responder feels alone in stress response. This usually comes about when others involved in an incident mask their feelings and deny any effect. Every responder must feel free to share the personal consequences of an experience. Warn your people that they can damage the effectiveness of an entire team if they suppress rather than process.

Delayed Stress

Delayed or cumulative stress manifests hours, days, or years after an incident. This is when responders frequently begin to exhibit classic characteristics of the "problem" employee. Let's take a look at some of the more common delayed stress symptoms.

As Table 8.2 shows, delayed stress symptoms fall into the same categories as acute responses. We've mentioned that the law enforcement supervisor must keep a close eye on responders immediately following an incident. You should also try to bear long-term effects in mind when dealing with individuals exhibiting problem behaviors well after an event.

Many of these symptoms affect job performance. Apathy, cynicism, or lack of concentration may all be misdiagnosed and mistreated as disciplinary problems. When you see these types of behaviors in otherwise professional, competent colleagues and subordinates, alarm bells should go off in your head. Are you dealing with a problem employee or an employee with a problem?

Both 9/11 and the Oklahoma City bombing in 1993 provided graphic examples of normal human response to horrendous events. In the wake of those incidents, indexes of stress-related problems in responders spiked

Table 8.2 Delayed Critical Stress Symptoms

Physical	Mental (Cognitive)	Emotional
Frequent and severe headaches	Intrusive mental images of the event	Marital or family problems
Sleep disorders	Poor concentration	Fear of event repetition
Sexual dysfunction	Nightmares or flashbacks of event	Constant depression
Substance abuse (drugs and/or alcohol)		Apathy and cynicism toward work
Loss of energy		Defensiveness about problems
Increased use of sick time		

immediately. We won't know the final toll of 9/11 on emergency responders for years. Unfortunately, it's a certainty that additional problems will arise.

But critical incident stress doesn't require an occurrence on those scales. It can result from a HazMat incident on the interstate. It can result from a botched robbery at the corner liquor store.

Strategies

So what can you do to reduce the impact of critical incident stress? While you cannot completely protect your people, there are several strategies you can use to minimize the effects of stress.

- Pre-event planning and training has been shown to have a major positive effect in preparing emergency personnel to more effectively deal with incident stress. If they know what they might face, they can better prepare for it.
- Working together as a team has been shown to provide positive effects for emergency responders. Law enforcement officers tend to work alone, but in critical incidents we are a team. We must be. Train as a team; respond as a team; debrief as a team. Firefighters can return to the firehouse and spend time together after an incident. Officers going back into service in their one-officer units do not have the same opportunity to debrief in a team setting. If you are the team leader (supervisor in charge) during an incident, take steps to make sure your officers spend time afterward in a group setting.
- Provide training to emergency response personnel in recognizing the symptoms and effects of critical incident stress. Demystify stress. Get it out in the open.
- Making support groups and professional counseling available to emergency workers has shown dramatic results in improving coping skills. Is counseling expensive? Sure it is. But it's money you can't afford *not* to spend.
- If you are the supervisor of a "nontraditional" responder or first-first responder you need to consider all of the above as well. Responders outside of public safety are more likely to suffer from acute stress in that they have been put in a position to deal with a "one time" situation outside of their everyday activity.

A responder suffering from postincident stress may be hesitant to discuss particulars of the event. The person could be embarrassed or there may be some review of the action under way. For the most part, therefore, counselors simply talk to responders about their own experiences. The most vocal proponents of stress counseling are those who have been there themselves. Simply hearing what others have experienced can be a major service.

The role of the peer counselor is most effective when the counselor relates his or her experiences to the individual who has just gone through the critical incident. More often than not, the person on the receiving end will be experiencing the same emotions and having similar experiences. The main point is for the recipient to realize is that he or she is perfectly normal, even while experiencing seemingly abnormal symptoms.

One more point needs to be made about peer counseling. It is not privileged communication. Unless the peer counselor can be classified into one of the accepted privileged professions (clergy, MD, psychiatrist, licensed psychologist, etc.) the conversation is discoverable in a court proceeding. That doesn't mean you shouldn't engage in peer counseling. You just need to be aware of that fact while you are doing it.

During an Incident

As a supervisor, there are steps you can take during a major event to reduce responder stress. These include:

- Providing effective management and control of the scene
- Making sure personnel take regular breaks
- Ensuring all personnel have adequate and nutritious food and beverages during extended events (avoid caffeine and sugar)
- Rotating and relieving workers regularly, making sure they move away from the scene and rest

Although we mentioned aftereffects of the Oklahoma City bombing, responders at that scene actually used many excellent stress-mitigating techniques. These included limiting the time search teams spent in the rubble to a maximum of 15 minutes at a time. Also, each searcher had access to a "defuser" on the way out. Defusing is a well-documented technique that helps take the edge off of acute stress at the scene by letting a responder talk to someone immediately. This is supplemental, however; it doesn't replace a full critical incident stress debriefing, which should take place as soon as possible after the incident.

After an Incident

Make it a policy to conduct an after-action review with all personnel involved, and encourage them to express feelings and opinions. This doesn't have to be an uncomfortable experience for those unused to sharing emotions. It's simply a venue for some much-needed venting. During this debriefing, remind your people that incident flashbacks are normal and that, among other things, they may initially have difficulty sleeping.

Conduct formal critical incident stress debriefings. Use an experienced and professional counselor, and conduct the debriefing as soon as practical after an incident.

And perhaps most importantly, closely monitor the comments, behavior, and attitudes of all personnel involved in the incident. Look for a change from "normal" preincident conduct. A formerly introverted person who is now the life of the party (or vice versa) should serve as a warning signal that something is awry.

Do everything possible to assist those having problems, and arrange for professional counseling, if required. In fact, it is a good idea to put officers who have endured a traumatic experience through counseling whether they want it or not. It certainly won't hurt, and it's likely to uncover problems of which the responder was unaware. Many responders are hesitant to request counseling. This is when you earn your money. The short-term easy route is to ignore the problem or not force the issue. Avoiding the issue does not serve the needs of your people. Make sure they get the attention they may need.

What is perhaps the worst thing you can do? Create a culture of suppression. Act as if nothing happened. Say things like "I got through it without any therapy. They can too." Awareness starts with you. If you want to shut your people down to dealing with stress, you can probably do it. If you want your people to process the incident so they will be prepared to handle the next one and the one after that, deal with stress openly. Remember our rule of tactical leadership: "Everything goes down lead."

Summary

Probably no group in American history has prided itself more on its toughness and strength than the U.S. Marine Corps. Yet in today's world, even the Corps recognizes the negative impact that stress can have on its Marines. They have developed a program around the phrase "It's OK not to be OK!" Other branches of the military are also addressing critical incident stress among their active duty and retired members. We owe it to the men and women we command and work with to do everything in our power to ensure their well-being, both physically and emotionally!

Review Questions

- Can you recall the types of events that can trigger critical incident stress?
- Could you recognize symptoms of acute stress in your responders?
- Could you recognize symptoms of delayed stress in your responders?
- Can you recall your options for lessening the impact of stress on your responders?

Emergency Operations Center

9

Objectives

The purpose of this chapter is to present a commonsense approach to adding or strengthening this level of response in your organization. When you complete the chapter you will be able to:

- Create an organizational chart that represents the initial response, command, and Emergency Operations Center (EOC) levels of the "concept of operations" for your organization.
- Explain the main purpose and function of the EOC.
- Describe the conditions under which an EOC would be activated.
- List the functional staff and section titles utilized in an EOC.
- Give a brief description of the role of each of the functional titles and sections.
- Describe how the EOC communicates with other levels of the organization during a crisis.

Active Shooter Scenario

Only 45 minutes have passed since the Director of Human Resources first heard the shots coming from a conference area of his department. After "getting out" and briefing responding officers, he has now arrived at the predesignated Emergency Operations Center (EOC) in the Administration Building. Even as he was briefing the Emergency Manager, new information was coming from the scene, and it didn't sound good. The security director had joined the unified command and has been forwarding information from the scene to the EOC. Numerous people have been shot including the shooter, who committed suicide as officers closed in to make an arrest.

After debriefing and assessing the mental state of the HR Director, the Emergency Manager assigned him to the Investigation and Intelligence Coordination Section. His knowledge of the scene, the employees in the building, and the procedures followed during events like a termination hearing made him a perfect fit for this section.

About 60 minutes into the situation, it was confirmed that several of the victims were dead, and others were wounded and had been transported to an area hospital. The shooter who had committed suicide as a police response team approached was in fact the Facilities employee who was being terminated. Identifications were being made that showed that numerous employees of the department as well as several applicants who were waiting for interviews were among the dead and hospitalized.

At this point, the Emergency Manager determined that the HR Director would be relieved from the EOC and escorted to the area hospital, where he was joined by a crisis counselor from his organization. Together they met with family members in an attempt to comfort and attend to their needs.

In later posttraumatic stress counseling sessions, the HR Director actually indicated that working with the trained professional during that time helped him with his grief and feelings of helplessness. He was involved and felt useful. Naturally, he was second-guessing his initial actions and overall responsibility as Director of the department. Over time he came to grips with the fact that he had taken and provided training in this area and that applying it had saved lives. He had no control over the intent of the shooter.

Subsequent to this event, his and other supervisors have been trained in "threat assessment," and an HR assessment team has been formed to evaluate situations that come to their attention from the field.

In his role in the EOC and after as an Agency Representative from the organization to the hospital, the HR Director was able to:

- Provide a firsthand briefing to the Emergency Manager.
- Give the Investigation and Intelligence Coordination Section a wealth of information on procedures and personnel, and access to the HR database.
- Calm and assure families of victims that the organization was concerned and involved in their recovery and grief.
- Recognize the need for counseling and provide it for others; and just as importantly, accept it for himself.

Introduction to the Emergency Operations Center

We have examined how individuals at any level of the organization can be called upon to function as first-first responders and how first responders can utilize the Seven Critical Tasks™ in the crisis phase of an incident. We also know that once stabilization occurs, we continue to build our decision-making team utilizing the Incident Command System (ICS) to establish a command post at or near the scene. The command post is responsible for resolving the incident and is made up of command-, supervisory-, and operational-level personnel. These are the folks whose day-to-day tasks include putting out fires, restoring public order, repairing IT failures, and so forth, depending upon their discipline. These groups make up the first two phases of response: the initial response and scene management.

The third level of response is at the administrative level in the form of an Emergency Operations Center (EOC). When the size, scope, and seriousness of an incident is beyond the ability of a field command post to address, an EOC may be activated. The EOC function may simply be a logistical support function for the command post or may address business continuity for the organization or community impacted by the incident. The EOC is comprised of a separate group of higher-level administrators who will respond when the business, service, or educational process of your organization or community is disrupted by a critical incident of any nature. It is the purpose of this group to maintain the mission of the organization and its good name in the face of an incident involving its employees, customers, and/or facilities. The EOC will play a coordination or support role in an event, *not a command* role. This is the group that will manage "business continuity" and/or implement the existing "continuity of operations" (COOP) plans to keep key processes of the organization functioning during a crisis. One of the challenges during a critical event is to keep the focus of the EOC members off what is happening in the inner perimeter and onto supporting the command operation with needs outside the outer perimeter.

If you walk into an EOC, the activities, sounds, and room layout will look strikingly similar to what you would find in a command post in a large-scale and protracted incident, particularly a command post that has been moved from the hood of the Incident Commander's car to an inside facility between the inner and outer perimeter. However, looks can be deceiving, as there are dramatic and fundamental differences that need to be understood by everyone involved in emergency management in your organization. First, the EOC should never be located inside the outer perimeter. Second, the entire focus of the EOC should be on managing the key business, educational, and/or service processes of the organization, not the resolution of the incident. The EOC also supports the command post with major logistical needs that are beyond their normal reach and with specific requests for assistance outside the outer perimeter. When you check the sign on the door, "EOC" or "Command Post," everyone in the system should be able to distinguish between the two and to describe the critical difference in the focus and activities that take place in each.

We want to say right up front that this chapter is oriented toward organizations, institutions, agencies and/or small to midsize municipalities, not large county, state, or major-city EOC operations. These large municipal agencies typically have dedicated EOC operations that are staffed full-time and may have millions of dollars invested in technology and communication systems. In the same way that your product or service is your main focus, preparing for and managing large emergency events is theirs. The purpose of the guidance offered here is to assist entities whose primary focus is on activities other than emergency management. Our undertaking is to assist you in understanding the value that an emergency operations center can give your organization and offer models of how it can be implemented and staffed without high-tech dedicated space and full-time personnel. That said, the "support" and "continuity of business" mission proposed in this section apply to all situations, large and small.

The first question is, who specifically functions at this level of management for your organization at the EOC? The easiest way to think of staffing this function is to identify those administrators who are responsible for maintaining the day-to-day business, educational, or service functions of your organization. Essentially, in a crisis, that is going to be the function we want them to accomplish in the EOC. The only difference is that they will be together in a structured environment utilizing the "functional" management principals of ICS. Depending upon the size of your organization, this group will typically be comprised of the vice presidents, associate vice presidents, and director- and assistant director-level personnel. These members will be running the functional sections of the EOC and should assign and train some key departmental staff to assist in accomplishing tasks. This is a comfortable assignment for these individuals because they bring the needed institutional knowledge with them. The initial discomfort of new NIMS-based titles and not operating in "committee mode" can easily be overcome through training and exercising.

The second question is, why would you want an EOC when most counties, cities, and states already have one? The reason certainly has nothing to do with competition, power struggles, or politics with local or state government. The governmental EOC is certainly concerned about every major organization in their jurisdiction and may even look at you as a "resource" for supplies, equipment, housing and/or feeding victims of a disaster, depending upon the resources you might have to offer. What they *cannot* focus on, however, is your business, educational, or service process. Only you are equipped with the staffing, knowledge, and experience to assure that the organization survives into the future.

In our experience, a separate EOC is the level of emergency management that is most overlooked by most nongovernmental institutions. We have encountered many reasons why an EOC is not included in the basic "concept of operations" design. Most prevalent is that the EOC functions and command functions are combined in a sort of stew. In other words, the administrators come together and get caught up in "what should be done at the scene" and "what we need to do at the broader level of business continuity" and then back to the scene concerns. Having their feet in two canoes, key administrators are always off balance in terms of their planning and execution, and they frequently make decisions regarding the scene that have already been executed or are contrary to what is being done because they are so removed from conditions on the ground.

We are talking about vice presidential and director-level personnel and their assistants, who will never turn a wrench, arrest a person, fix an IT failure, or decontaminate a building but can get fascinated with the scene. This is common and understandable because most of us who get to this level are Type A, know we need to do something, and see the fire, contamination, or shooting as the problem we should be addressing. It is more exciting to think of what should be done next at one of these scenes than it is to consider, plan, and execute setting up alternative space with the appropriate supplies and equipment so that we can conduct the necessary business or educational process that was driven from the affected building(s). The problem is, the latter is essential to the long-term survival of the organization, and you already have qualified operational-level people in place resolving the scene.

Failure to set up and recognize the EOC as separate from scene command is generally attributable to a lack of understanding of the NIMS structure. Organizations need to mirror what occurs at local and state governmental level, as it is time tested and compliant with NIMS standards. Using traditional non-NIMS titles such as "Emergency Response Committee" and institutional titles will also contribute to confused levels of management responsibilities. As a requirement for public institutions and a "best business practice" for private ones, we need to understand NIMS structure, drop our institutional titles at the EOC door, and adopt the common terminology and structure that our mutual aid partners from the public sector will understand and use. This is not to say that we drop our institutional knowledge at the door. The EOC is staffed in a multidisciplinary manner, and when you look around the room and spot an "expert" in the area you are looking for, you need to tap into that regardless of the function in which that person is currently engaged.

When Would You Activate an EOC?

The size, scope, and **seriousness** of an incident are the best determinants in making the decision to activate the EOC. When an incident is of a size, or grows to a size, that it will disrupt the day-to-day operations or good name of the organization and/or surrounding community, then you need to consider activating the EOC.

A health crisis that is starting to affect staffing levels, a facility failure that will take a key building off line, a mass-casualty incident, an IT failure that brings down key systems, an active-shooter or hostage event, weather-related events that disrupt the community—these are but a few examples that would precipitate the need for an EOC.

There are other cases where an incident may not have an active scene at your location but will still rise to the level of disrupting the operations or having the potential to damage the reputation and good name of the organization.

You could have a group of executives or students taken hostage, or worse, in a foreign country. In this case, there is not a scene to initially respond to and manage, but the implications for the organization are clearly going to be disruptive. You will have the media spotlight on you and have to work with federal authorities as they investigate any links to terrorism. You will have key functions of the organization missing key leadership personnel. You will have to deal with the emotional damage of the hostages, your other employees, and the families of the hostages. Legal issues, medical coverage, insurance, and possibly supporting a response team who will travel to the country are just a few of the possibilities that lie ahead.

Work stoppages, even absent violence on a picket line, can present challenges that will require the EOC to be activated. Staffing, providing services, safety issues, contingency planning, legal issues, and media inquiries will require continuous attention.

Product liability, class action lawsuits, internal corruption cases, fraud, and other threats to the mission, values, and good name of the institution can be best managed at this level.

Another key issue in determining when you would set up your EOC is timing. Rarely will you activate all three or four (later we will discuss the role of the Executive Policy Group) levels of management simultaneously. We know that we will initiate the 7 Critical Tasks at the moment of discovery of an incident and move to scene management once we have achieved stabilization. So these phases come very rapidly.

The executive phase of an incident response will typically lag a bit. As soon as possible, usually around the time of stabilization, when further casualties and property damage have been averted, notifications go to the CEO or designee. Life/safety is always the first priority, and first responders are always understaffed and under pressure in the first few minutes of an incident. While this can cause delays in notifications beyond the expectations of the executive staff, life/safety has to be the first concern at the scene. As we will discuss in detail in the next chapter, the CEO may activate the full Executive Policy Group (typically 3–6 persons) or designate a person for policy issues almost immediately upon notification. This will aid the Incident Commander at the scene with policy issues that arise. However, the EOC still may not be activated. In fact, the EOC will probably be activated in less than 10 percent of incidents that you will deal with, as the overwhelming majority of incidents will be resolved at the scene without major disruption to the key processes of the organization.

It is natural that gathering information and making damage assessments will take some time. Once the information has been gathered and evaluated, the Emergency Manager and the Executive Policy Group can make a decision on the impact the incident will have on critical day-to-day operations. If it appears the impact will be, or is, significant, then a decision to activate will be made. It would not be unusual for an hour or more to pass before activation, as circumstances continually change on the ground. Information from the scene seemed to indicate "the building would be back on line soon." Then chemical contamination was discovered, and it appears this key facility will be "down for up to multiple days." A structural defect was discovered, and it could be months before it can be mitigated. Again, size, scope, and seriousness remain the drivers of this decision.

On the other hand, it could be apparent from the outset that the EOC will be needed. A light plane crashes on your organization's property, causing damage and claiming lives; a loud explosion is heard, and parts of a building blow out; or a straight-line wind storm or tornado strikes. In these types of incidents, the enormity and impact of the incident is felt and recognized by all levels of management. What you hope for is that the planning, training, and exercising you have conducted were recent and powerful enough to guide the actions of each group of responders and managers. Delays, confusion, and inappropriate responses can be fatal at this point.

What does "activating the EOC" mean? Is it always the same, and if not, why not? These are all questions we hear frequently and that you need to consider as you plan your response. What are the activation "triggers"?

- The Incident Commander (IC) may, in the initial notification to the Emergency Manager and/or CEO, recommend the activation of the EOC. This would be a case where conditions on the ground and the experience of the IC make it apparent that the incident is going to disrupt critical functions of the organization.
- The more traditional trigger would be: The Emergency Manager and the CEO confer, and based upon information from the scene, and hopefully, predetermined thresholds, make the call to activate.

Very often when we talk about setting up an EOC, or even a command post for that matter, there is a tendency to think about a full-blown implementation with 20 to 30 people involved and all the sections fully staffed. Because of this "all or nothing" approach, we often wait too long because we do not want to overreact, "cry wolf," and impact large numbers of people unnecessarily. This type of thinking can cause a delay and negatively impact the work of this group. So what can you do to avoid either a delay or the potential inconvenience, and what are the activation "models"?

One of the first considerations should be to direct the Technical Support Unit to prepare the predesignated facility for activation. This would include setting up the electronic equipment (computers, projection, video, etc.), positioning the tables (we will give you a design later in this chapter), put table tents with section titles on the tables, and set out guides, checklists, ICS forms, and position titles. This will save time and confusion if partial or full activation is ordered.

If an immediate call-up is not needed, then notify the key personnel to be on call to the EOC. This will alert team members to gather materials and prepare them for activation, while also allowing them to continue with normal business functions.

You should also consider a partial implementation with three to five key members if it appears the incident will have a minor impact or is not currently impacting but could produce a major impact if certain variables come into play. This would give the advance team a chance to functionally "preplan" for the disruptive outcomes with minimal interference to the business routine of the larger group. Team members will learn valuable lessons and improve their skills with each one of these limited call-ups.

A full call-up would be needed for large-scale events that could threaten the key processes of the organization. You should have trained and exercised adequate numbers of people (20 to 40 in a large organization) in the functioning of an EOC and identified key personnel to fill the leadership positions within the center. It may take a fully staffed EOC to get ahead of an incident in your planning and execution. Remember, the very survival of your organization could be at stake.

If and when it becomes apparent that the incident is going to be continuing for 24 hours or more, then it will be necessary to break into at least two teams and move to 12-hour shifts.

Inasmuch as the EOC must have the ability to flex with the needs of the incident, you can reduce the size of the personnel commitment over time.

You may eventually move to a model where you schedule one or two briefing sessions per day regarding ongoing activities, and plan or activate any contingencies that might arise.

Location, Structure, and Process of the EOC

We will detail the organizational structure and individual functions of the EOC later in the chapter. But first, let's spend a few minutes discussing the facility itself.

You should predesignate at least two sites that would be suitable for this function. The primary site is typically in the organization's administrative building, and the secondary site could be blocks or miles away and/or in a building owned by another organization altogether. You need a secondary site in case the primary site is in the proximity of the shooter, fire, chemical, flood, or whatever the cause is, and cannot be safely accessed and utilized. This was the case on September 11, 2001. The New York City Office of Emergency Management had a predesignated EOC in the World Trade Center complex. However, it was deemed unsafe for utilization due to the close proximity to the incident. This proved a wise decision as the damaged building housing the EOC collapsed at 5 p.m. on September 11, 2001.

The physical setup of the EOC will contribute to, or detract from, the effectiveness of the process. Often when we are training, our clients will say, "Let's go visit our new EOC," and we find ourselves hoping on the way over that we don't walk in and find the President's old conference table put to a new use.

"The conference or round table is the enemy of effective emergency management" is a common mantra in our training. As we discussed in the chapter on ICS and command post operations, separating the "functional" sections is critical to efficiency and effectiveness. Later in the chapter you will see an illustration of the EOC setup showing the room with tables around the outside perimeter that are separated from each other. This layout is a major change for individuals who have grown up in the world of round-table committees. The challenge is that most of us in organizations outside of professional emergency responders are used to the committee model. We don't necessarily like committee meetings and discussing everything to death week after week, but we're used to it.

Even students who have seen the value of setting up the room according to the plan as depicted in Figure 9.1 in training and exercises may fail to utilize that configuration during an actual incident. When you arrive at the EOC, others have already pushed the tables together and are discussing the event, and you don't want to seem "pushy." Inertia then takes over and things just never seem to get set up properly. It is the job of every person in the system to advocate for following the training they have been given, using all the tools available, and following the policy of the organization. Having an NIMS-based plan and then failing to follow it opens up the organization and its leadership to litigation.

The problem with round-table management is we can predict what is going to happen. When you are eyeball-to-eyeball across the table, the conversation will lapse into an operational discussion: "What we should do next?" "No, I think it should go this way." Everyone has an opinion, so the discussions can last quite a while without any decisions or, worse yet, any action taking place. Who is thinking of resource needs, safety issues, tracking costs, and contingency planning should plan A fail and/or the situation get worse? These discussions may fit perfectly into our comfort zone but will not allow us to get ahead of the events in terms of our planning and execution.

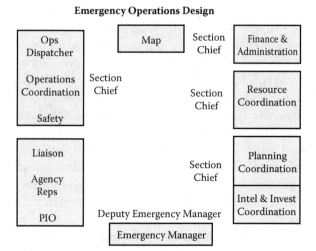

Emergency Operations Design

Figure 9.1 EOC design.

In our training, we often run an exercise where we divide the participants into the functional sections of a command post or EOC and have them "pre-plan" a significant but familiar event. We hold interaction between the separated sections to a minimum and give them a total of only 30 to 35 minutes to put an entire plan together and report back. We call it planning in 30 minutes versus 30 meetings. At first it is uncomfortable because people don't know what is being said or planned in the other sections. But quickly they get focused on just their section's task, and things begin to hum. These plans must include:

- A complete schedule for the event in question
- A complete list of resource needs
- Multiple contingency plans if facilities should fail or weather prevents plan A
- Safety issues
- Information for public and internal consumption fleshed out
- An intelligence plan

All of this in 30 to 35 minutes with everything documented by a Scribe at each section. That is the power of functional management.

Individuals tell us they have been responsible for this event for 10 to 15 years and have never thought of all the issues identified in the 30-minute exercise. We also ask them what would happen if we were around a conference table, and they tell us that the group would "still be arguing about a single issue," and then would go back over the same issue at the next meeting.

Maintaining the key business and service functions of the institution is too critical to rely on a round table or committee type of process. The ICS

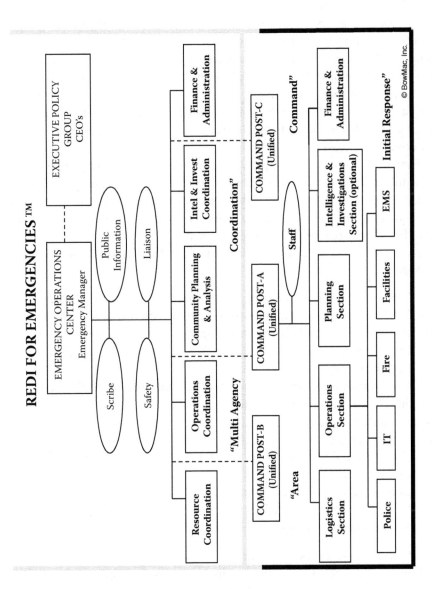

Figure 9.2 Fully evolved organizational structure.

functional management structure has proven itself over 30 years in these types of circumstances.

In the introduction of this chapter, we indicated that we were focusing on nongovernmental organizations and/or smaller municipal jurisdictions that do not have and cannot support full-time staffs or a fully dedicated high-tech Emergency Operations Center. On one hand you need a predesignated space for both the primary and secondary EOC, and on the other hand, the infrequency of these types of "call-ups" makes it impractical for most to dedicate space for this use only. You will need to find an area in some department of the organization that meets the needs that are spelled out herein and can be configured quickly when the EOC is activated. A clear understanding, supported at the CEO level, has to be in place that indicates the EOC has priority over other facility uses in every case.

Figure 9.2 shows a design that you could use for a multipurpose room.

Think of each of the rectangles as separate tables, or groups of tables, pushed together to give each of the sections working space. The section chiefs are in chairs in the middle, and the staffs are positioned on the outside near the walls, which are used for charts and the like.

Some of the criteria you should consider for the predesignated site would be:

- Adequate size for 50 to 60 people; not that you will have that many in the room, but you will want open space to reduce noise and confusion.
- Moveable tables and chairs; we recommend you mark the floor with a subtle but permanent pattern for EOC design above to facilitate a quick changeover.
- Bare walls and/or white boards that can be used to display status charts, flip chart paper, or to write on
- No conference table
- Emergency generation for power, heat, and air conditioning
- Ideally a small room off to the side for Agency Representatives from key mutual aid agencies
- Multiple "nonpublished" phone jacks
- Proximity to a small kitchen area and bathrooms as this becomes very important in long-term events

Access to basic technology is important, as long as it does not dominate the human interaction and decision-making process. Technology should assist, not drive the process. Keep in mind that in a major incident, technology may become useless due to lack of power, cellular communications, and so forth. Always back up "new technology" with paper-and-pencil capabilities. Minimally, you should have the availability of:

- Six to eight laptop computers with VOIP capability and wireless phone cards for Internet access
- Extra batteries and chargers for the laptops
- One or two LCD projectors
- Cell phone chargers for the most popular models used by the organization
- An "old-fashioned" overhead projector
- A multiple-line portable phone system that can quickly be set up with at least two incoming unpublished lines for return phone calls
- A lockbox or storage cabinet containing supplies for the operation, including table tents with section titles, and position titles on tags or vests
- Guides and checklists, like those found in Appendices A and B of this book for each functional position
- Copies of continuity of operations/business plans for each critical department
- Emergency resource information, electronically available if possible
- Pens, pencils, legal pads, and chart markers
- Wall charts for tracking personnel and equipment requests
- Facility information, if not electronically available, such as MSDS (Material Safety Data Sheet) information and floor plans for each of your buildings
- Up-to-date occupancy assignments, if not electronically available

Basic EOC Functional Roles and Who Should Fill Them

Early on, we indicated that the EOC is staffed with administrators who are comfortable with managing all facets of the organization. They will be leaving their institutional titles at the door and adopting NIMS-compliant titles. This is done not only to demonstrate compliance with NIMS to some higher authority but also to create comfort with other mutual aid and responding agencies who will recognize the structure and process you are using. It's worth repeating that although you leave your day-to-day title at the door, you will need your institutional knowledge. You may be requested to leave your original designation and move, temporarily or permanently, to another section because they need your expertise and/or access to your department's data.

The following is a listing of the key functional NIMS titles and a description of their mission that we advocate for the EOC. The Federal Emergency Management Agency (FEMA) and others recommend that you use different titles for the EOC than are used in the command post. To have Logistics at command level making requests to Logistics at EOC level would soon become a nightmare. Inasmuch as the EOC is a coordination rather than command entity, we have included "coordination" in the titles.

In this section we will overview each of the key positions, their mission, and the skills set you should consider as you make appointments. In Appendices A and B, you will find an additional job description along with a checklist of tasks.

Emergency Manager

Mission

Organize, direct, and coordinate the EOC. Offer support to scene command. Provide/seek policy advice from the Executive Policy Group. Remain strategic, and keep focusing participants on the action plan. Manage consequences caused by the incident. Oversee continuity of operations and recovery efforts. Maintain the focus of the EOC away from "scene resolution."

Skill Set

This person needs to have excellent leadership and communication skills. He or she will be creating and communicating the big picture for the entire EOC. It is important to remember that given the mission of the EOC to run the organization in the face of a disruptive incident, it is not necessary for this person to have an expertise in the specific nature of the incident. In fact, being an expert in that area could become a distraction for the Emergency Manager and hence the EOC itself. The ability to be strategic and not get caught in the weeds is critical.

Deputy Emergency Manager

Mission

Assist the Emergency Manager by monitoring and mentoring EOC staff and section activities. Ensure that EOC staff and section chiefs stay on task and don't freelance or overlap. Assume the Emergency Manager position when he or she is temporarily unavailable. Comply with directives of the Emergency Manager. Help maintain EOC focus on scene support, consequence management, and continuity of operations issues. Orchestrate regular briefings from section chiefs.

Command Staff

Scribe

Mission The Scribe is part of the Emergency Manager's staff. This individual is expected to do the following: Chronologically document pertinent information on all significant actions, decisions, directives, and communications. Significant means an impact on life, safety, or property, a financial impact, a change in operational tactics, or an action or communication that could be controversial or challenged at a later time. Assure that the Emergency Manager is aware of critical information (game changers) such as listed earlier. Assist in gathering all documents, charts, maps, and notes from the EOC for event documentation.

Skill Set   This person should have the ability to multitask and will have to record and listen for content at the same time. Administrative assistants and executive secretaries who are used to "guarding the door" of the Emergency Manager are excellent, as they know the issues that will be important to this individual. The Scribe will need to keep a written or electronic log of the critical information received, decisions made, and actions taken.

Public Information Officer

Mission   The Public Information Officer (PIO) is a member of the Emergency Manager's staff. This person is expected to do the following: Represent the "face" of the organization during times of crisis. Gather event-related information from the Emergency Manager, section chiefs, and EOC command staff. Organize information into a presentable format, and seek signed approval of the update from the Emergency Manager before presenting it to the media. Coordinate media releases with command post personnel as directed. Provide periodic updates to the media, the EOC personnel, and EPG staff. Establish a media staging area. Provide rumor control by disseminating factual information.

Skill Set   The PIO should be unflappable and a polished speaker who projects a good image to the public. Once selected, this person needs to have specific training in dealing with the media, writing press releases, and so on. We strongly recommend that the CEO does not fill this role in the response stage of the event where you have a fluid and volatile situation. The CEO can exercise this role during the recovery stage when all the facts are in and verified and leadership is needed to set the tone for the future.

Safety Officer

Mission   The Safety Officer is a member of the Emergency Manager's staff and is expected to do the following: Ensure an ongoing assessment of hazardous environments. Coordinate consequence management and continuity of operations safety efforts. Implement measures to promote responder safety during EOC-related operations. Exercise authority to stop any unsafe action that threatens the life/safety of personnel. Review all plans from the

Operations Coordination and/or Planning Coordination Sections for safety concerns. Be proactive.

Skill Set This person should have some background in health and safety. An understanding of OSHA and other safety standards would be extremely helpful. A strong personality is also essential, as they are the only people who can stop a plan or action in its tracks. Observation, listening, assessment, and communication skills are essential if they are going to be effective in saving lives and preventing injuries to responders.

Liaison Officer

Mission The Liaison Officer is a member of the Emergency Manager's staff whose duties are to: Identify necessary support agency personnel and make them available to the EOC. Establish support agency work areas, and monitor EOC operations to identify current/potential interorganizational problems. Periodically update Agency Representatives with approved information, and maintain an activity log of all related transactions. Note: Ensure that key agency and organizational representatives have the authority to speak for, and/or make decisions for, their parent agency or organization on all reasonable matters.

Skill Set This person needs to have the skills of a professional "party planner." It is critical that Agency Representatives be made comfortable and given the accommodations to carry out their functions appropriately. People in your organization who always seem to know someone at whatever organization you mention are perfect for this position, as they already have a network of contacts.

Operations Coordination Chief

Mission This person's responsibilities include the following: Directly manage all consequence-related operational activities, such as scene support, consequence management, continuity of operations, and restoration of normal operations. Obtain resources through the Resource Coordination Section. Obtain information, intelligence, and action plans from the Planning Coordination and Intelligence Sections.

Skill Set This individual must possess the ability to direct and control others with clarity and decisiveness. He or she needs to assess and prioritize work flow and coordinate with other individuals and sections in the EOC. He or she will need to communicate effectively with the Safety Officer and trust that person's judgment when he or she deems that actions or plans may be unsafe. This person also needs to be able to delegate as well as reach out to other sections, like Planning Coordination for long-term needs and the Intelligence Coordination Section for critical information.

Planning Coordination Chief

Mission   Oversee the development of continuity of operations and recovery plans. Create action plans as directed by the Emergency Manager and/or Operations Coordination. Be proactive and predict long-term needs. Anticipate contingencies by asking, "What if?" and plan for them. Monitor ongoing conditions. Maintain safety awareness for nonresponders.

Skill Set   This person must think strategically and direct others in the section to focus on long-term, not immediate, needs. He or she needs to delegate and subdivide tasks among the team members, as well as request assistance from Resource Coordination, Intelligence Coordination, and the Safety Officer. Report writing and review skills are critical.

Investigation and Intelligence Coordination Chief

Mission   Perform an ongoing assessment of information and intelligence critical to the incident. Collect, coordinate, and disseminate relevant national and local information to the scene, Intelligence Section, and EOC staff as appropriate. Provide operational and strategic information to the Emergency Manager and the Planning Coordination Section to guide the development of action plans.

Skill Set   This person needs strong investigative and management skills. He or she must have strong ties to, and contacts within, the organization, the community, and other agencies at state and local level. Being detailed oriented and possessing good report-writing and review skills are important. He or she needs to be able to sort out fact from fiction, and cite sources for documentation. The ability to communicate effectively with other sections in the EOC and at the scene is critical. He or she should have a technical orientation and utilize electronic searches internal to the organization, as well as external tools. Finally, he or she must be able to safeguard sensitive information and have an understanding of "need to know" principals within the organization.

Resource Coordination Chief

Mission   Order, document, and stage all resources needed to facilitate incident consequence management, continuity of operations, and scene support. Provide alternate facilities, supplies, communications, food services, and information technology support. When not actively filling actual requests, be proactive in anticipating and researching availability of resources that may be needed in the future.

Skill Set Good management skills with an orientation toward detailed documentation are critical. This individual will need to subdivide tasks with the team, and manage the flow of requests from other sections within the EOC and occasionally from the Logistics Section at the scene. Documentation and situational awareness are essential to avoid duplication of, and/or dropping of, important requests.

Finance and Administration Coordination Chief

Mission During major incidents requiring consequence management and/or continuity of operations, record incident costs for reimbursement, record personnel time records, record incident-related compensation claim requests, and approve and process emergency purchase orders. Advise Resource Coordination of approved emergency vendors and other sources of supply.

Skill Set This person needs a background in finance, purchasing, and payroll. He or she will need authorization to access electronic data from the organization's finance and human resource files. Familiarity with the requirements and documentation standards of the organization's insurance company for reimbursement is important. This individual also should know the documentation standards for claims during a "declared emergency" situation at state and federal level.

Functional Process of the Emergency Operations Center

It bears repeating that one of the keys to a high-functioning EOC is the physical layout and design of the room, which does not include the conference table. We have witnessed centers where every person is wearing a function identification vest or name tag, but they are around a large table with multiple Agency Representatives from participating organizations, and they all have a phone and radio in front of them. When the Emergency Manager or another section chief would alert "the room" about a game changer, you could watch everyone independently radio a message to his or her organization and then pick up their own phones. It wouldn't be long before someone at or near the scene would start reporting on "independent action" being taken by several agencies and general chaos in terms of coordination of the agencies.

In most of these cases you could make two interesting observations. One was that while the sign on the door said "EOC," everyone was thinking and acting too close to "scene command." Second, everyone was thinking "operationally" instead of carrying out the function on their tag or vest, and worse yet, they were doing it as independent agencies. The result of this is that instead of feeling supported, the scene commanders felt smothered and not in control of their own scene. This is not only frustrating; it is downright dangerous for the personnel close to the scene. This said, we need to examine the logic behind the EOC room layout and the interactions within the room as well as with other layers of the response and management of the incident.

A reexamination of the recommended design suggests a logic that facilitates communication and work flow within the EOC. Remember also that the emphasis of this chapter is aimed at nongovernmental organizations and/or smaller jurisdictions that lack large full-time staffs, dedicated space, and a high-tech environment. It is also recommended when the primary function of the EOC is business continuity for the organization or community. When the primary function is logistical support, a facility with fixed workstations for individual departments may be more appropriate. This design represents the setup of a multipurpose facility with moveable tables that can be quickly configured like the design in Figure 9.2.

Because there is a rationale to this setup, we would actually recommend that you "label" the floor in some permanent way so that the room can be organized quickly and consistently. There will be enough confusion during a crisis; you don't need to guess or just randomly shove tables around the room and then start to work. If you have trained and exercised using this configuration, then it is important to maintain that consistency or people will feel strangely "out of place" and not get into flow quickly.

Notice a few things about this design:

- The Emergency Manager will be positioned behind the table at one end with a view of the room. This will allow him or her to be more strategic than if he or she is moving around the room. The EOC Scribe should be seated with the Emergency Manager, and if they are going to be effective, the Emergency Manager must limit movement.
- The Deputy Emergency Manager will be moving freely in the center area to and from the table to communicate with and supervise the activity of the sections. It is important that he or she can see work product and hear discussions so duplication of effort can be minimized.
- Staff personnel will sit on the outside or wall side of the tables, and the section chiefs will have a chair on the inside near the open space. This accommodates communication with the Deputy and Emergency Manager. Walls will be used for charts that can be easily seen by other section personnel. This cuts down on shouting back and forth to check status of requests and the like between sections. Bare walls are also an important feature.
- The Investigations and Intelligence Coordination and the Planning Coordination Sections are close to each other and could be combined.

We advocate separate sections if staffing permits, as often planning overwhelms the intelligence function when combined.

- If a map is going to be introduced, it should be *projected* at the opposite end of the room from the Emergency Manager's table. You want it visible from all areas of the room so people don't gather around it and lapse into operational discussions.
- Sometimes a separate area adjacent to the EOC can be set up for Agency Representatives. It is our experience that in the nongovernmental EOC environment, there are fewer Agency Representatives invited in. This is attributable to the fact that the organizational EOC is more narrowly focused than the governmental one, so the separate area is not as critical.

Notice also the positioning of the functional areas in the EOC in Figure 9.2:

- The Investigations and Intelligence Coordination Section is located near both the Emergency Manager and the Planning Coordination Section. This facilitates the handling of written request slips for information that will often come from the Emergency Manager and planners. Also, when staffing is an issue, intelligence functions will fall to the planning personnel. It is recommended that you designate a person in the section for that task.
- The Resource Coordination Section is located between the finance and planning functions. This accommodates the natural need for planners to request the availability of personnel, supplies, and services from the section to complete their planning requirements. Because the personnel in the Administration and Finance Coordination Section are familiar with vendors, emergency purchasing, and pricing, they are a valuable asset to the resource personnel.
- The Operations Coordination Section is positioned near the map so they can be updated on areas to avoid, perimeters that restrict movement, facilities in and out of service, and so on, as they are identified by command at the scene. They will also control communication out to the field through their Operations Dispatcher, so there is a single voice directing consequence-related operational activities.
- The PIO, Agency Representatives (if any), and Liaison Officer (if appointed) are in close proximity so that the PIO can coordinate information with other agencies when necessary. The PIO is also in close proximity to the Emergency Manager, who will need to approve and sign all releases.

Communication and Interaction in the EOC

Within the EOC, there is a flow of interaction that we sometimes call the "dance of the room." Earlier, a metaphor was used that the Incident Commander was like the conductor of an orchestra. The same is true for the Emergency Manager in the EOC. If you come early to the theater, you will hear "noise" not music as the orchestra tunes their respective instruments. Once the conductor gains control, the noise is turned into beautiful music. The same is true for the EOC. There is a "warm-up" period in the first 30 to 40 minutes when individuals are trying to get briefed on the details of the incident, assess what the impact on the organization might be, and determine what each section should be doing to start the process. But there comes a time when the noise and confusion turn into a hum and individuals are busy at the various sections on specific tasks. That is the "music" you want to hear in the EOC. It's also like a group of friends who are out to eat; it's noisy and can be confusing during the cocktail time as everyone is trying to catch up. But once the meal is served it quiets down, and the conversation is much more controlled.

So how do the Emergency Manager and Deputy Emergency Manager move the group past the noise and start to make music? One of the early tasks is to make sure everyone is reminded of what the mission of the EOC is and is not. Once assignments have been made and individuals have used the checklists and job descriptions to brief themselves on the specific tasks of their staff or section, then the Emergency Manager needs to clearly state that mission in an initial briefing of the entire team. "Remember folks, we have competent people managing the scene, and while we don't yet have all the information we may need, our mission is different from theirs. It is our job to keep the organization running in the face of what is going on, to support and *not* duplicate the efforts at the scene, and to protect the good name of this organization. In that regard, I have Intelligence Coordination working on the information piece. What I need is for each section (based upon what you know) to anticipate what *impact* this situation might have on our total operations and, within the scope of your section's responsibilities, do some initial planning and research. I will then have you report back to the team, and I will make section assignments as appropriate. You have 15 minutes." This type of leadership in the initial stage of formation will go a long way toward getting past noise and establishing the credibility of the Emergency Manager.

The next briefing would typically be a specific one based upon intelligence information and ideally from someone who was originally at the scene and is now moving into a position in the EOC. Once delivered, the section chiefs and staff would be called upon to give the impact assessment from the perspective of their assigned duties. This will bring the room up to date with the event and the potential disruption that could be caused to the key processes of the organization. Even as the briefings are in progress, the Emergency Manager or Deputy can make assignments as key points are delivered. To the PIO, "As soon as we complete this briefing, I need you to prepare a press release." To Planning Coordination, "I will need you to prepare a long-term plan for moving operations back into the facilities once they have been declared safe." And so on.

With the EOC and its sections focused on specific tasks, the Deputy will now start to work the room, moving from section to section making sure that each chief has properly tasked the section members and that the focus is appropriate and within the job description and not in conflict or overlapping what another section is doing. This will leave the Emergency Manager free to think strategically: "Where will this situation be in three to four hours?" "How can we support the command post operations?" "What policy issues might arise, and how do I present them to the Executive Policy Group?" "Is there a possibility this could go on overnight, and will I need to staff a second shift?" The Emergency Manager constantly needs to remind him- or herself to stay strategic. This will assist in focusing the EOC as a whole.

There will also be periodic briefings conducted by the Deputy where the section chiefs are either called to the back where the Emergency Manager is located, or they will do them from their section table for the benefit of the entire room. If there is conflict or overlap between sections, then the more private rear-of-the-room briefings are appropriate so that the Emergency Manager and Deputy can get things back on track. There are also times when the entire group should be brought up to date on what everyone is working on currently, as well as the status of the operations and planning. This where some overlap presents itself as you will typically hear that the Planning Coordination Section is working on some plan that Operations already has in motion or has completed. This usually happens early in the event and is an indication that the Planning Section Chief needs to move the focus farther out in time. This should be controlled as a "briefing" and not a "discussion," and a time frame should be given: "OK, listen up everyone. Starting with Intelligence, then Operations, I need a briefing on what you are currently working on and have accomplished since the last briefing. *Two minutes,* please!" Generally this is done at increasing intervals starting with 30 to 40 minutes in the first few hours and then every couple of hours as things slow down.

There will also be interaction between the various sections as they work through their tasks. The whole purpose of "functional management" is to eliminate duplication of effort. If you are the Emergency Manager and want to see a 10-day forecast, no one can stop you from calling the Weather Bureau, but if everyone worked that way you would find them asking, "Doesn't the right hand know what the left hand is doing down there?" as they will already have fielded requests from Intelligence and Operations. Use the functional assets and insist that others do as well. This is how we are able to plan a complex event in our training classes in 30 minutes instead of 30 meetings; everyone is concentrating on their piece of the puzzle. We strongly recommend that you use written request slips when you are seeking intelligence information, planning activities, and/or resources. Typically these request slips will flow from:

- The Emergency Manager to the Planning Coordination Section and the Investigation and Intelligence Coordination Section seeking long-term plans or information
- Operations Coordination to the Planning Coordination Section, Investigations and Intelligence Coordination Section, or the Resources Coordination Section
- The Public Information Officer to the Intelligence Coordination Section seeking to vet rumors and verify facts or issues raised by the press
- The Planning Coordination Section to the Resource Coordination Section and Intelligence Coordination Section asking them to research available space, equipment, supplies, and other information needed in long-term planning

Use a multipart form so that both the requester and the provider remember what, when, from whom, and why something was requested and what its priority is. The provider should give feedback to the requester when the task is completed.

While it is the job of the Deputy to mediate differences and/or disagreements between sections, much of this can be avoided if the section chiefs take the initiative to go to the other sections and either request or offer assistance. "How can we support you?" "I wanted you to know that we're working on a long-term plan for _____. Let me know when you need it." This is all part of the "dance" of a functioning EOC.

EOC Communication, Internal and External

We have said it before in this book, and it always comes up in training that "communication is the first thing to go in an emergency." We covered many of the communication channels and methodologies within the EOC in the last section. It is essential that the mission and updates on the individual tasks be communicated effectively if the EOC is going to reduce the impact on the organization's critical processes.

That leaves the question of how the EOC communicates with the other layers of response and management, as well as the outside world. Remember that part of the mission is to protect the good name of the organization with the public and other agencies/organizations with which we interface. This means we need clear policies, effective channels, good training, reliable electronic systems, executed memorandums of understanding (MOUs) with other organizations, and exercises that test these things.

We will explore the lines of communication with the Executive Policy Group (EPG) in the next chapter, but there are a number of issues that will impact the EOC and its effectiveness if they are not handled properly. Our experience tells us that the EPG usually feels like they are out of the loop in terms of knowing what is happening at the scene and in the EOC. This group is composed of three to five of the top leadership of the organization led by the CEO, and they feel enormous pressure and responsibility to make sure the organization does the right things fast. They will be getting inquiries from VIPs internal and external to the organization as well as press inquiries, and a good flow of facts is necessary. We will expand on communication methods in the next chapter, but there are some traps you need to avoid if you are the Emergency Manager.

The first trap is that lacking timely and accurate information, they will want the Emergency Manager to report to their site. This is a trap because once you allow this to happen, it becomes like the game of "capture the flag" we used to play, and you will become a captive of the group for a long period of time. When this occurs, they then request other persons to appear as well, and soon the event is being managed and supported out of the Executive Policy Group and not the command post or EOC. The best solution to avoid this is a combination of training and exercising where they witness how busy the EOC is and avoid leaving it leaderless, along with the assignment of an Agency Representative from the EPG to EOC as eyes and ears that can keep them informed. This, in combination with an electronic log such as is found in BowMac's "REDI for Emergencies" software that allows all levels and functions to post timely data, will give this group the information they need to make quality policy decisions and handle high-level inquiries that would otherwise distract the functioning of the EOC.

The functional areas of the EOC should also establish direct links with their counterparts at the command post. The IC should be able to request assistance from the Emergency Manager, Operations at command level can request support from Operations Coordination at EOC level, the PIO and Intelligence Coordination will certainly need eyes and ears at the scene, and so forth. The key is that all of this needs to be set up in advance and practiced during exercises if it is going to work in live events.

Summary

The Emergency Operations Center is a necessity for all organizations of any significant size. It needs to be separate from the Command Post, away from the scene and staffed with individuals who have been trained. While the EOC need not be a "dedicated facility" it should be pre-designated, equipped with appropriate technology, and have backup power generation. The administrators and support staff functioning at this level need to maintain a focus on supporting (not micromanaging) the efforts at the scene, and continuity of operations for the organization. In order to be NIMS compliant and operate at maximum efficiency the physical set up must support "functional" management principles rather than round table committee design. The EOC will operate long after first responders have completed their jobs and gone home as they will be tasked with coordinating the recovery efforts for the organization's facilities and personnel.

Review Questions

1. Why would an organization want to set up an EOC when one already exists at the local or regional governmental level?
2. How does the focus of the EOC differ from that of the Command Post?
3. Who in the organization is best suited to staff the EOC?
4. Why is the physical setup of the facility important?
5. Why do the titles of the EOC positions differ from those in the Command Post?
6. How does the EOC communicate with other levels of the response and management of an incident?

The Executive Policy Group

10

Throughout the years in training first responders, inevitably the issue of the Executive Policy Group and their role in an emergency arises. When the question "Do you want the top elected official, president of the university, CEO of the organization, involved in your incident?" is posed, the answer is almost always a resounding "No!" When the top executive has appointed a group of individuals to assist him or her in emergency response, their involvement can become very helpful or totally disrupt incident response. The reality is that their involvement may be crucial to your success. Their position places responsibility for the outcome and the continuity of business directly upon them.

The hesitancy to have them involved in an incident usually results from experiences when the top executive or his or her designee attempted to run the incident or assume the role of Incident Commander. This misunderstanding of responsibility is usually directly attributable to a lack of clarification of the top executive's actual role in an incident. They know they have a role, and if it isn't clarified for them, they will become involved in the operational aspects of the incident. In this chapter, we will attempt to clarify that role. To every first responder we recommend ensuring that your top executive reads this chapter and has a clear understanding of his or her role and responsibility.

Keeping this in mind, let's go back to our scenario involving the president that was presented in the Introduction.

It's been 35 minutes since the president first heard an explosion in one of the organization's buildings next to her office. After being thrust into the role of a first-first responder, the last half hour has flown by. In that time, the president has done the following:

- Notified 911 of the blast and its location.
- Being on-site in the off hours, she responded to the scene and secured the perimeter as well as she could using some bystanders and the overtime personnel who escaped from the building. This prevented several nonemergency personnel from entering the building to attempt an unwise rescue. Given that there was a secondary explosion, this simple act may have saved several lives.
- As ranking person on-scene, the president was in charge of the scene up to the point of the arrival of the fire department and for a short

time was actually serving in unified command with the Incident Commander from the fire department sharing information on the facilities and the like.

- The president then assigned the shift supervisor who escaped the building as her replacement on-scene.
- At that point, she made a number of notifications to key organizational personnel—the Emergency Manager, the Director of Facilities, and her Executive Assistant. She indicated that she wanted immediate notifications made to the organization's Emergency Operations center (EOC) team and the Executive Policy Group that they were being operationalized.

It was now 45 minutes into the situation, and the president returned to the headquarters building. Key personnel who had been notified or heard of the incident via the media were beginning to arrive. In the absence of the Emergency Manager, the president directed that the predesignated EOC facility be operationalized. Several EOC technical support personnel worked to set up the facility.

Twenty minutes later, the Emergency Manager arrived, and after a short briefing the president then moved to the pre-designated facility for the Executive Policy Group one floor above the EOC. The EOC support unit had activated the electronic Incident Event Log, and the president posted a description of the events up to that time. While unusual that initial information would come from someone in the Executive Policy Group, it was absolutely appropriate as the president was part of the initial response and scene command before arriving back at headquarters.

Posting this information on the incident log allowed others at EOC level to brief themselves on the incident. Shortly thereafter, other information started coming in from the scene regarding injuries and damage. There were reports of serious injuries, and a number of individuals were still unaccounted for.

Members of the Executive Policy Group started to arrive, and eventually all five members—the COO, CFO, Executive VP of Operations, legal counsel, and the president were present. The president appointed her Executive Assistant as the Scribe for the group and sent another assistant to the EOC as an Agency Representative for the Policy Group.

Even before the entire group was assembled, the work, which would carry on for days to come, began. Many decisions needed to be made to set the tone of the organization's response to this incident over the next few days.

We will discuss the function of the Executive Policy Group in depth and look at some of the decisions that our president and the Executive Policy Group needed to make in this incident. But first, let's look at the approximately one-and-a-half-hour journey of our president.

1. Because the incident occurred in off hours when there were only a handful of individuals at work on a special facilities project, some of whom were contractors, the president was in the unique position of being a first-first responder and initiated many of the Seven Critical Tasks™ that have been discussed in earlier chapters.

2. Once a degree of stabilization had taken place and public safety responders were on-scene, she then found herself as the Incident Commander. There were no pronouncements, vests, or formalities, but in fact she was in consultation with the Incident Commander from the fire department, and he had jurisdiction over the facilities, personnel, and other resources in the game. So for that short 20 to 30 minutes, the reality was that she was in unified command as the organization's Incident Commander.

3. She then executed a "change of command" by appointing the Shift Supervisor to work with the fire command and returned to head-quarters to oversee the implementation of the remainder of the NIMS-based "concept of operations" as per prior planning and training. Extricating herself from the scene as quickly as possible was critical to the overall response of the organization. Too often, individuals get enamored with the scene, and the larger issues of the response are ignored or delayed.

4. The president recognized quickly that the size, scope, and seriousness of the situation would require activating the EOC and the Executive Policy Group as quickly as possible. She made notifications from the scene while transitioning to headquarters.

5. She directed the initial setup of the EOC and Executive Policy Group facilities, and from her unique position in this event published the initial briefing.

6. She then settled into her "natural" position as head of the Executive Policy Group where she would continue to function well into the future.

Who would guess from looking at a static NIMS/ICS chart of positions that someone at the head of an organization could take that journey and fill all of those roles. Many individuals say to us, "Just tell me where I should report and what function to do when I get there. I don't need to know all the rest." Wouldn't it be nice if it was that simple? But it's not.

The head of this organization had taken the time to go to training and fully grasp the "concept of operations" for the organization. She also spent time going through some mental preparation where she visualized herself responding to various scenarios. It was this knowledge and mental preparation that propelled her through all of these steps, probably saving lives, property, and financial losses for the organization.

All of that and her "designated" emergency management role is just beginning, so let's examine the role and function of the Executive Policy Group.

Executive Policy Group Overview

The Executive Policy Group (EPG) in any organization should be kept very small and include the top four to six individuals that surround the CEO of the organization, plus a trusted executive assistant who will serve as the Scribe and a second trusted assistant who will serve as an Agency Representative to the EOC.

This group sets the tone for the organization's long-term response and needs to be strategic in its thinking. When they convene as a group, they will gather together apart from the EOC or command post operations, typically in the CEO's conference room. Notice that this is the only time when a round or conference table is advocated in managing a crisis. The nature of EPG's work dictates discussion, face-to-face interaction, and knowledge of all the inputs that go into the final decisions that will be disseminated to the other levels of the emergency response.

Decisions on closing business, municipal, educational services, and/or manufacturing processes are paramount and must be made as quickly as possible. Articulate these decisions as clearly and quickly as possible to allow EOC and command levels to plan and implement effectively. In a campus environment for instance, the closing of all or part of the educational process, or all or part of the campus, has enormous impact upon the decision making at command post and EOC level. A decision to cancel the educational process can quickly become "the campus is closed" as the information passes from person to person. The actions associated with closing a campus are dramatically different from those of canceling classes. Valuable time can be lost due to the confusion.

Continuity of operations (COOP) during an emergency is a primary concern of the executive policy group. An excellent example of this occurred during the BP crisis in the Gulf of Mexico. As large an incident as this was, and considering the impact the incident could have on the future of the company, top executives could not be drawn to the "scene." They needed to ensure that the corporation continued operating. A designee was assigned to the incident. However, the principal task of the Executive Policy Group involved keeping the company's administrators focused on a much larger scope of the company's operation, beyond events in the Gulf of Mexico.

Other policy decisions may be related to notification procedures for families of employees, customers, or students injured or killed in the event; release of sensitive information to the public; and level and tone of the response. Other kinds of decisions involve whether employees or others should be negotiated with or arrested for minor crimes such as trespass, whether to repair or replace facilities, and/or whether to continue a line of business or educational discipline or eliminate it.

Delayed decision making frustrates the other levels of response and often leads to independent actions being taken by command or the EOC levels that later are deemed inappropriate by the Executive Policy Group because they are contrary to the policy decision that was eventually made. When this happens, friction develops between the levels of management that can be extremely counterproductive and even dangerous if allowed to continue. The Emergency Manager and/or Incident Commander may stop requesting policy decisions, even though their "sixth sense" tells them to. Members of the Policy Group may start making "operational" decisions, even though they are far removed from actual conditions on the ground.

There are numerous reasons that policy decisions can be difficult and/or delayed. Some of the most common in our experience are:

- Lack of timely information coming to the Executive Policy Group: When there is not an efficient flow of information from the EOC and/or the field, Policy Group members often feel as though they are being kept in the dark purposefully or otherwise. The longer the delay, the more frustration develops.
- Inaccurate information due to distortion, misunderstanding, and/or conflicting sets of data at scene command and EOC levels: Conflicting times, numbers of injured, types and seriousness of injuries, who was injured (employee, customer, student, names), affected facilities, and level of damage can all be problematic.
- Failure of the Policy Group members to train and/or a lack of understanding of their role in the greater concept of operations.
- Failure to have prepared themselves for likely scenarios through discussion and the types of decisions they will have to make in each.

When the frustration reaches a certain point, there is a tendency for the Executive Policy Group to do one of several things:

- Go to the predesignated command post, EOC, or, worse yet, the scene. This brings them into a less than ideal venue for thoughtful decision making, and there is a tendency to begin to manage operational details rather than lead through setting direction and tone for the response. Consider the scenario described in the beginning of this chapter. Had the President of the organization failed to have recognized her role in the incident and remained at the scene, none of the described activities involving the Executive Policy Group would have occurred or at best they would have been unnecessarily delayed.

- The other option is to bring the Emergency Manager and/or Incident Commander into the Policy Group's domain. This usually has results as previously described. The Emergency Manager or IC becomes trapped, and the discussions move from policy discussions to operational discussions on how and what to do next. The EOC and/or command post is left without its leader, and the true function of the Executive Policy Group is diluted.

Communication Models

Numerous times we have said that communication is one of the first things to go in a crisis. And continued communications issues can sink the ship. Following are a number of models that we have seen for communication between the Executive Policy Group, the EOC, and the scene command post:

1. Historically the Public Information Officer (PIO) was tasked with keeping the Executive Policy Group informed because of the close relationship and trust built up by day-to-day contact between the PIO and the top executives of the organization. The PIO will be operating out of the EOC in a major event and will typically have boots on the ground at the scene, so he or she is positioned to gather information at the appropriate levels. This model of having the PIO do the briefings seemed to make sense because of the task and trust. However, we have found the PIO to be too busy to be effective when tasked with keeping the Policy Group properly informed. Every time the PIO phones or delivers information to the Policy Group on breaking information or critical decisions, he or she risks missing other information that should be forwarded as well. The PIO also has gaps of time when he or she is preparing, gaining approvals for, and delivering press releases. The incident itself and the decisions being made regarding the event simply do not stop during these gaps.
2. Some organizations have the Executive Policy Group send an Agency Representative to the EOC and/or command post so that critical information can be transmitted back to the Policy Group. We have observed that this is an improvement over using the PIO but still produces gaps in information. Some of these gaps can be caused by the sheer volume of information being processed in the EOC and the ability of the Agency Representative to multitask. Gaps also occur during the time that the Agency Representative is actually briefing the Policy Group by phone or in person. Once again, the incident does not stop. The Agency Representative must also be familiar with the "functional management" positions in the EOC and where to

obtain and verify information before forwarding it to the Policy Group. Key sources would include the Emergency Manager's Scribe, the Investigative and Intelligence Section, and the PIO.

3. A third model would involve using a running electronic log such as that found in BowMac's "REDI for Emergencies III" software program. It feeds information onto a secure scrolling log that identifies the exact time and from where the information came, by ICS position, and provides a method of communicating with that person if verification is necessary. While no one runs to the computer in the first minutes of an incident, most organizations have a call taker and/or dispatch person for safety/security operations who can initiate the log. There is always a delay between the initial response and the activation of the EOC and Executive Policy Group. Part of the setup process should be getting the log online. Having this tool available with accurate on-scene accounts of injuries, transports, damage reports, logistics, closings, and so on allows for better decision making at all levels. A tool like this, combined with an Agency Representative from the Policy Group, will go a long way toward reducing the tension that can arise between levels of the management and response. The electronic log also serves as a briefing tool at all levels of the event. Only in training do we all arrive in our functional areas at once. People come in random intervals as they receive notifications and travel from meetings, home, and so forth. Much valuable time is spent in briefings (which typically become more and more abbreviated) that could be spent on decision making. The log provides a method for a "self-brief" with actual times and data, which reduces repetitive questions and false assumptions. This option may be negated during a major incident due to a lack of power and the like but should be considered whenever possible.

4. The most efficient method we have observed involves a combination of numbers 2 and 3. Using an electronic log and appointing an Agency Representative to the EOC provides backup for an electronic failure and a direct method of verification or clarification of critical data.

Preparation

The Executive Policy Group should take steps ahead of an actual event to prepare itself for quality decision making in an actual pressurized event. As we have mentioned, training and exercising are critical to establishing the connections between the levels of the response and management and testing how your organization's communication system functions. But there is more.

The Executive Policy Group needs to carve out time at regular intervals to prepare it to function at peak efficiency during an event. A common question asked is, "How and what can we prepare for the unknown?" After the initial training and exercising, the Policy Group should have a good sense of both the types of issues that they will grapple with and how difficult it is to start from scratch in formulating good policy decisions under pressure. They should also have a sense of how important it is to make quality decisions quickly that will allow the EOC and command levels to proceed smoothly.

Often the first time through an exercise (hopefully) or an event, Policy Group decisions that could be routine are difficult because members of the group have not visited established protocols and policies of the institution in some time. This means they need to start by asking:

- How has this been handled in the past?
- What's the worst-case scenario for this event?
- Do we have established protocols for this?
- Is this already part of a continuity of operations plan somewhere in the organization?
- Who should make these notifications?
- What are the thresholds for staying open or closing in this case?

In our day-to-day world, decisions like this can be pondered for hours until an ideal policy is hammered out. Continuing this deliberative process in a pressurized, fast-moving crisis can have dire consequences, as we have discussed previously.

So what can we do to prepare?

- A good place to start is to prioritize the hazards faced by your organization. Your Emergency Manager, or whoever is in charge of your NIMS-based planning, will already have a hazards analysis completed. Take that list and organize it into categories such as "similar events" that would require similar decision making, and/or events that are most likely to occur, and/or difficult or catastrophic events that would challenge you the most. There is no magic formula here, and you cannot take on all the events at one time, so we suggest that you apply some logic to the process that makes sense to you and your organization. This way you can break up the tasks among the participants and/or scheduled work sessions.
- For each of the hazards, or groups of hazards, you can project the types of policy decisions that will need to be made. Be careful here not to fall into operational decision making like, "What facilities could we use to house those personnel or that process?" Your task is to predetermine the conditions that would cause you to issue a policy

decision to cancel a critical process, close a facility, or move the process/personnel to some other site. It will be the task of the EOC to explore the details of suitable sites, as well as plan and execute the process for the move or shutdown.

- This means you will be looking at "thresholds" for your decision making. For instance, in an influenza event, what would be the percentage of personnel affected that would cause you to close facilities, move to a "work at home" process, or move to the continuity of operations planning tools for maintaining "critical operations"? Having thresholds established in advance for critical functions, operational capability, service capacity, and/or workforce impact will make decision making during an actual event quicker and more effective.

Executive Policy Group Preparation Work Flow

- Select and categorize potential hazards.
- Brainstorm organizational consequences.
- Discuss threshold levels related to consequences.
- Anticipate policy decisions.
- Record for the future.

Conducting regular sessions where various scenarios related to potential hazards and the potential policy decisions related to thresholds are addressed will be invaluable in protecting the personnel and viability of the organization during a crisis. You will find the first few work sessions the most difficult (actually they will be similar to the process of trying to create policy decisions during a critical event), but as the first few hazards are worked through, the process will smooth out and similarities of outcomes between differing types of events will become evident. This planning process will become the model for your process during an event. Additionally, your decision making during an event will be accelerated, due to the fact that you have considered the thresholds and resulting options in advance.

CEO of the Executive Policy Group

Mission

Organize and direct the Executive Policy Group. Insulate EOC staff from distractions caused by outside political inquiries, and keep "need-to-know" VIPs informed and up to date regarding the impact of the incident on the organization and community. In collaboration with legal advisors and jurisdictional leaders, make policy decisions related to continuity of operations (COOP).

Skill Set

This person is either the CEO of the organization itself or has been appointed by the CEO to head this group of top executives. The group could be comprised of the COO, CFO, executive vice president, legal counsel, and so on. Typically it would be comprised of four to six persons.

Structure of the Executive Policy Group

Most of our discussion so far has surrounded a large event where the entire Executive Policy Group has been assembled.

This is only one model for activation. Let's look at the possibilities and other models:

- **No Executive Policy Group:** As we know from previous chapters, events vary in size, scope, and seriousness, and only a few rise to the size that requires an EOC to be activated. Many resolve themselves in the first few minutes and do not even require the establishment of a scene command post. In such cases, a notification may have been made to the CEO or designee per organizational policy, but the activation of the Policy Group was not requested nor instituted by the CEO.
- **Designated Policy Person:** The incident did not resolve itself, and a scene command post (unified or not) was established to resolve the incident. A notification was sent to the CEO, and a request was made, or mutual agreement was reached, that policy decisions could be needed due to the nature of the event. Size, scope, and seriousness did not dictate that the event would abnormally affect routine operations of the organization, so the EOC was not activated. Because of the request, however, a "go-to policy person" was designated by the CEO, therefore activating the Policy Group. The CEO instructed the go-to person to get a briefing and keep his or her "personal communication device" on during the normal course of the workday so that immediate contact could be achieved by the Incident Commander at the scene.
- **Limited Executive Policy Group:** The incident was of sufficient size and scope that during the notification from the scene, a request was made to the CEO to activate both the Executive Policy Group and the EOC for support. It was clear there would be an impact on routine operations, but less than catastrophic, and the CEO ordered minimal staffing for both functions. This resulted in the EOC being activated and staffed with four to six key personnel, and the Executive Policy Group being staffed with a Scribe and a few members whose skill sets matched those of the incident.

- **Full Executive Policy Group:** The fourth model is that of full activation, due to the predictable impact the event will have on normal operations of the organization. This would require the full activation that we discussed earlier in this chapter.
- **Full to Limited Executive Policy Group:** We may also find that during an incident we may flex the Executive Policy Group from a full activation in the first few hours to that of two or three smaller teams that will track the event through time. We always have to be mindful that when we fully activate any level, we may find ourselves moving into 24-hour, multiday operations that can burn out our capability if we fail to do succession planning.

Once again, we see the flexibility and adaptability of NIMS/ICS to grow and shrink in relationship to the size, scope, and needs of an event.

Another consideration in structuring the Executive Policy Group is to subdivide the team into task forces, each related to a different policy decision. This way we can address immediate decision-making needs and start to get ahead of the event by anticipating future policy needs and requests. One of the carryover habits of our round-table committee-oriented decision model is that often we have the whole group involved in each decision being made. By assigning individuals in teams of two or three to take on a specific task, the discussion will be dramatically reduced, leading to faster output. The CEO can then approve and implement the policy or call for a brief and present and revise it according to the broader feedback received. Either way, separation of tasks reinforces the need for efficiency and is consistent with the "functional management" model equated with NIMS/ICS structure.

Traps

As we have alluded to, there are many traps in which the CEO and members of the Executive Policy Group can find themselves:

- **Rushing to the scene:** The fire, chemical spill, roof collapse, or whatever the crisis is always going to be more compelling than the conference room off the CEO's office. There will be a tendency for individuals in leadership positions to want to go to the scene, and they will always have excellent rationale for doing so: "show of support," "get a firsthand look at what is happening," and on and on. If this occurs, valuable time needed to anticipate and make policy decisions is being lost. Other levels of management in the system need you to be in place and available to set the tone of the response and to make key policy decisions. We will never tell a CEO that he or she can't go to the scene; *however*, we will say that if you make that choice, then designate someone else as the head of the Executive Policy Group until you are in a position to fill that role, and be prepared to accept that person's decisions on policy matters. By going to the scene, recognize that you may be out of position and may not be able to fully execute your true duties.

During the first crucial hours following the terrorist attack on the World Trade Center, Mayor Rudy Giuliani gathered his Executive Policy Group together. Their leadership was crucial during this horrific event. However, for a few brief minutes they were almost removed from any role in the incident. They had decided to respond closer to the actual scene. Recognizing that the EOC established at #7 World Trade Center might be too close, they responded to a building at 75 Barclay Street. When the South Tower collapsed, they found the site they had selected on Barclay Street too close. They had to be extricated from the site by following two janitors through a maze of underground tunnels to exit onto Church Street to continue their efforts. Their desire to respond closer to the scene for all the above "good" reasons almost rendered them totally ineffective. This desire is a common consequence of responding to the scene.

- **Becoming overly involved with the scene:** In today's era of technology, there is another way the Policy Group can go to the scene without leaving the predesignated site. Through live video feeds and monitoring of emergency radio frequencies, unfolding events can be evaluated without being exposed. Overexposure is the antithesis of our earlier concerns regarding lack of information needed to make good decisions. You are now drawn into the scene and the minute-to-minute decisions that are being made by professional responders from public safety, facilities, or health services. While this is fascinating on one hand, it will dramatically limit your ability to get ahead of the event in your thinking and can draw you into micromanagement of the event.

- **Trying to achieve full consensus:** Routine day-to-day habits die hard, and there is a tendency to want to arrive at the absolute "best" decision. Inevitably it will require more time, information, and discussion, possibly pushing the Incident Commander or Emergency Manager to take an independent action absent your policy decision. You may have to make a series of less than optimal decisions with clearly articulated thresholds that would force a new decision. "Right now we will remain open; however, if two or more additional facilities go down, then we will be forced to consider closing operations for an undetermined period of time."

- **Taking of Hostages:** Sometimes in an effort to gain more insight, the Policy Group will request the physical presence of the Emergency Manager and/or Incident Commander and/or the Public Information Officer. What inevitably happens is that discussions expand beyond the original scope of policy. These key personnel are now absent from their own management duties, and the Policy Group degrades into a third and competing Operations Section making decisions on how and what to do next. This can become a train wreck for the entire structure, as activities already in play are changed by actions based on information separated by too much distance from conditions on the ground.

Summary

The Executive Policy Group and its functions are a critical component in the "concept of operations" for all organizations. Like the other functions in the NIMS/ICS structure, its members are working at the level and doing the functions that mirror their day-to-day work in the organization. In this case, it is making policy decisions, setting the tone for the response, keeping the organization focused on its mission, and maintaining the good name of the organization with its partners and the public while ensuring the survival of the organization itself.

This function needs to be internalized by the key executives of your organization. They need to know where to report (and where not to go), what to do when they get there, where to get critical information, and how to communicate their decisions effectively. This means training and preparation are needed; institutional hazards, thresholds and potential policy decisions have been discussed and documented, and familiarization of the organizations Continuity of Operations Plans are reviewed and understood.

Review Questions

1. How does the role of the Executive Policy Group differ from that of the EOC?
2. What are the different "communication models" for the EPG and what are the benefits and/or limitations of each?
3. What are the various "structural models" for the EPG and when would you apply them?

Appendix A: ICS Task Checklists

All Incident Command System (ICS) positions and functions have specific duties. Unless you implement ICS responses on a regular basis, you're unlikely to remember all of the tasks. Therefore we have included a summary of those tasks, by position and function, that you are most likely to use, in a checklist format. There are approximately 140 potential functions/positions in a fully operationalized ICS model. We have included those most likely to be used for the overwhelming majority of critical incidents you may respond to. If the structure is started correctly with the positions/functions included here, it can be built upon and expanded to include any or all of the other areas requiring staffing.

Although these checklists can serve as an aid and reference when using the Incident Command System, there is no substitution for training and hands-on experience.

The following pages cover each of the positions and functional areas discussed in Chapter 6.

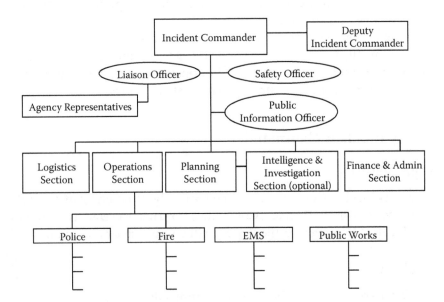

Figure A.1 ICS command structure.

Incident Commander

Responsibilities

The Incident Commander (IC) is charged with the overall responsibility for all incident activities, including the development and implementation of the Incident Action Plan, and approval and releasing of resources.

Normally, the first-responding supervisor to the scene will assume the role of IC, and if relieved, will be reassigned to another position.

Checklist

- If first supervisor to respond, take action to stabilize the scene by initiating the "critical tasks."
- Assess the situation if first to assume command, or obtain briefing from the prior Incident Commander. Fill out ICS 201 for next briefing.
- Select and establish an appropriate command post.
- Approve all information released to media and approve plan for returning to normal operations—the termination phase.
- Select appropriate functions to establish the Incident Command System; issue ICS identification badges, which correspond to the specific function assigned.
- Determine whether a unified command structure with assisting agencies is necessary.
- Conduct initial briefings of command and section chiefs and request that an Incident Action Plan be developed, with specific objectives, for review and approval.
- Brief all command post personnel on the Incident Action Plan.
- Continually review and update the Incident Action Plan with staff.
- Authorize and approve release of information to news media sources and approve plan for returning to normal operations.

Deputy Incident Commander

Responsibilities

The Deputy Incident Commander is a member of the command staff. He or she is appointed to assist the Incident Commander for a major event. In the absence of the Incident Commander, the Deputy will assume interim command.

Checklist

- Obtain briefing from the Incident Commander.
- Assist the IC as directed or where appropriate.

- Assume interim command when the IC is unavailable or absent from the command post.
- Verify execution of Incident Commander's directives and compliance with the Incident Action Plan.
- Serve as "systems manager" to:
  - Assure that all command post personnel function in their specific role.
  - Assure the smooth flow of information throughout the command post operation.
- Request that participating agencies provide liaison personnel or Agency Representatives to the command post when appropriate (this may be delegated to the Liaison Officer).
- Review situation or status reports, journals, and other data for accuracy and completeness.
- Ensure that all unit logs are submitted to the Incident Commander in a timely manner.

Safety Officer

Responsibilities

The Safety Officer is a member of the command staff. He or she is responsible for monitoring and assessing hazardous and unsafe situations and developing measures for assuring personnel safety. The Safety Officer will correct unsafe acts or conditions through regular lines of authority, although he or she may exercise emergency authority to stop or prevent unsafe acts when immediate action is required.

The focus is on responder safety, not community safety, which is left to the Planning Section.

Checklist

- Obtain briefing from the Incident Commander.
- Identify and mitigate hazardous situations
- Review the Incident Action Plan for safety implications.
- Monitor operational activities for potential danger or unsafe conditions.
- Exercise emergency authority to immediately stop or prevent unsafe acts or conditions when appropriate.
- Initiate preliminary investigation of accidents within the incident area.
- Monitor stress levels of involved personnel.

- Participate in planning meetings.
- Maintain a log of all activities.
- Prepare ICS Form 215A when appropriate

Public Information Officer

Responsibilities

The Public Information Officer is a member of the command staff. He or she is responsible for the formulation and release of information regarding the incident to the news media and other appropriate agencies and personnel as directed by the Incident Commander.

Checklist

- Obtain briefing from the Incident Commander that includes any limits on information release.
- Establish a single and separate incident information-briefing center, if possible.
- Obtain copies of all media releases pertaining to the incident.
- Prepare information summary on media coverage for specific command post personnel.
- Obtain approval from the Incident Commander for the release of information to the news media.
- Conduct press briefings and news releases as appropriate. Post all news releases in command post for review.
- Arrange for meetings between news media and incident personnel upon direction of the Incident Commander.
- Provide escorts for the media and other officials as necessary.
- Make information about the incident available to incident personnel.
- Maintain a log of all activities.

Liaison Officer

Responsibilities

The Liaison Officer is a member of the command staff. He or she is responsible for initiating mutual aid agreements and serves as the point of contact for assisting and cooperating agencies. This could include Agency Representatives and other jurisdictions in which mutual aid agreements are initiated, that is, fire service, emergency medical services, public works, and so forth.

Checklist

- Obtain briefing from the Incident Commander.
- Provide a point of contact for assisting mutual aid Agency Representatives.
- Identify Agency Representatives from each jurisdiction including communications link and location of all personnel assigned to assist with the incident.
- Handle requests from command post personnel for interagency contacts.
- Monitor incident operations to identify current or potential interorganizational conflicts or problems.
- Provide information to appropriate governmental agencies.
- Maintain liaison with the command center of other agencies involved in the incident.
- Provide agency-specific demobilization information and requirements.
- Maintain an activity log.

Agency Representative(s)

Responsibilities

The Agency Representative is a member of the command staff and reports to the Liaison Officer, or in the absence of a Liaison Officer, directly to the Incident Commander. He or she is assigned to the command post from another agency and is vested with full authority to make decisions on all matters affecting the activities of the agency represented. Only one representative from each agency involved should be assigned to the command post.

Checklist

- Receive briefing from the Liaison Officer or Incident Commander.
- Assist with the development or implementation of the Incident Action Plan, as appropriate.
- Provide input on the availability of resources from their agency and provide technical expertise where appropriate.
- Assist and cooperate with all command post personnel in matters regarding their agency's involvement.
- Monitor the well-being and safety of their agency's personnel assigned.
- Advise the Liaison Officer of special requirements of their agency.
- Report periodically to their agency on incident status.

- Participate and assist in demobilization planning. Ensure that all personnel and equipment are accounted for and that all reports are completed before leaving the command post.

Operations Section

Responsibilities

The Operations Section is responsible for the management of the operational units directly related to incident "stabilization" and "resolution." It is also responsible for assisting in the development of the Incident Action Plan, with specific responsibility for formulating the tactical objectives and operational strategies (operational component to Incident Action Plan) for bringing about incident resolution.

Checklist

- Assist in the development of the Incident Action Plan (operational component).
- Manage the tactical situation.
- Execute the operational component of the Incident Action Plan, with approval of the Incident Commander.
- Direct and control the tactical deployment of field elements assigned through the Operations Section, which includes Mission Unit Leaders.
- Will assist the Logistics Section in providing all resources (equipment, supplies, and personnel) to field operations for incident resolution.
- Ensure that appropriate reports are completed for Operations Section activities.
- Assist with demobilization planning for returning to normal operations.

Operations Section Chief

Responsibilities

The Operations Section Chief is responsible for the management of operational units related to incident "stabilization" and "resolution." He or she is responsible for assisting in the development of the Incident Action Plan, with specific responsibility for formulating tactical objectives and operational strategies. The Operations Section Chief will supervise and direct tactical operations and release resources as required. He or she also will make expedient changes to the Incident Action Plan based on field developments and with concurrence of the Incident Commander.

Checklist

- Obtain briefing from the Incident Commander.
- Supervise and direct the activities of all assigned Operations Section personnel.
- Assist in the development of the Incident Action Plan (operational component).
- Coordinate Operations Section activities with other field command post units.
- Prepare and recommend operational plan changes and revisions to the IC.
- Issue operational orders to implement directives of the Operations Section Chief and Incident Commander.
- Advise the Incident Commander on the readiness of tactical teams for deployment.
- Select or recommend staging area locations, perimeter assignments, evacuation strategies, and resource requirements/availability to the field commander.
- Provide frequent incident status briefings.
- Ensure personnel prepare after-action reports.
- Prepare an activity log, and assist in planning for return to normal operations.

Operations Dispatcher

Responsibilities

The Operations Dispatcher will report to the Operations Section Chief and will serve as communications coordinator for radio and telephone traffic at the command post.

Checklist

- Serve as communications coordinator for radio and telephone traffic for the Operations Section.
- Direct field units by radio or telephone as authorized by the Operations Section Chief.
- Coordinate communications activities with other operational agencies involved.

- Maintain a personnel and vehicle status board to assist the Operations Section Chief.
- Monitor deployment of and depletion of personnel and vehicles and advise the Operations Section Chief.
- Maintain a dispatch log.

Staging Area Supervisor

Responsibilities

The Staging Area Supervisor reports to the Operations Section. He or she is responsible for establishing and maintaining a location where personnel and equipment can be staged to provide support and resources to the field commander.

Checklist

- Obtain briefing from the Logistics Officer.
- Assist in selecting a location that is appropriate for staging vehicles and personnel and can be properly secured.
- Establish a staging area layout, and post signs to ensure area can be easily identified.
- Determine support needs for equipment, feeding, sanitation, and security.
- Maintain a status log and report resource status changes or shortages as required.
- Supervise the safeguarding and security of all personnel and equipment.
- Demobilize the staging area in accordance with the plan developed for return to normal operations.
- Maintain an activity log.
- Prepare and maintain ICS Forms 211e and 211p.

Mission Unit Leaders

Responsibilities

Mission Unit Leaders—for example, Special Weapons and Tactics (SWAT), Canine Unit, Mounted Unit, and Hazardous Materials Response Unit—will report to the Operations Section Chief. They are responsible for conducting specific tactical objectives as assigned by the Operations Section Chief and formulated under the Incident Action Plan. They are also responsible for operational deployment and supervision of assigned personnel only within the scope of their mission.

Checklist

- Obtain briefing and mission assignments from the Operations Section Chief.
- Review assignments with team and assign tasks.
- Direct, supervise, and monitor execution of tasks/mission.
- Coordinate activities with other field elements and Mission Unit Leaders as required.
- Maintain an activity log.

Planning Section

Responsibilities

The Planning Section is responsible for the collection, evaluation, and dissemination of information to measure the size, scope, and seriousness of the incident and to assist with development, implementation, and updating the Incident Action Plan.

It will be responsible for identifying technical specialists to assist in planning "incident resolution" strategies. Examples of specialists would be psychologists, environmental scientists, structural engineers, and industrial chemists.

The Planning Section may also activate the following units when appropriate: Situation Unit, Documentation Unit, Resource Unit, Medical Unit, and Demobilization Unit.

Checklist

- Prepare contingency plans for the incident.
- Project various operational plans, which may be needed to resolve the situation.
- Conduct danger assessment in affected area for personnel and the general public.
- Prepare a plan for evacuation and repopulating of evacuated areas, where appropriate.
- Assess and prepare estimations of factors affecting escalation or de-escalation and, at the request of the Incident Commander, perform field observations such as situation damage/injury/casualty estimates.
- Prepare a plan for returning to normal operations and a coordinated plan for the reassignment of all incident personnel (activation of Demobilization Unit, if required).

- Prepare appropriate ICS forms as necessary: IAP Cover, ICS 202, ICS 203, ICS 206 (Medical Unit), ICS 207 (Resources Unit), and ICS 221 (Demobilization Unit).

Planning Section Chief

Responsibilities

The Planning Section Chief is responsible for the collection, evaluation, and dissemination of information to measure the size, scope, and seriousness of the incident and to assist with the development, implementation, and updating of the Incident Action Plan. He or she identifies technical specialists to assist in planning "incident resolution" strategies.

Checklist

- Obtain briefing from the Incident Commander.
- Prepare contingency plans.
- Based on projections, develop plans for long-term operations
  - Prepare estimates of incident escalation and de-escalation at request of the Incident Commander/unified command.
  - Prepare situation damage/injury/casualty estimates.
- Develop plans to correct any condition observed that may cause danger or is a safety hazard to personnel and/or the general public.
- Prepare a plan for returning to normal operations.
- Maintain an activity log.

Documentation Unit

Responsibilities

The Documentation Unit is a member of the Planning Section. It is responsible for maintaining a written log (command post journal) of all incident events and for keeping appropriate command post personnel updated on significant developments.

Checklist

- Obtain briefing from the Planning Section Chief.
- Maintain a command post journal, which will include time, activity, and action taken.

- Periodically distribute a situation report to command post personnel.
- Gather incident-related information from other command post personnel for entry into the journal.
- Refer pertinent information to the Public Information Officer.
- Maintain custody of all documents prepared for briefing the Incident Commander; ensure that the date, time, and all persons present for the briefings are properly recorded.
- Assist the Planning and Intelligence Section in developing a plan for returning to normal operations.

Situation Unit

Responsibilities

The Situation Unit is a member of the Planning Section. It Is responsible for the collection, processing, and organizing of all incident information and for keeping appropriate command post personnel updated on significant developments. It Is also responsible for maintaining an updated map of the incident location or area.

Checklist

- Obtain briefing from the Planning Section Chief.
- Maintain an updated map of the incident location, which when displayed for all command post personnel will depict:
  - Affected area or location
  - Inner and outer perimeter locations
  - Scene command post location
  - Staging area location
  - Areas requiring evacuation or already evacuated
  - Location of assisting agency personnel or specialists
- May assist in developing future projections of incident growth and intelligence information.

Intelligence and Investigations Section (Optional)

Responsibilities

This section is responsible for ensuring that all investigative and intelligence operations, functions, and activities within the incident are properly managed, coordinated, and directed. This function may be located:

- Within the command staff
- In a unit within the Planning Section
- In a branch within the Operations Section
- In a separate general staff section. If activated as a section, the Intelligence Section Chief will head it.

Checklist

- Obtain briefing from the Incident Commander.
- Collect, process, analyze, and appropriately disseminate intelligence.
- Perform intelligence analysis and field observations:
  - Identification of high-risk locations
  - Identification of individuals inciting violence
- Deploy and supervise personnel as needed to gather and assess intelligence information.
- Maintain an intelligence file on specific hazardous locations and for individuals advocating and/or participating in violations of the law.
- Obtain photographs and sound and video recordings of incident activities where appropriate to assist command post personnel in developing an operational response plan.
- Direct that coverage of all television and radio broadcasts be monitored.
- Conduct a thorough and comprehensive investigation.

Logistics Section

Responsibilities

This section is responsible for requesting and/or providing facilities, services, and all resources required for the safe and successful resolution of the incident. The following units may be activated if required:

- Telecommunications Unit
- Medical Unit
- Food Unit
- Supply Unit
- Facilities Unit
- Ground Support Unit
- Technical Specialists Unit

A Unit Leader who will report to the Logistics Section Chief will head these units.

Checklist

- Determine with the Operations, Planning, and Intelligence Sections the size, scope, and seriousness of the incident and immediate or anticipated resources required for incident resolution.
- Request, maintain, and control selected equipment, supplies, facilities, and other services required by the Operations Section. Provide security for the command post, staging area, and other sensitive areas as required.
- Arrange for and provide meals and refreshments for all incident personnel in coordination with other section officers. (Activate Food Unit if required.)
- Maintain a visible chart of resources requested and advise the Operations Section of estimated time of arrival or the unavailability of the resources requested.

Logistics Section Chief

Responsibilities

The Logistics Section Chief is responsible for providing facilities, services, personnel, and other resources required to assist in the safe and successful resolution of the incident. He or she will participate in the development and implementation of the Incident Action Plan and will activate appropriate elements of the Logistics Section as necessary.

Checklist

- Obtain briefing from the Incident Commander.
- Plan and coordinate the activities of the Logistics Section and supervise assignment of personnel.
- Evaluate with the Operations, Planning, and Intelligence Sections the current size, scope, and seriousness of the incident and plan necessary logistical support for field operations.
- Provide, maintain, and control selected equipment, supplies, facilities, and services required by the Operations Section.
- Assign security for command post, staging area, and other sensitive areas, as required.
- Coordinate and process requests for additional resources.
- Maintain a visible chart of resources requested and advise the Operations Section of arrival of resources for deployment. The logistics chart should display information as follows:

- Resources requested (available/unavailable)
- Time requested
- Estimated time of arrival
- Resource "staged" location and available
- Descriptive data regarding resource—size, numbers, capabilities, and ratings.
- Provide for meals and refreshments for all incident personnel.
- Maintain an activity log.

Finance and Administration Section

Responsibilities

This section reports to the Incident Commander and is responsible for all financial and cost analysis aspects of the incident. Subordinate finance functions may include the Time Unit, Procurement Unit, Compensation Claims Unit, and Cost Unit.

Checklist

- Obtain briefing from the Incident Commander.
- Activate necessary elements (time unit, procurement unit, compensation claims unit, and cost unit) to support Finance Section activities.
- Provide input in planning sessions on financial and cost analysis matters.
- Assist the Logistics Section with procurement of equipment, supplies, and other resources needed for incident resolution.
- Ensure that all personnel time records are maintained and transmitted to agencies assisting with the incident.
- Participate in demobilization and incident termination planning sessions.
- Prepare an incident-related cost analysis as requested by the Incident Commander.
- Respond to and evaluate incident-related compensation claim requests.
- Maintain an activity log.

Appendix B: EOC Task Checklists

Emergency Manager

Responsibilities

The Emergency Manager is charged with the overall responsibility for all emergency incident activities, including the development and implementation of the Incident Action Plan, demobilization of resources, and oversight of the termination and recovery phase.

Normally, the designated Emergency Manager will assume the lead role unless an incident-related specialist is more qualified. If relieved, the Emergency Manager will be reassigned to Deputy Emergency Manager. Based on the size, scope, and seriousness of the incident, an Emergency Operations Center (EOC) may be established by the Emergency Manager.

Checklist

- Classify level of threat.
- Select and establish an appropriate EOC.
- Assess the situation and obtain briefing from emergency services personnel at the scene.
- Select appropriate functions to establish the Incident Command System and issue EOC identification badges that correspond to the specific functions assigned.
- Conduct initial briefings of command staff and section chiefs, and request that an Incident Action Plan, with specific objectives, be developed for review and approval.
- Brief all command post personnel on the Incident Action Plan.
- Continually review the Incident Action Plan with staff and update as necessary.
- Approve all information released to the media.
- Approve plan for the termination phase and the return to normal operations.

Deputy Emergency Manager

Responsibilities

The Deputy Emergency Manager is a member of the command staff. A Deputy Emergency Manager is appointed to assist the Emergency Manager during a major event. In the absence of the Emergency Manager, the Deputy will assume interim command.

Checklist

- Obtain briefing from the Emergency Manager.
- Assist the Emergency Manager as directed or where appropriate.
- Assume interim command when the Emergency Manager is unavailable or absent from the emergency operations center.
- Verify execution of the Emergency Manager's directives and compliance with the Incident Action Plan.
- Serve as "systems manager":
  - Assure that all EOC personnel function in their assigned role.
  - Assure the smooth flow of information throughout the EOC operation.
- Request that participating agencies provide liaison personnel or Agency Representatives to the EOC when appropriate (this may be delegated to the Liaison Officer).
- Review situation or status reports, journals, and other data for accuracy and completeness.
- Ensure that all unit logs are submitted to the Emergency Manager in a timely manner.

Safety Officer

Responsibilities

The Safety Officer is a member of the command staff. He or she is responsible for monitoring and assessing hazardous and unsafe situations and developing measures for assuring response personnel safety. The Safety Officer will correct unsafe acts or conditions through regular lines of authority, although he or she may exercise emergency authority to stop or prevent unsafe acts when immediate action is required.

Checklist

- Obtain briefing from the Emergency Manager.
- Assist in the formulation of the Incident Action Plan.

- Monitor operational activities and assess potential danger or unsafe conditions.
- Exercise emergency authority to immediately stop or prevent unsafe acts or conditions when appropriate.
- Monitor stress levels of involved personnel.
- Maintain a log of all activities.

Public Information Officer

Responsibilities

The Public Information Officer is a member of the command staff. He or she is responsible for the formulation and release of information regarding the incident to the news media and other appropriate agencies and personnel as directed by the Emergency Manager.

Checklist

- Obtain briefing from the Incident Commander.
- Establish a single and separate incident information briefing center, if possible.
- Obtain copies of all media releases pertaining to the incident.
- Prepare information summary on media coverage for specific command post personnel.
- Obtain approval from the Emergency Manager for the release of information to the news media.
- Provide press briefings and news releases as appropriate. Post all news releases in the EOC for review.
- Arrange for meetings between news media and incident personnel upon direction of the Emergency Manager.
- Escort media and other officials as necessary.
- Maintain a log of all activities.

Incident Log/Scribe

Responsibilities

The Scribe is a member of the command staff. He or she is responsible for maintaining a written log (EOC journal) of all incident events and for keeping appropriate EOC personnel updated on significant developments. The Scribe is also responsible for maintaining an updated map of the incident location or area.

Checklist

- Obtain briefing from the Emergency Manager.
- Maintain an EOC journal that includes time, activity, and action taken.
- Periodically distribute a situation report to EOC personnel.
- Gather incident-related information from other EOC personnel for entry into the journal.
- Refer pertinent information to the Public Information Officer.
- Maintain custody of all documents prepared for the Emergency Manager briefing; ensure that the date, time, and all persons present for the briefings are properly recorded.
- Maintain an updated map of the incident location that will depict:
  - affected area or location
  - inner and outer perimeter locations.
  - scene command post location
  - staging area location
  - areas requiring evacuation or already evacuated
  - location of assisting agency personnel or specialists
- Assist the Planning and Intelligence Sections in developing a plan for returning to normal operations.

Liaison Officer

Responsibilities

The Liaison Officer is a member of the command staff. He or she is responsible for initiating mutual aid agreements and serves as the point of contact for assisting and cooperating agencies. This could include Agency Representatives and other jurisdictions in which mutual aid agreements are initiated, for example, fire service, emergency medical services, and public works.

Checklist

- Obtain briefing from the Incident Commander.
- Provide a point of contact for assisting mutual aid Agency Representatives.
- Identify Agency Representatives from each jurisdiction including communications link and location of all personnel assigned to assist with the incident.
- Handle requests from command post personnel for interorganizational contacts.
- Monitor incident operations to identify current or potential interorganizational conflicts or problems.

- Provide information to appropriate governmental agencies.
- Maintain liaison with the command center of other agencies involved in the incident.
- Maintain an activity log.

Agency Representative(s)

Responsibilities

The Agency Representative is a member of the command staff and reports to the Liaison Officer, or in the absence of a Liaison Officer, reports directly to the Incident Commander. He or she is assigned to the command post from another agency and is vested with full authority to make decisions on all matters affecting the activities of the agency represented. Only one representative from each agency involved should be assigned to the command post.

Checklist

- Receive briefing from the Liaison Officer or Incident Commander.
- Assist with the development or implementation of the Incident Action Plan, as appropriate.
- Provide input on the availability of resources from their agency and provide technical expertise where appropriate.
- Assist and cooperate with all command post personnel in matters regarding their agency's involvement.
- Monitor the well-being and safety of their agency's assigned personnel.
- Advise the Liaison Officer of special requirements of their agency.
- Report periodically to their agency on incident status.
- Participate and assist in demobilization planning. Ensure that all personnel and equipment are accounted for and that all reports are completed prior to leaving the command post.

Operations Section

Responsibilities

The Operations Section is responsible for the management of the operational units directly related to incident "stabilization" and "resolution." It is responsible for assisting in the development of the Incident Action Plan, with specific responsibility for formulating the tactical objectives and operational strategies (operational component to Incident Action Plan) for bringing about incident resolution.

Checklist

- Assist in the development of the Incident Action Plan (operational component).
- Continuously appraise and evaluate the tactical situation.
- Execute the operational component of the Incident Action Plan, with approval of the Incident Commander.
- Direct and control the tactical deployment of field elements assigned through the Operations Section, which includes Mission Unit Leaders.
- Assist the Logistics Section in providing all resources (equipment, supplies, and personnel) to field operations for incident resolution.
- Ensure that appropriate reports are completed for Operations Section activities.
- Assist with demobilization planning for returning to normal operations.

Operations Section Chief

Responsibilities

The Operations Section Chief is responsible for the management of operational units related to incident "stabilization" and "resolution." This individual is responsible for assisting in the development of the Incident Action Plan, with specific responsibility for formulating tactical objectives and operational strategies. He or she will supervise and direct tactical operations and release resources as required. He or she also will make expedient changes to the Incident Action Plan based on field developments and with concurrence of the Incident Commander.

Checklist

- Obtain briefing from the Incident Commander.
- Supervise and direct the activities of all assigned Operations Section personnel.
- Assist in the development of the Incident Action Plan (operational component).
- Coordinate Operations Section activities with other field command post units.
- Prepare and recommend operational plan changes and revisions to the IC.
- Issue operational orders to implement directives of the Incident Commander.

- Advise the Incident Commander on the readiness of tactical teams for deployment.
- Select or recommend staging areas locations, perimeter assignments, evacuation strategies, and resource requirements/availability to the field commander.
- Provide frequent incident status briefings.
- Ensure that personnel prepare after-action reports.
- Prepare an activity log, and assist in planning for return to normal operations.

Operations Dispatcher

Responsibilities

The Operations Dispatcher will report to the Operations Section Chief and will serve as communications coordinator for radio and telephone traffic at the command post.

Checklist

- Serve as communications coordinator for radio and telephone traffic for the Operations Section.
- Direct field units by radio or telephone as authorized by the Operations Section Chief.
- Coordinate communications activities with other operational agencies involved.
- Maintain a personnel and vehicle status board to assist the Operations Section Chief.
- Monitor deployment of and depletion of personnel and vehicles and advise the Operations Section Chief.
- Maintain a dispatch log.

Mission Unit Leaders

Responsibilities

A Mission Unit Leader—for example, Special Weapons and Tactics (SWAT), Canine Unit, Mounted Unit, and Hazardous Materials Response Unit—will report to the Operations Section Chief. He or she is responsible for conducting specific tactical objectives as assigned by the Operations Section Chief and formulated under the Incident Action Plan. He or she is also responsible for operational deployment and supervision of assigned personnel only within the scope of their mission.

Checklist

- Obtain briefing and mission assignments from Operations Section Chief.
- Review assignments with team and assign tasks.
- Direct, supervise, and monitor execution of tasks/mission.
- Coordinate activities with other field elements and mission unit leaders as required.
- Maintain an activity log.

Planning Section

Responsibilities

The Planning Section is responsible for the collection, evaluation, and dissemination of information to measure the size, scope, and seriousness of the incident and to assist with developing, implementing, and updating the Incident Action Plan.

The Planning Section will be responsible for identifying technical specialists to assist in planning "incident resolution" strategies. Examples of specialists would be psychologists, environmental scientists, structural engineers, and industrial chemists.

Checklist

- Deploy personnel to gather and assess intelligence information.
- Provide intelligence information relating to specific hazardous locations and for individuals advocating and/or participating in violations of the law.
- Obtain photographs and sound and video recordings of the incident where appropriate and assist command post personnel in developing operational response plan.
- Monitor all television and radio broadcasts related to the incident.
- Assess and prepare estimations of factors effecting escalation or de-escalation and, at the request of the Incident Commander, perform field observations such as:
  - identification of high-risk locations
  - identification of persons inciting violence

- situation damage/injury/casualty estimates
- weather and environmental conditions

• Prepare a plan for returning to normal operations; conduct personnel danger assessment in affected area and a coordinated plan for the reassignment of all incident personnel.
• Prepare a plan for repopulating of evacuated areas, where appropriate.

Planning Section Chief

Responsibilities

The Planning Section Chief is responsible for the collection, evaluation, and dissemination of information to measure the size, scope, and seriousness of the incident and to assist with the development, implementation, and updating of the Incident Action Plan. He or she will also identify technical specialists to assist in planning "incident resolution" strategies.

Checklist

- Obtain briefing from the Incident Commander.
- Provide briefing on incident size and scope to all Planning and Intelligence personnel.
- Deploy and supervise personnel as needed to gather and assess intelligence information.
- Maintain an intelligence file on specific hazardous locations and for individuals advocating and/or participating in violations of the law.
- Obtain photographs and sound and video recordings of incident activities where appropriate to assist command post personnel in developing an operational response plan.
- Direct that coverage of all television and radio broadcasts be monitored.
- Prepare estimates of incident escalation and de-escalation at request of IC, by performing intelligence analysis and field observations:
  - Identification of high-risk locations
  - Identification of individuals inciting violence
  - Estimate of crowd size and type
  - Situation damage/injury/casualty estimates
- Report to the Safety Officer or take immediate action for any condition observed that may cause danger or is a safety hazard to personnel and prepare a plan for returning to normal operations.
- Maintain an activity log.

Logistics Section

Responsibilities

This section is responsible for requesting and/or providing facilities, services, and all resources required for the safe and successful resolution of the incident.

Checklist

- Determine with the Operations, Planning, and Intelligence Sections the size, scope, and seriousness of the incident and immediate or anticipated resources required for incident resolution.
- Request, maintain, and control selected equipment, supplies, facilities, and other services required by the Operations Section.
- Provide security for the command post, staging area, and other sensitive areas as required.
- Arrange for and provide meals and refreshments for all incident personnel in coordination with other section officers.
- Maintain a visible chart of resources requested and advise the Operations Section of estimated time of arrival or the unavailability of the resources requested.

Logistics Section Chief

Responsibilities

The Logistics Section Chief is responsible for providing facilities, services, personnel, and other resources required to assist in the safe and successful resolution of the incident. He or she will participate in the development and implementation of the Incident Action Plan and will activate appropriate elements of the Logistics Section as necessary.

Checklist

- Obtain briefing from the Incident Commander.
- Plan and coordinate the activities of the Logistics Section and supervise assignment of personnel.
- Evaluate with the Operations, Planning, and Intelligence Sections the current size, scope, and seriousness of the incident and plan necessary logistical support for field operations.
- Provide, maintain, and control selected equipment, supplies, facilities, and services required by the Operations Section.

- Assign security for command post, staging area, and other sensitive areas, as required.
- Coordinate and process requests for additional resources.
- Maintain a visible chart of resources requested and advise Operation Section of arrival of resources for deployment. The logistics chart should display information as follows:
  - Resources requested (available/unavailable)
  - Time requested
  - Estimated time of arrival
  - If "staged" give location and availability
  - Descriptive data regarding resource—size, numbers, capabilities, and ratings
- Direct that meals and refreshments for all incident personnel be provided.
- Maintain an activity log.

Staging Area Supervisor

Responsibilities

The Staging Area Supervisor reports to the Logistics Section Chief. He or she is responsible for establishing and maintaining a location where personnel and equipment can be staged to provide support and resources to the field commander.

Checklist

- Obtain briefing from the Logistics Section Chief.
- Assist in selecting a location that is appropriate for staging vehicles and personnel and can be properly secured.
- Establish a staging area layout and post signs to ensure area can be easily identified.
- Determine support needs for equipment, feeding, sanitation, and security.
- Maintain a status log and report resource status changes or shortages as required.
- Supervise the safeguarding and security of all personnel and equipment.
- Demobilize the staging area in accordance with the plan developed for return to normal operations.
- Maintain an activity log.

Communications Unit Supervisor

Responsibilities

Under the direction of the Logistics Section Chief, the Communications Unit Supervisor is responsible for providing technical support and developing a plan for the effective use of incident communications equipment, testing and repair of equipment, and supervision of the communications center (if established).

Checklist

- Obtain briefing from the Logistics Section Officer.
- Prepare and implement an incident radio communications plan.
- Ensure that communications center and equipment are operational.
- Set up telephone and public address system (if required).
- Provide technical support to:
  - Evaluate the adequacy of communication systems in operation.
  - Determine the geographical limitations on communications system.
  - Evaluate equipment capabilities.
  - Inventory equipment availability.
  - Anticipate problems with equipment during incident .
- Maintain inventory of all communications equipment.
- Maintain an activity log.

Security Unit Supervisor

Responsibilities

Under the direction of the Logistics Section Chief, the Security Unit Supervisor will coordinate all activities of the security unit and supervise assigned personnel.

Checklist

- Prepare and submit for approval a security plan for the command post (EOC), staging area, and other facilities as needed.
- Provide necessary security for staging area to safeguard equipment and personnel.
- Provide personnel for securing the command post, staging area, and other areas as directed.
- Provide security escorts to accompany dignitaries to secure areas.

- Ensure that security posts are manned.
- Issue passes to authorized personnel to tour secured area.
- Deny entrance to unauthorized personnel.
- Notify the Logistics Section Chief of individuals requesting to visit command post or other secured areas.
- Maintain an activity log.

Personnel Group Supervisor

Responsibilities

The Personnel Group Supervisor reports to the Logistics Section Officer. He or she is responsible for evaluating personnel requirements. He or she also maintains a master listing of personnel assignments and performs timekeeping functions.

Checklist

- Obtain briefing from the Logistics Section Chief.
- Coordinate activities of the personnel to meet the anticipated needs of the Operations Section.
- Maintain a reserve of personnel to meet the anticipated needs of the Operations Section.
- Maintain timekeeping and assignment location records for all personnel including mutual aid, volunteers, and so on.
- Maintain the following special files and logs:
  - Overtime card file
  - Assignment file
  - Schedule of personnel reassignment or release
- Brief relief personnel on incident status.
- Maintain personnel resources status board and account for all personnel upon initiation of the termination phase.

Finance Section

Responsibilities

This section reports to the Incident Commander and is responsible for all financial and cost analysis aspects of the incident. Subordinate finance functions may include the Time Unit, Procurement Unit, Compensation Claims Unit, and Cost Unit.

Finance Section Chief

Checklist and Responsibilities

- Obtain briefing from the Incident Commander.
- Activate necessary elements (time unit, procurement unit, and compensation claims unit and cost unit) to support Finance Section activities.
- Provide input in planning sessions on financial and cost analysis matters.
- Assist the Logistics Section with procurement of equipment, supplies, and other resources needed for incident resolution.
- Ensure that all personnel time records are maintained and transmitted to agencies assisting with the incident.
- Participate in demobilization and incident termination planning sessions.
- Prepare incident-related cost analysis as requested by the Incident Commander.
- Respond to and evaluate incident-related compensation claim requests.
- Maintain an activity log.

Appendix C: Using the DOT Emergency Response Guidebook

You've probably seen the little orange book at some time or another. We are going to try and convince you that, beyond being a handy reference tool, the Department of Transportation *Emergency Response Guidebook* (DOT ERG) is a critical part of your practical equipment—right up there with your gun and your radio.

The ERG coverage in your HazMat class might have been one of those segments that caused your eyes to glaze over. When we've taught classes to hazardous materials ICs and other experts from the fire service, we've had these professionals ask us why we are able to get law enforcement responders to listen to us. We believe it's *because* we're not experts. It's because we focus on need-to-know information for critical decision making.

And one of the most need-to-know elements for HazMat is the ERG! The ERG is simply one of the best tools you can have available that will help you make those correct decisions. But first you've got to make it available to all of your responders, and then they have to know how to use it.

The federal government publishes the ERG every three years. It is available to your department for free. You can probably get as many copies as you need through your local emergency management coordinator. There should be one in the glove box of every emergency unit right next to that pair of binoculars. (Remember the rule of thumb? If you can't cover the scene with your thumb, you're *too close!*)

We are going to go through the book quickly from front to back and briefly discuss the purpose of each conveniently color-coded section. Everybody likes color coding.

A quick aside: The term "dangerous goods," which you see on the cover, is simply the Canadian equivalent of "hazardous materials."

For the latest information about the ERG, or to obtain a searchable electronic version, go to http://www.phmsa.dot.gov/hazmat/library/erg.

Briefly, the ERG sections are:

- White: How to use the guide and identification tips
- Yellow: Substances listed by universal four-digit identification numbers

- Blue: Substances listed alphabetically
- Orange: Hazards and response strategies
- Green: Initial isolation distances

You might want to have a copy of the ERG handy as we discuss each section. That's the best way to see what we're talking about.

White Pages

Among other things, the white pages tell you how to use the book. They also include samples of the placards you might see on some loads. You should at least be able to recognize the colors and numbers of these placards. There is also a cheat sheet of the nine hazardous materials classes. The other handy bit of information here are silhouettes of common trailer and tanker types. This is critical to knowing whether a load is under pressure, liquid, or solid.

The top of page 1 gives you the big three things to remember:

- Resist rushing in!
- Approach the incident from upwind.
- Stay clear of all spills, vapors, fumes, and smoke.

Yellow Pages

The yellow pages give you a numeric listing of chemicals by their four-digit identification numbers. This is where you look if you have a placard with a number (1013, 2811, etc.). There are 75 pages of chemicals here. Would you guess that this represents all of the chemicals produced in North America? Not by a long shot! The ERG covers only the most commonly transported quarter of that staggering total.

Finding the chemical name is interesting information, but essentially useless. What are you supposed to do about it? Once you find a chemical in this section, you'll notice that it may or may not be highlighted. Based on that you turn to one of two sections for help:

- No highlighting on entry: Whether or not the substance is on fire, use the associated guide number to turn to the orange section, which we'll discuss shortly.
- Highlighted entry: If the substance is *not* on fire, turn to the green section for isolation distances. If it *is* on fire, turn to the orange section.

Why? Some substances are more dangerous when burning, and some are more dangerous when not burning. For example, the entry for "poisonous, flammable gas" (ID 1953) requires an isolation zone of 1 km if it's on fire, but up to 11 km if it's *not* on fire. Good information, don't you think?

Blue Pages

The blue pages give you an alphabetical listing of the thousands of commonly transported substances. Again, there is a four-digit ID and a guide number associated with each.

This section also includes highlighted entries. You use highlighted entries just as you do in the yellow section (depending on whether the substance is burning).

Orange Pages

This is the meat of the book. This is where you find the information you need to make public safety decisions. And because you always make those decisions based on the substance released, you always come to the orange pages through either the yellow or blue section.

This section gives you the data you need to assess risks and provides response guidelines. If you want to take proper action, do what the orange pages tell you to do.

Information for each guide number is always contained on two facing pages. That makes the book easier to handle in the dark with a flashlight.

At the top of each orange page is a guide number associated with every substance listed in the ERG. (Obviously, there are fewer guide numbers than substances. Many substances call for the same response.) Next to the number is a general description of the nature of the substance—for example, flammable liquid, explosive, mixed load, and so on.

Remember the two primary HazMat threats we discussed earlier? The potential hazards area of each guide number gives you that primary threat: fire/explosion or health. It's in big print right up front because it's the most important information.

One thing that you should note is that every one of these guide pages recommends wearing SCBA. Most recommend a chemical suit. And how many of you have these available? Your best defense is distance!

It's not unusual to have no idea at all what you're dealing with. You can still respond appropriately. In this case, turn to the first guide in the orange section, number 111. Use these guidelines to provide a safe response until the exact substance can be identified.

Green Pages

Turn to the green pages to find isolation distances for releases that do not involve fire. Note that this section divides releases into small (200 liters or less) and large (more than 200 liters). For the non-metric-literate, 200 liters is about 50 gallons. When in doubt, assume a large spill.

The other big consideration is time of day. You will notice that isolation zones for spills at night are frequently three or four times as great as those during the day. This is largely due to the difference in atmospheric conditions. A specialist should, if at all possible, decide on the actual size of the isolation zone and whether to evacuate or shelter-in-place.

Index

Page references followed by *t* or *f* refer to tables or figures.